First Catch
Your Peacock

First edition: 1980
This revised paperback edition: April 1996

© Bobby Freeman 1980, Y Lolfa Cyf., 1996

This book is subject to copyright and may not be reproduced
by any method, except for review purposes, without the
prior, written consent of the publishers.

ISBN: 0 86243 315 0

Photography by Keith Morris, Stuart Ladd, and by
permission of the National Library of Wales.

Printed and published in Wales
by Y Lolfa Cyf., Talybont, Ceredigion SY24 5HE;
tel. (01970) 832 304
fax 832 782
e-mail ylolfa@netwales.co.uk
internet http://www.ylolfa.wales.com/

BOBBY FREEMAN

Her Classic Guide to Welsh Food

First Catch Your Peacock

For Jamie, Isabella, Robert and Daniel

Contents

Preface to 1996 Edition

LOOKING BACK NOW to the time I originally put together the material and knowledge I had acquired about traditional Welsh food and drink into the first edition of this book, I am struck by the unprecedented changes which have taken place since. This revised edition reflects these developments through the addition of new material, without, I hope, impairing the quality of the original which to my delight had sufficient appeal to create the demand for this new edition.

I began writing it in Cardiff in the summer of 1976, chained reluctantly to the typewriter and the city throughout that long, hot summer. . . but it was to be the end of 1980 before publication was effected. There were delays due to major re-writing to reduce the material to fit the publisher's decreased purse, followed by a further and traumatic delay when he collapsed into insolvency just as the book was actually in page proof. After all the delay, I was driven by an urgent conviction that the book deserved publication, for nothing like it had been attempted before on the subject of Welsh food. Three months later a partnership with the printers, with my publishing-inexperienced self at the sharp end of marketing, sales and publicity, got the work into the bookshops. Never a gambler, I was so desperate to see it in print that I risked staking my slender 'old age' savings on it. (I didn't increase them much, but at least recouped them.) Many good people whose judgement I valued backed me up and helped during this difficult time: Alan Davidson of Prospect Books; Wyn Thomas, then MD of Lear's Bookshop, Cardiff, who gave it a splendid launch; Richard Binns; and the late Jeremy Hadfield, who efficiently lessened the distaste I felt for promoting my own book by taking the bulk of it over. Much has altered in that respect, too – no-one would think anything of self-publication today, indeed, it has become quite the thing to do.

In the decade or more I had been delving into the subject I

Organic yoghurt production at Rachel's Dairy, Aberystwyth. Photo by Keith Morris.

was endlessly told that there was 'no such thing as Welsh food'. I chose the tantalising title (the inspiration of a literary-minded publicist friend) to make people think again. 'An absurd title for a serious work', I was then admonished – but it worked, didn't it?

Since then we have had two major TV series on traditional Welsh food – the first made for the Welsh language channel, S4C, faultless in its evocation of times past, inspired I was told by this book; the second by BBC Wales about contemporary Welsh food, presented by the innovative and indefatigable Gilli Davies.

I have over 30 years in Wales behind me now – from the time in the early 1960's, when Pembrokeshire was 'another world' (gone now) as far removed from the life of big towns and cities as you could then hope to get in mainland Britain. As a caterer I found the difficulty of obtaining locally-grown vegetables, not to mention unheard of items like peppers and aubergines, frustrating. Now the former are grown locally! Many items had to come by post – sea salt from Elizabeth David's Pimlico shop, for example. So I made the most of local produce – oven-baked bread, top quality meat, locally-caught fish, crab and lobster, and laverbread. The organic vegetable-growing and on-farm cheese-making were a long way off then, the idea of Welsh wine was frankly risible, and the number of notable restaurants very small. I have seen the pattern of shopping in Wales radically altered, from the spread of wholefood and speciality food shops to even the smallest rural towns, to the arrival of the large supermarkets which have made the more 'exotic' food items available even to the remoter areas. I am well aware of their threat to the survival of small shops, especially in rural areas, but at the same time note the consequent improvement in local shopping and a new enthusiasm for different foods and tastes, as well as the beneficient effect upon restauraunts in their vicinity. Open-air markets flourish and WI stalls have become a welcome addition to most weekly markets.

The revivers of the old rural industries were the ones who began the creation of interest in Welsh food products – a lukewarm interest in the beginning, it has to be said. It also has to be said that most of the interest came from outside, rather than within Wales. Official bodies which might have provided effective help held back, or studiously ignored, part and parcel of the former refusal to believe that good, even exciting, food could come from Wales. What everyone was enamoured with at the time was exotica from 'abroad'. Ever ready to champion a lost cause, I have a groaning remembrance of the disdain with which both English and Welsh media met my enthusiasm for the burgeoning Welsh food revival. I must have been a great irritant to them.

But bit by bit notice was taken. What a sense of achievement and excitment one felt when the organic vegetable-growers and on-farm cheese-makers succeeded in getting their produce into, first London, then the supermarket chains. I like it when I observe my London-based daughter casually adding a Welsh cheese to her weekly haul from her local Sainsbury's, and now one of the Dyfed cheeses sells under Safeway's own-brand label. It's progress, of course, but it has been achieved at the cost of their chosen way of life, for by now they have all had to become efficient business-people.

And so, at last, the official promotional bandwagon got going. Now there are more foods and food products made in Wales than can possibly be listed here, and they are being added to all the time.

In addition to the original stalwarts of organic produce, you can now have chocolates from Pembrokeshire, Gwynedd and South Glamorgan, wines from eleven Welsh vineyards, Welsh whisky, escargot, bottled water, smoked fish and cheese, oysters, cockles, mussels and the enigmatic laverbread, venison, ice-cream, sauces, pies, breads, cakes and biscuits, preserves, sweets. . . and, well, you name it, Wales now produces it. The range even extends into institutional catering: when Welsh hospitals began to convert to frozen patient meals they needed to look no further than the Welsh mining Valleys.

And what of the old dishes? Are they still being made as an unselfconscious part of daily life? In the rural areas at least, by the farming and small townsfolk they are. There's still the old fondness for cakes of all kinds, richly made with butter and eggs in defiance of health warnings. People living along the west Wales coast are still gathering and boiling their own laverbread, and only the other day I was offered real 'home-cured' (i.e. extremely fatty bacon) in a Fishguard shop – where they were also doing a brisk trade in bulk muesli, dried fruits, porridge oats, fresh fish and vegetables.

I have been living again in west Wales for over ten years now. It's different – less of an adventure than it was, but still a good place to be.

Newport (*Trefdraeth*), Pembrokeshire, June 1994.

Acknowledgements

So many helped, often in small but valuable ways, with the preparation of both this and the first edition, that to list them all would be difficult. I thank everyone who gave so willingly of their time to talk, make suggestions and give recipes. For the research: the staff of the National Library of Wales, (Mr G M Griffiths, former Keeper of MSS and Records, and Dr M I Williams, former Keeper of Printed Books) and Brynmor Jones, the Welsh Librarian, Cardiff Central Reference Library.

My thanks are also due to Ieuan Griffiths, for translating the Mati Thomas MS, the late Maxwell Fraser, and Ben Owens, former Keeper of MSS, NLW.

BOBBY FREEMAN   March 1996

11

METRIC AND IMPERIAL EQUIVALENTS

Weight/Solids

15 g	½ oz
25 g	1 oz
40 g	1½ oz
50 g	1¾ oz
75 g	2¾ oz
100 g	3½ oz
125 g	4½ oz
150 g	5½ oz
175 g	6 oz
200 g	7 oz
225 g	8 oz
250 g	9 oz
275 g	9¾ oz
300 g	10½ oz
325 g	11½ oz
350 g	12 oz
400 g	14 oz
425 g	15 oz
450 g	1 lb
500 g	1 lb 2 oz
600 g	1 lb 4 oz
700 g	1 lb 9 oz
750 g	1 lb 10 oz
1 kg	2 lb 4 oz
1.2 kg	2 lb 12 oz
1.5 kg	3 lb 5 oz
2 kg	4 lb 8 oz
2.25 kg	5 lb
2.5 kg	5 lb 8 oz
3 kg	6 lb 8 oz

Volume/Liquids

15 ml	½ fluid oz
30 ml	1 fl oz
50 ml	2 fl oz
100 ml	3½ fl oz
125 ml	4 fl oz
150 ml	5 fl oz (¼ pint)
200 ml	7 fl oz
250 ml (¼ litre)	9 fl oz
300 ml	10 fl oz (½ pint)
350 ml	12 fl oz
400 ml	14 fl oz
425 ml	15 fl oz (¾ pint)
450 ml	16 fl oz
500 ml (½ litre)	18 fl oz
600 ml	1 pint (20 fl oz)
700 ml	1¼ pints
750 ml (¾ litre)	1½ pints
1 litre	1¾ pints
1.2 litres	2 pints
1.5 litres	2¾ pints
2 litres	3½ pints
2.5 litres	4½ pints
3 litres	5¼ pints

OVEN GUIDE

The thermostatic dials on some electric
cookers are marked in Centigrade.
These correspond to Fahrenheit
and gas markings as follows:

°F	°C	Gas mark	Temperature
250	130	½	Very cool
275	140	1	Very cool
300	150	2	Cool
325	(160	3	Warm
	(170		
350	180	4	Moderate
375	190	5	Fairly hot
400	200	6	Fairly hot
425	(210	7	Hot
	(220		
450	230	8	Very hot
475	240	9	Very hot

Introduction

A TRADITION OF WELSH COOKERY has long been denied by the Welsh (and the English, too), almost always on the grounds that it lacks sufficient distinction from that of the rest of Britain and Ireland to merit separate recognition.

But there are other touchy, emotive reasons: the effects of a self-denying Puritanical religion and much past hardship understandably colour Welsh attitudes to their native cookery. Even today a discussion of the subject is apt to generate a surprising amount of heat – I have been treated to more than one lecture on the frivolity of studying the history of Welsh food! It is this contrived indifference which is perhaps one of the reasons why so little has been written down about Welsh cookery – for the lack of written records is so notable that one is bound to comment upon it.

This has much to do with the fact that the traditional dishes were passed orally from mother to daughter, and since the Welsh have good memories for the spoken word, it would be seldom necessary to write the recipes and methods down. Mati Thomas prefaces her collection of very old Welsh recipes, a prize-winning National *Eisteddfod* entry of 1928, with the declaration that she wishes to make a written record of the old dishes of the latter part of the 18th century from the memories of old people, while they were still alive to recall them for her.

This manuscript collection is, as far as I know, unique as a record of traditional Welsh recipes, old cooking methods and comment upon the frugal lifestyle of the small independent or tenant farmers who characterised the Welsh rural scene from medieval times to practically the present day. For only under the economic pressures of our times are the small farms in Wales at last disappearing into large farming units.

Those who might have written Welsh recipes down, the *uchelwyr* (gentry), did not do so because after the Act of Union

1536, when English law and language superseded that of Wales, Welsh country mansions were run firmly on English lines. Their kitchens thus cooked in the English style.

The English presence within Welsh life was in any case already there, for many of the great houses, and earlier still, the Norman castles, were occupied by Anglo-Norman and English nobility and gentry. Cooking generally tends to come down from the top, from the tables of the rich, becoming simplified as it adapts to less money and less sophisticated cooking facilities (often achieving a new elegance from this very simplicity). Clearly this did not happen in Wales: the country's traditional cookery grew out of the life of the farming folk and peasants – and there it stayed, remaining remarkably intact.

I can trace no more than a few standard sauces, such as *béchamel*, with no real Welsh connection, as having come down to ordinary households. They would have been acquired and made by local women who had worked as cooks and kitchen staff in the *plas* (mansion). 'Teifi Salmon Sauce' is often quoted in Welsh collections, from the same influence I'm sure, but this is not a sauce at all. The enormous quantity of butter the recipe calls for is the clue to its 18th century origin, when butter was used by the wealthy as a cooking medium.

One of the reasons why Welsh cookery has been so confusing to trace is that many recipes for English dishes have found their way into Welsh collections and been passed on and on without question until they were attributed to Wales. Mostly these are recipes for dishes copied out of best-selling later Victorian cookery books (though I have found a few from Mrs. Maria Rundell's long-selling 'New System of Domestic Cookery') 1806 first published in England but sold of course in Wales as well; eventually the copied recipe is assumed by later generations to have been mother's own and proudly produced as a 'very old Welsh recipe'.

Of the few books which were written in the Welsh language in Victorian times for instruction in cookery and household management, most follow the English pattern and English cookery. Of those who do include a few Welsh dishes one feels they are there more as a record than with any desire to create enthusiasm for continuing a Welsh tradition as such.English cookery writers haven't bothered overmuch about Welsh cookery, either. It's assumed that *bara brith*, Welsh Cakes, leeks and Welsh Rarebit are its sum total. To add to the lack of recognition for Welsh cookery, many dishes which properly belong to Wales, like flummery and pikelets, have become completely divorced from their Welsh origin, and occasionally one finds a little Welsh dish tucked away amongst an English collection, under an English name.But there are two notable exceptions in the other direction – dishes which found their way into English cookery, their Welsh names corrupted to an English spelling. *Llymru*, the jelly-like dish of oats from early Welsh peasant cookery, spread to all parts of the British Isles as 'flummery', its humble Welsh origin completely forgotten by the time it was taken up and embellished for the dinner tables of the rich. Pikelets are familiar enough by their English name and it puzzled me for years how they came to be included in so many Welsh collections. The name is thought to be another corruption from the Welsh – *bara pyglyd*. 'Pitchy bread' was another name for these yeast pancakes which resemble the thicker English crumpet (cooked in rings) in their mixture. But most of the more recent recipes in Wales have become muddled with the pancake and lightcake recipes and are now egg and soda mixes. Thus all the (sometimes exceptionally beautiful) handscribed recipe collections which were compiled in Welsh country houses in the 17th, 18th and 19th centuries are no different from their counterparts compiled in English mansions and do not contain a single reference to traditional Welsh dishes or methods of cooking.

Nor does it appear to have occurred to any of the writers of cookery books in the Welsh language to make any attempt to encourage the recognition of a Welsh culinary tradition. Most of the books are devoted to instruction in cooking in English style; there are a few traditional Welsh recipes, but included one feels for reference purposes rather than as an attempt to keep an old tradition alive.

There is, though, one exception. Augusta Hall, though English by birth, was brought up at Llanover near Abergavenny in Gwent. She was a zealous champion of everything Welsh, and as Lady Llanover, wife of Baron Llanover – Benjamin 'Big Ben' Hall – became an enthusiastic patron of Welsh culture, and renowned for her hospitality. The Llanover estate was ostentatiously run on Welsh, not English lines, and some Welsh dishes were prepared in the Llanover kitchens with their famous motto:

Da i bawb cynhildeb yw
A thad i gyfoeth ydyw
(Thrift is beneficial to all
and is the father of wealth)

In 1867 Lady Llanover published her remarkable views on cookery and nutrition in *The First Principles of Good Cookery*, which ends with an appendix of recipes. About a dozen of them are for traditional Welsh dishes, amongst them the Welsh Salt Duck, one of the few references I have been able to find to what is a most successful and unusual dish.

My own involvement with Welsh cookery began a hundred years after Lady Llanover's *Good Cookery*, in the early 1960's, when I had already got my little hotel and restaurant going in Fishguard. One day I decided to play a hunch and try serving a few traditional Welsh dishes to the tourists. This was a completely new departure in those day. It was an instant success and so we wanted to increase our repertoire. I was very anxious to get the dishes right and very conscious of the disadvantage of being English. It was then that I began to discover how difficult it was to find out about Wales' traditional dishes.

There wasn't much in print; a few little recipe collections were all I found then, notably *Croeso Cymreig* (A Welsh Welcome) published by the Wales Gas Board. But their recipes were neither authenticated nor explained, and to make head or tail of them at all one needed either a Welsh rural background or a more profound knowledge of old British cookery than I then had.

Thus began a long search to authenticate Welsh cookery. I was hampered by many things, not the least a complete lack of the Welsh language; by a lack of academic training; but most of all by the baffling refusal from those I questioned to admit that there was such a thing as Welsh cookery!

In recent years I have been helped enormously by the increase of well-researched books on British cookery in general and on Welsh cookery in particular, the most important of which is undoubtedly the collection compiled from the memories of old people by Mrs S Minwel Tibbott of the Welsh Folk Museum, St Fagan's, under the title *Welsh Fare*.

The *Laws of Hywel Dda* (Howell the Good – a medieval Welsh Prince who brought unity to the whole of Wales and codified the different laws of its various kingdoms and princedoms into one universal law) reveal much about the importance of foodstuffs and their value, as well as giving a picture of what was available in Wales during the time between the departure of the Romans and the Norman conquest. From them we learn for example that white beasts with red or black ears (cattle which may have been brought from Italy in Roman times) were greatly prized (the honour price fixed for the Lords of Dynefwr, capital of the old princedom of Deheaubarth, was for as many of these cattle 'as will extend, the head of one to the tail of the other, from Argoel to the palace of Dynefwr, with a bull of the same colour for every score').

The *Laws* also tell us that the Welsh princes had a staff of professional hunters to assist them; hunting was restricted to species and season – stags from midsummer to the beginning of winter; then for a short time, wild swine; and from February to midsummer again was the time for hunting hinds.

It was in this period, too, that the noted speciality of later times in Wales, goat hams, began to be prepared.

The Welsh medieval poets often seem to have more to say about love and war, mead and wine than food – until you examine the charming *Bwyd y Beirdd* ('Food of the Bards'), an early, poetic good food guide, recording in verse the food and wine the medieval Welsh poets received in the homes of the Welsh nobility as they toured Wales on their *clera*. Their vivid descriptions of the hospitality they received include details of the tableware as well as the food and wine. One of my favourites is this:

Eight sorts of mead for the table
Eight dishes in twofold adorned it

Eight sorts of sauces – eight piping hot
Eight sorts of wines and delicacies.

Guto'r Glyn, writing of Dinas Mawddwy, mid 15th century. Food of the Bards *by Enid Roberts.*

Dafydd ap Gwilym wrote often in praise of the Glamorgan vineyards which were still flourishing in his time after having been planted 900 years before by the Romans. After a shaky start in the 1970's, during which vineyards were planted in various parts of south Wales, to flourish for a time and then be abandoned, usually because their ageing owners could no longer cope with the work, Wales now has several well-established vineyards, producing excellent white wines in the main, though there are now a few reds becoming available. Restaurateurs in Wales have naturally been delighted to be able to offer these on their wine lists.

From the same region as one of these present day vineyards came the famous 'peaches of Troy' – gift of the Marquis of Worcester from his summer house at Troy, near Monmouth, to Charles I just before the Civil War, and amongst the first peaches to be grown in Britain. For years these peaches puzzled social commentators blind to the fact that 'poor, wet Wales' was capable of growing anything other than leeks: the wrong Troy was assumed and all speculated how even so rich a man as the Marquis could afford the swift conveyance of such perishable fruit across Europe to London. . .

A pleasing side-effect of the new fast roads is the highlighting of little, formerly obscure places which have especially lovely names. The Gwent Troy is one of them – the dual carriageway linking the M4 with the Ross Spur and the M5 to Birmingham is known as the Mitchell Troy Bypass.

Regional and geographical differences

...almost all the population lives on its flocks and on oats, milk, cheese and butter.

Giraldus Cambrensis, 1188

This assessment of Welsh eating habits in the later Middle Ages is customarily interpreted as disparaging. But it is in fact a valuable observation which reveals the dependence in the upland areas, which form the greater part of Wales, upon meat and animal products in the absence of grain and a variety of vegetables (leeks and cabbages are the only two cultivated vegetables named in The *Laws of Hywel Dda*).This condition characterised the Welsh diet from the earliest times, in contrast to the cereal-bulked pottages which were the basis of the diet of the common people in the lowlands of Britain. Potatoes were then still unknown in Britain, so for the Welsh meat was of immense importance, its use extended by root vegetables, leeks and cabbage. Thus the earliest *cawl*, pronounced 'cowl' – broth, stew (see pp 108-9) was of meat (usually bacon, reflecting the Celtic dependence upon the pig) and vegetables only. In the 18th and 19th centuries the composition of *cawl* was virtually reversed, since meat had all but disappeared from the broth, which by then depended heavily upon potatoes for its content.

The inhabitants of the British Isles in early times ate according to the prevailing geographical and climatic pattern. Thus the upland areas of northern England and Scotland, as well as Wales, were restricted by the cold and wet to growing oats only as a cereal crop; while rye, barley and wheat could be cultivated in the cleared forests of the lowland areas.

People living near the coasts of northern and western Britain would have included seaweed in their diet. There would have been nothing odd in this, for in prehistoric times it was common practice to eat land weeds – indeed the reaping of weed seeds along with cereal grain, in order to ensure some kind of harvest if the cultivated grain failed, was continued in the remoter areas of Britain until late medieval times, as did the grinding of corn on hand querns long after powered mills had taken this task over in lowland areas.

We can see Wales as part of the British whole in the evolvement of early eating habits due to climate and geography. As elsewhere, the rich and fertile lowland areas were influenced by the Roman and Norman invaders and their more sophisticated eating habits, while the remoter and sparser upland areas were left to their more primitive devices. In Wales, where the native Celtic population was finally forced to retreat away from the productive coastal areas and into the wilder hinterland, there was a greater concentration of the preservation of the old ways with food. This persisted through to the end of the 19th century, and in a few isolated areas actually to the present day where the 'fire on the floor' and the old pot-crane, steam kettle and wall-oven can still be in use – though these remarkable exceptions cannot be expected to last much longer in their original surroundings.

In the upland areas in Wales the diet was restricted by what could be grown and reared and gleaned from the woodlands and hedgerows. This would be frugality rather than poverty: before the enclosures and the rape of the land by the Welsh squires at the end of the 18th and the beginning of the 19th centuries, most of the agricultural land in Wales was farmed by small tenant farmers, who were able to maintain themselves with sturdy self-reliance, if not in affluence, at least well above the poverty-line.

There would almost always be a cow or two, for milk, cheese and butter; certainly pigs and a few hens, and in coastal or river areas fish – indeed it is interesting to note that the Welsh labouring classes, according to John Burnett in *Plenty and Want*, were better fed than their English counterparts when the first British national food enquiry was conducted in 1863.

Significantly, the whole of the small farms' gardens were given over to vegetable-growing, seldom to flowers. Though they are fast catching up, the Welsh never devoted themselves to flower gardens as the English did.[1]

With this fairly spartan but extremely healthful upland living can be contrasted accounts like those of Dr James Williams, revealing the comparative affluence of life on a reasonably well-to-do farm in the lush Teifi Valley, where hard work and long hours were amply compensated by plenty of good wholesome food which often rose to heights of glory in the hands of a capable cook.

What seem to me to emerge are two distinct strains of traditional Welsh cookery: the broths and the porridges and yeast-baked bread and and bakestone cookery evolved from the ancient

---

1. Gwyn Williams: *The Land Remembers*.

Celtic styles, much of which does not appeal to today's palates, and the addition of pies and cakes and girdle scones coincident with the industrial revolution. From this came the great movement of population in Wales, together with an influx of workers from other parts of Britain and beyond, and the introduction of commercial flour, cheap sugar and chemical raising agents – most of these we enjoy today.

Regionally in Wales there are few culinary differences. They do not amount to much more than lobscouse being largely a north-Walian dish, and the use of goose-blood (echoing the primitive bleeding of cattle which could not be spared for killing at the end of winter) in pies and a pudding confined to certain areas of mid-Wales. This points to an exceptionally strong tradition, especially when one considers the oral transference of the dishes and the poor communications which existed in Wales until the coming of the railways.

The only region which has a strongly-marked difference from the rest of Wales is Gower, where a number of dishes which are not found elsewhere developed: 'whitepot', 'dowset', 'souly cake', and the use of pumpkins. Sometimes here different names were given to dishes endemic to the rest of Wales. This is explained by the long-standing, cross-channel exchange of trade and workers with Somerset and Devon, affecting both the food and the language of this lovely little peninsula which occurs so unexpectedly between industrial Swansea and Llanelli, and was, until the coming of the railway in the late 19th century, virtually self-contained.

A movement of people always has its effect upon cookery, as the invaders or emigrants will tend to retain their own style and specialities if they can continue to obtain the necessary ingredients. These eventually become mingled with the traditions of the region or country in which they have settled, and this is what happened in Gower. Whitepot (*whipod*) is a Devon dish; souly cake, which on Gower celebrated the old Welsh year's All Souls' Day (12 November), seems to have a connection with the West country 'pop dolly' and was probably imported from there by workers settling in Gower; while pumpkins do not appear to have been grown anywhere else in Wales except Gower, where they were a distinct speciality. Some people incline to the belief that emigrants from Gower took their pumpkin recipes with them to North America and established the pumpkin-pie tradition over there.

Again, those who emigrate to foreign lands tend to return home on visits with, or to send back recipes from, their adopted country: the Welsh are particularly good at retaining their links with home, which is why, I think, Welsh Women's Institute recipe collections contain so many American and Canadian dishes.

What do confuse sometimes are the different Welsh names given to the same dish. For those who have no knowledge of the Welsh language this can be a great puzzle, and even when some familiarity is acquired the different words used in north and south Wales, the mutations and the variance of words used by different dialects still create misunderstandings.

A good example of this is the bakestone bread which in the hands of a skilled Welsh cook can be made to rise despite the improbable conditions, called variously: *bara planc, bara crai, bara cri, bara trw'r dŵr,* according to district and dialect. Occasionally the same name is given to different dishes, as with *dowset,* which can mean either a savoury pie, or a sweet pie (see pp 191-2): both are Gower specialities. And of course there is the confusion caused by dubbing a Welsh name·on an English dish.

Celtic cooking comparisons, fuels, etc

The similarity of conditions naturally resulted in many basic similitudes between early Welsh cookery and that of other Celtic countries which go to make up the British Isles. A preoccupation with the staple crop oats, affects the traditional cookery of Scotland, Ireland and Wales, with more or less the same results: the Welsh *brŵes/brywes* turns up as *brose* in Scotland, and the Welsh *sucan* as *sowans* in Ireland and in Scotland, but all three developed their individual specialities, too. Salt duck is exclusive to Wales (did they salt it to tenderize an old bird or simply to keep it for a few days?), and though bakestone (griddle) cookery is common to all three Celtic countries, it seems the Welsh have extended its use further than the others – from scones and pancakes and quick-breads of all kinds (plain and curranty) to fruit-tarts and apple-cakes. And there is nothing in the bakestone tradition of either Ireland or Scotland to approximate Wales' traditional Welsh cakes (*pice ar y maen*), also equally exclusively baked in Wales in the alternative Dutch oven.

Comparisons are sometimes drawn between the Celtic cookery of Wales and that of the other Celtic country across the Channel – Britanny – whose language is so similar to Welsh that their onion-sellers used to have little difficulty in conversing with the Welsh when they came over in their jaunty berets with their onion-strung bicycles. This long-standing trade is now almost over as a result of EC regulating. The Bretons share the Welsh love of pancakes, though their *crêpes dentelles* are perhaps daintier, more sophisticated than most Welsh *crempoq*, and they have a spicy currant loaf, *morlaix brioche*, similar to the Welsh *bara brith*. They also love leeks, and the combination of bacon, onions and potatoes so frequently encountered in Wales (though the Bretons add garlic) – and they like buttermilk with such a dish, too. Again, there's a Breton 'butter cake' resembling the Anglesey *slapan*, though this is made on the bakestone, not in a tin, as is the Breton cake. In northern Spain, where we are among Celts again, *caldo* is a close cousin to *cawl* and highly esteemed, especially when made with pork; and the Welsh idea of pouring buttermilk over potatoes, especially the little early ones, boiled in their tissue-thin skins (*tatws llaeth*) is just as popular with the farming folk of Galicia.

There are interesting similarities in the cookery of parts of northern Germany with that of Wales. Along the North Sea coast, in the region of Schleswig-Holstein, a sailors' stew of onions and potatoes with fish, beef, or both, is called *labskaus*. (The north of England lobscouse became so absorbed into the cookery of north Wales that it acquired a mock Welsh spelling (*lobsgows*) and is popularly assumed to be a traditional Welsh dish. But it is not: in old English *lob* meant sheep, *scouse* soup.)

As with Wales there was a dependence in this region of northern Germany upon herring, fresh and salted, a liking for spicy cakes, goose, onions with lamb or mutton, and bacon and potato dishes – though in Germany they tended to include eggs with these dishes which the Welsh never did. Here, too, there is a beer soup which closely resembles the Brandy Broth of Wales.

And farther afield still, in lands vastly different from Wales in climate and culture, there is a dish similar to one of Wales. The middle-eastern Sheep's Head Broth is a valued dish; but the Welsh *cawl pen dafad*, made in the same way but with the addition of oatmeal dumplings, is not; for it is ineradicably associated with times of extreme poverty, when the sheep's head would be given to the farm labourer by his employer, out of compassion for the worker's struggle to feed a large, growing family. The meal was enjoyed none the less, but to make it when times were better would be unthinkable.

Many of the old Welsh dishes and some of the traditions associated with food have survived surprisingly strongly into the present day, despite the obvious killer, progress. Like the Sunday rice-pudding which most Welsh housewives make as well as another dessert, seldom realising that they are carrying on a Welsh tradition, and the *cawl* which appears as a matter of course for school dinners in Wales.

With the passing of the ancient fires on the floor and the old, neat, coal grates which replaced the open hearths and were such a feature of the little miners' terrace houses in the Valleys, have gone the old ways with food. Conditions dictate cookery methods and it is not easy (in some cases impossible) to reproduce the old dishes on modern gas or even solid fuel cookers.

Cooking in those primitive conditions in Wales must have required great skill and involved back-breaking work. When I've talked to Welsh people about the old cookery the men have recalled it with relish, but their women have said very little, their silence more revealing than words.

Mati Thomas's description of farm life in the 1870's gives us a clear picture of conditions then for women:

'Cleanliness was of prime importance in the preparation of food, the kneading bowl, basins, plates and spoons, which were of wood, were as white as ivory. . . the brass and copper pans were polished to mirror perfection. The wooden pails had their bands polished like silver. . . The only method of heating was an open grate, and the fuel would be peat, wood, fern or even cattle manure. They were not aware of the existence of coal, except in the areas where this was found' (notably along the coasts of south Pembrokeshire and Carmarthenshire). 'Oil and gas stoves did not exist in any form. Taking into consideration all the handicaps associated with the preparation of food in the olden days the meals were very appetising. Every girl in those days could bake oatmeal bread, make puddings from shelled oats, and could prepare porridge.'

Another fuel, which Mati does not mention, was culm – a mixture of anthracite dust and shattered coal with clay, made into briquettes. It was exported from Hook, Saundersfoot and possibly Nolton Haven, in south Pembrokeshire, where there were small, near-surface mines.

One of the skills possessed by earlier Welsh cooks which has most impressed me was their management of fuel in conditions when the kind of fuel and its successful control, and not the stove, governed the cooking and was responsible for its style. Many of the old dishes are difficult if not impossible to achieve today, for we are in a sense disadvantaged by fuels which leap obediently to the turn of a knob. How can a cook with these fuels be galvanised into a morning's baking because the wind's just right for the stove, when every day the gas or electric cooker registers the same exact temperatures? And never, ever, goes down low enough to enable a pot to be left to look after itself with any safety?

The line 'and the gorse blazing gaily beneath it' in the poem about *cawl* is not just poetic fancy, but fact. The area the poet is writing about, the wild, windswept moor behind the rock-bitten coast of Pencaer, by Strumble Head, is a mass of gorse, a glory of yellow bloom all summer long and providing plenty of serviceable fuel supply: gorse burns with a hot, clear flame, much valued by the cook for certain kinds of cooking. Peat and culm provided slow, banked heat for long cooking, when the pot had to be left all day, while good, steady-glowing peat or coals were best for the bakestone.

Welsh foodstuffs and their history

If we look at the ways in which the Celts grew and dealt with their crops and livestock, we can trace the development of the Welsh style of eating from its very beginning, through Roman and medieval times to the Industrial Revolution and the present day.

1. Cereals By the time of the early Celtic Iron Age, spelt (obtainable from Dove's Farm organic producers), clubwheat (mutants of earlier varieties found in their wild form in areas of Asia Minor) and barley were the foremost cereals. During the Bronze Age barley became the major cereal. Primitive grinding by hand produced a harsh, hard, branny bread baked on the hearthstone: sometimes fat or honey would be employed to hold the coarse dough together.

The idea of oven-baked bread began when the Celts inverted their clay domes over the dough on the hearthstone, thus enclosing the warmth from the stone and keeping some of the steam inside the small bun-like loaf, resulting in a slight rise in the bread. This method survives in Welsh bakestone breads, and in the use of the pot-oven, to this day.

The next stage in Celtic breadmaking was to introduce fermentation – the Celts of Spain and Gaul had learned how to encourage fermentation by adding beer barm to their dough, producing a lighter bread than that of the Greeks and Romans, and it is entirely reasonable to suppose that the British Celts did likewise.

By Roman times, the distinction between brown and white bread was being made; thenceforth white bread has always been considered superior, in earliest times served solely for consumption by the rich and noble – as a mark of distinction. In Wales, when the *ffwrn fach* (pot-oven – see p.94) was employed, according to Mati Thomas, it was almost always used to bake white bread. When eventually the greatest proportion of the Welsh were driven into the uplands, where barley, oats and rye were the foremost crops, the distinction between brown and white bread tended to be more pronounced in Wales than England.[2]

The barley-bread tradition was strongly established in Wales during the Middle Ages, and continued to the end of the 18th century. Rye bread was also made but was not liked; according to Mati Thomas it was eaten solely for its medicinal value. Wheaten bread was little known, even amongst the gentry in some parts of Wales until the end of the 18th century, and even when it had become more common, there were still areas, such as Cardiganshire, where it was little known.

By the end of the 17th century spiced fruit cakes were being baked on the bakestone, and also pitchy bread (*bara pyglyd*), bread cakes of a leavened batter of flour and milk. These became popular in the west Midlands, where their Welsh name was corrupted to pikelets.[3] The recipes for these appear regularly in Welsh collections, almost always under their corrupted name, thus unfortunately giving little clue to their Welsh origin.

Pottage, the earliest-made dish of meat, herbs (i.e. green vegetables), bulked with some kind of cereal and cooked together with water in one pot over heat to produce in all its variations a semi-liquid spoonmeat, had by the medieval period divided into pottages containing meat and vegetables as well as cereal, and those composed entirely of cereal, i.e. porridge. In Wales either oats or barley went into the porridge, which was capable of endless variations (see p.230). At its simplest it was merely oatmeal and water, but was sometimes flavoured – in Wales with leeks rather than onions as the former grew more easily, in the Welsh climate.

The Welsh were to develop pottages without cereal bulking, as a true meat and vegetable broth, because of the poor supply of grain in upland Wales.

Llymru was another Welsh oatmeal dish – fine oatmeal steeped in water for a long time, the liquor strained off and boiled while being continuously stirred until it was almost solid, something

---

2. C.Anne Wilson: *Food and Drink in Britain*, p.231.
3. C.Anne Wilson: *Food and Drink in Britain*, p.239.

like the modern blancmange. A coarser version, *sucan*, was made with the soaked husks and leavings from oats that had been ground, the upper layer being skimmed off for *llymru*. *Llymru* was considered a wholesome and nourishing dish of the highest order and was eaten with milk or honey or beer; with wine by the gentry, for as flummery it spread from Wales into Cheshire and Lancashire and eventually throughout Britain. In the late 17th century the name had been extended to cover a form of sweet jelly flavoured with cream or ground almonds, a popular dessert for entertainments and far removed from the dish of simple sustenance originally devised by the Welsh in the crude conditions of a cottage kitchen, which in later cookery books was distinguished from the elegant party confections as 'oatmeal flummery'.

But *sucan* was often intensely disliked because it provided immediate filling but little sustenance. In north Pembrokeshire and south Cardiganshire it was called *uwd* or *uwd sucan*; James Williams remembers from his border farm a few miles from Cardigan:

> *Uwd* was the cooked juice of strained oatmeal. . . [it] was taken out to the haggard and the fields in huge tin milk dishes, in which it had set into a quivering brown blancmange. Everybody helped themselves to it, using wooden spoons and basins, adding to it either beer or cool fresh milk from the dairy. To supplement it, there were stacks of home-made bread well-spread with salted butter. This was a most sensible midday repast, for the men and women were back at work within a quarter of an hour, a valuable saving of time when most harvests were not safely gathered in till dark.

The special stick for making *llymru* in Wales varied in size and shape and had many different names according to region: *myndl* in Montgomeryshire; *mopran* or *pren llymru* in Caernarfonshire, and *wtffon* or *rhwtffon* in Merionethshire.[4]

Some Welsh recipes, for *llymru*, such as that from *Lloyd George's Favourite Dishes*, specify soaking the meal in a mixture of buttermilk and water:

---

4. S.Minwel Tibbott: *Welsh Fare*, p.53.

'2 lbs oatmeal
buttermilk and water

Mix oatmeal with sufficient buttermilk and water to make a liquid
consistency. Leave for two nights. Afterwards rinse through a hair
sieve, let it stand and pour off the surface water. Simmer in a brass or
enamel saucepan for 40 minutes and keep stirring. Serve with sweet
milk and salt.'

2. Milk, cheese and butter Celtic wealth was measured in
cattle up to and throughout the medieval period, thus butter
and cheese made from cows' milk was more usual in Wales,
although there is plenty of evidence of the use and value
attributed to ewes' and goats' milk. In Wales the custom of
wintering cattle on the stubble and fallow fields around the
village and farm, and taking them up at sowing-time into high
summer hill pastures (*hafod*) had been established possibly well
before the Roman conquest, and although not exclusive to Wales,
the practice of transhumance played a more enduring and
important part in Welsh rural life than elsewhere, as was well
attested in the *Laws of Hywel Dda*.

It was at the *hafod*, or smaller hill-farm, that the butter and
cheese were made, the butter churns being devised to be the
right size to take oatcakes as made in the kitchen of the lower
farm (*hendref*) for delivery at the *hafod*, where they would be used
to return the newly-churned butter. This custom continued in
Wales until well after the end of the 18th century.[5] (My mother,
incidentally, who was born at the turn of the century, came from
a north Wales family with upper and lower farms.) A lot of the
hardship in rural Wales was brought by the rapacious activities
of the Welsh squires and the collapse of the lesser Welsh gentry
in the late 18th century, which forced the farming folk out of
their lower farms to live year-round in the *hafod*, which was ill-
equipped for winter habitation nor able to support the family
with all its needs.

Butter-making was almost certainly introduced to Britain by
the Celts, who understood churn-making and what happened

---

5. C.Anne Wilson: *Food and Drink in Britain*, p.140.

when milk was agitated.[6] They also knew how to produce salt. Butter was the earliest substance which could be employed as a spread to make the early crude breads more palatable. After the Roman withdrawal and the drastic reduction in olive oil supplies, butter became the prime cooking medium in Britain ('boil in butter', was the injunction) and for hundreds of years to come served as almost the only sauce for vegetables and pulses (see Recipe, One, Teifi Salmon Sauce).

By the early medieval period salt was a customary constituent of cheese-making in Wales, an advance on the earliest methods of soured milk cheese. The *Laws of Hywel Dda* reveal that Welsh cheese spent some time in a brine solution: when arranging a divorce 'to the wife belong the meat in the brine, and the cheese in the brine; and after they are hung up they belong to the husband; to the wife belong the vessels of the butter in cut, the meat in cut and the cheese in cut. . .'

The Welsh had an early passion for roasted, or toasted, cheese – *caws pobi* (*caws* cheese, *pobi* roasted), the forerunner of what became known eventually as Welsh Rarebit. From medieval times there are numerous references to it, and by Tudor times it had become something of a national dish. References to Welsh efforts to trade for the hard cheeses, especially of Cheddar, they coveted for roasting, confirm that the acidity of the soil in such a large part of Wales produced milk more suited to making soft cheeses of whole, or at least only semi-skimmed milk matured for a short time; though this is not to say that hard, well-matured, less rich cheeses were not made in some places. The poem in dialect by Dewi Emrys contains the line (in translation) '. . . and a hunk of a fine old cheese', yet the soil in that part of west Wales is notoriously acid – hence the proliferation of lime kilns along that coast. But perhaps the cheese was made from ewes' milk, always specified as an alternative to Cheddar for *caws pobi* because of its sharp-flavoured hardness.

Nevertheless, Welsh skim-milk cheese never achieved the open notoriety of the ill-famed skim-milk cheese of Essex and Suffolk, fit only for feeding labourers and the poor, though in

6. C.Anne Wilson: *Food and Drink in Britain*, p.140.

late medieval times Thomas Tusser listed cheese 'full of hairs' as faulty: said to be a failing of Welsh and Scottish cheese.

The Welsh weakness for *caws pobi* was recorded in Henry Tudor's reign by Andrew Boorde, in his *First Boke of the Introduction of Knowledge*, 1547, 'I am a Welshman, I do love *cause boby*(sic), good roasted cheese'. But Boorde himself was not Welsh – he was born at Cuckfield in Sussex. However, with a Welsh king on the throne of England, there had been a considerable invasion of the English Court by Welshmen, not always too popular, as indicated by the famous tale of St Peter tricking the Welshmen out of Heaven, amongst the *Merrie Tales of The Wise Men of Gotham* recorded by Boorde:

> Fynde wryten amonge olde jestes how God made St Peter porter of heven. And that God of his goodness suffred many men to come to the kyngdome with small deservyng. At which tyme, there was in heven a grete company of Welchmen which with they rekrakynge and babelynge trobelyd all the others. Wherefore God says to St Peter that he was wery of them and he would fayne have them out of heven. To whome St Peter sayde, 'Good Lorde, I warrent you that shall be shortly done'. Wherefore St Peter went outside of heven gayts and cryd with a loud voyce, 'Cause Babe! Cause Babe', that is as moche as to say 'Rosty'd chese!' Which thynge the Welchmen herying ran out of heven a grete pace. . . And when St Peter sawe them all out he sodenly went into Heven and lokkyd the dore! and so aparyd all the Welchmen out!

In the mountainous parts of Wales, skimmed ewes' and goats' milk cheeses continued to be made from the 17th century through the 18th century. In the Vale of Glamorgan fat ewes' milk was added to skimmed cows' milk for cheese. In 1662 Welsh cheese was described as 'very tender and palatable' and the dairy farmers of the Vale of Glamorgan exported cheese to Bristol and other Somerset ports. Dairies in north Wales supplemented the Cheshire cheese actually made in that county with a facsimile cheese of their own production, which they sent to Chester in large quantities to help meet the demand for this economical cooking cheese.[7]

The border counties of Wales were supplying the English gentry with cattle as early as the 14th century, and from the end of the 17th century the drovers' routes from west and mid-Wales

---

7. T.Fuller:*English Worthies*, quoted in *Food and Drink in Britain*, p.161.

to the markets of the Midlands, the North and London were well established.[8] A logical outcome of the droving of large numbers of cattle, sheep and sometimes geese (the animals were shod with metal shoes and the geese's feet with tar and fine sand) to the main English markets, was that some drovers seized upon the opportunity to set up in London in the fast-growing business of selling milk from dairy shops from cows kept within the city, now grown too large to be supplied with fresh milk from the surrounding countryside.

In time the Welsh dairymen, mostly from west Wales (70% were from Cardiganshire) dominated the London dairy trade until about 45 years ago, when the big amalgamations took place. What had begun as an opportunity for a drover to set up in business for himself was later to provide an escape from rural poverty, particularly in the 1930's, for Welsh relatives back home – for the little dairy businesses were handed down from generation to generation.

The coming of the railways attracted a large contingent of Welsh dairymen to the Paddington district to deal with the bulk milk supplies as they arrived from Wales.

None of the Welsh dairymen were represented by the taking-over dairy giants; they had all been in quite a small way of business, with just four or five cows providing a bare living. But when the mergers came it was these small dairymen who formed the nucleus of the workforce of the big dairies.

As always, links with home in rural Wales were tenaciously maintained, many London-Welsh retaining their language of home. . . a friend reports a lady in Blackfriars as speaking English with a pure south London accent, and Welsh in the true lilt peculiar to Tregaron.

Salting plentiful summer-butter well to ensure it kept throughout the winter was customary throughout Britain, but perhaps because the Welsh had learned about acquiring salt very early on through their early Celtic ancestors, and had a good

---

8. Prof.Caroline Skeel, M.A., D.Litt.:*The Cattle Trade Between Wales and England from the 15th-19th Centuries.*

source of home-produced salt (by the end of the 17th century the practice of making 'salt upon salt' by boiling either brine from the springs of Worcestershire and Cheshire, or Nantwich rock-salt brine, with seawater in the river mouths of north Wales was well established),[9] they salted their butter to a degree that now takes some acceptance by palates accustomed to the blander butters of England and new Zealand – for the saltiness of Welsh butter has persisted to the present day in brands like *Shir Gâr* and *Ymenyn Cymru* and is one of the reasons for the unfortunate prevalence of heart-disease in Wales.

Most Welsh butter made only short journeys to market, though Glamorgan butter was shipped across the Bristol channel. Butter's importance to the poor was immense; they ate it as they had always done, as a relish upon bread, and as long as fasting days were kept, butter was eaten with salt fish.[10] The fact that butter was such a commonplace in 17th- and 18th-century diet may account for the Welsh custom of drenching pancakes with butter. In the houses of the rich the liberal buttering of practically all food was reflected in their stylish cookery in what was literally the golden age of butter in English cookery, and to which we owe the classic English melted-butter sauce we treasure still.[11]

Buttermilk was a much loved and valued drink in Wales; from what Welsh people have said to me and I have read, it seems to me more so than in England at least. Above all, its healthful quality was recognised. When I wanted to talk to Welsh country people about the old foods I found my best passport was a bottle of proper buttermilk from a farm churning of butter, for it both let me in and opened up the memories.

3. Poultry and eggs   In early medieval times geese and hens were already important in Wales, and subject to several laws in Hywel Dda's codification which acknowledged their different temperaments: geese could be summarily executed if found

---

9. C.Anne Wilson: *Food and Drink in Britain*, p.48.
10. C.Anne Wilson: *Food and Drink in Britain*, p.48.
11. C.Anne Wilson: *Food and Drink in Britain*, p.166.

damaging standing corn, or corn in barns, but hens, if discovered in a flax garden or barn were to be restored to their owner on payment of no more than an egg.

Goose-feather beds are ineradicably associated with memories of hilltop Welsh farms: the larger feathers were employed in the kitchen – the wing-pinion for sweeping the hearth, and the smaller wing feathers for brushing flour or oatmeal during baking.

Dovecotes formed part of the medieval castle in Wales; the idea was brought by the Romans, who also introduced hens, guinea fowl, pheasants, partridges and peacocks to Britain. Wild pigeons, simply roasted, are still a part of Welsh country people's diet. Wild pigeons (*colomennod*) were trapped and later shot for the pot. In medieval times small wild birds were roasted in the street on Anglesey, and the catching of starlings (*drudwen*) when they were boys, is recalled by men now in their 70's – not for food, for the sport. But geese were already being kept by the Celts before the Romans came, probably the greylag variety, still our main domestic goose.[12] Goose remains popular in Wales as a festive bird, though there is now nothing especially Welsh in the way it is cooked.

There are no indications that the use of eggs in cooking developed along any special lines in Wales, but the absence of egg-dishes in the traditional recipes and the popularity of pancakes suggests that they were customarily stretched to go a long way, because they were seldom available in abundant supply, at least not to the household, since eggs were marketable.

4. Meat By tradition, Welsh society is essentially a pastoral one, its development linked to animal-husbandry rather than cereal cultivation. A semi-nomadic people of early times with strong tribal customs were not persuaded to settle into homesteads until the 11th century, when the Welsh princes introduced them to the laws of inheritance.

The early Celtic tribesmen of Wales counted their wealth in

---

12. C.Anne Wilson: *Food and Drink in Britain*, p.105.

cattle, the most valuable being the white beasts with red or black ears mentioned in the *Laws of Hywel Dda*. But for eating, their enduring preoccupation was with the pig, which they had learned to preserve in salt during the early Iron Age, when salt workings were established around the British coast. The pig was the most popular salting animal as it took less salt than any other meat and moreover stayed more succulent. Even the humblest peasant could usually manage to keep a few pigs and be able to kill at least one a year.

The Romans, too, were fond of pork and soon pigs in Britain were being penned and fattened on grain to supply the Roman armies: at the great legionary fortress at Caerleon, pork was second only to beef in the soldiers' diet.[13]

In the early Dark-Age settlement of Dinas Powys in Glamorgan pigs are calculated to have accounted for 61% of all the meats eaten there.[14]

The *Laws of Hywel Dda* pay the expected attention to pigs – a foodgift from a Welsh township to the King included a sow 'of three winters three fingers thick'. Penalties are listed of instant death for pigs found in woods and spoiling the cornfields, and their value, which was high: 'the three animals of equal worth in the herd at all times' (i.e. thirty pence each) were a herd boar, the principal swine of a herd, and a sow marked for the King's *gwestfa* (entertainment due paid by the freeman to the King twice a year). The *Laws* also make reference to the feast of St John of the Swine (*Gwyl Ieuan y Moch*) on 29 August, occurring during the period when the acorns begin to fall in the woods.

As always in these early times, geography dictated diet; gradually as more open country emerged from deforestation more sheep and goats were kept, and with so much of Wales an upland area suitable for little else but sheep and goat-grazing, these two animals soon became closely associated with native Welsh food. Goat-keeping for milk and flesh, especially of the kids, went on much longer in Wales, with goat hams becoming

---

13. C.Anne Wilson: *Food and Drink in Britain*, p.66.
14. C.Anne Wilson: *Food and Drink in Britain*, p.71.

known as 'hung venison'.[15] Mutton hams were also treated in the same way. Wild cattle and bears survived longer in Wales (and Scotland) in the remote forests, but by late medieval times native bear-meat was no longer available. The *Laws of Hywel Dda* regulated the hunting of wild animals in medieval Wales.

Celtic cooks learned how to prepare meats by potboiling with hot stones, sometimes followed by a roasting within a dome of red-hot stones, but the introduction of metal cauldrons was not only to revolutionise Celtic cookery but remain a basic method of cooking in Celtic regions almost to the present day. The Romans introduced the mass-produced round-bellied iron cooking-pot to Britain, and in the late Roman era British smiths hit on the idea of combining the principle of the tripod with the round-bellied pot and created the three-legged cauldron. But in Wales the earlier principle of suspending the iron pot from chains above the fire endured just as long, and a few fireplaces with a crane-controlled suspension for the pot remain in use in the present day.

The *Laws of Hywel Dda* recognised the cauldron's importance in that the Court smith was not expected to make the Royal cauldron without proper payment, although he did other smithy work purely for his keep.

In Elizabeth's reign Welsh mutton was already a preferred favourite, along with that of Norfolk and Wiltshire. Thomas Moufet, a physician of the time, is explicit: 'The best mutton is not above four years old, or rather not much above three; that which is taken from a short, hilly and dry feeding is more sweet, short and wholesome than that which is either fed on rank grounds or with pease-straw (as we perceive by the taste); great, fat and rank fed sheep, such as Somersetshire and Lincolnshire sendeth up to London, are nothing so short and pleasant in eating as the Norfolk, Wiltshire and Welch mutton; which being very young, are best roasted; the elder sort not so ill being sudden (boiled) with bugloss, borage and parsley roots.'

The inferior Somerset sheep were fortunate for the Welsh who drove their superior breed to Bath, to barter for the hard Cheddar

15. C.Anne Wilson: *Food and Drink in Britain*, p.31

cheese they coveted for their *caws pobi*. The most prized breed today is still the small Welsh Mountain Sheep, sought after in Europe as well as Britain, strongly marketed by one of the new such schemes, in this case 'Welsh Lamb Enterprise'.

The long-standing export trade in surplus cattle between Wales and England had its roots in the supply of cattle to Court and Church in the early 14th century (in 1312 the King required 700 oxen from the Chamberlains of Carmarthen and north Wales, and in 1317 the Bishop of Winchester bought fat cattle for the household of the Chancery). By the 15th century Welsh cattle were provisioning the English army in France, and the droving industry was an established factor in the Welsh economy. The trade was mainly in store cattle – lean animals to be fattened on the rich pastures of the English Midlands, Essex and Kent.

The Civil War nearly put a stop to droving in the mid 17th century, but a special decree in 1645 gave the drovers free passage along their special routes, which by the 18th century were being chosen to avoid the ruinous toll-gates. Anglesey cattle had to swim the often turbulent Menai straits, and some went by boat across the Bristol channel from Tenby and Cardiff or across the Severn river to Bristol. The colour of the cattle varied, the most famous being the Welsh Black, a breed now increasingly seen again in Wales. Herds of three to four thousand were commonplace as drovers from different areas joined up at regular meeting-places. Cobbett reported meeting 2,000 cattle from Pembrokeshire between Cirencester and Cricklade en route for fairs in Sussex.[16]

5. Fish and shellfish Early man in Wales found fish and shellfish of all kinds a useful not to say essential item of diet, once they devised the means of catching and collecting them. Wales' long coastline and many fast-flowing rivers ensured a plentiful supply of both freshwater and sea fish, and the predominantly rocky shores were a natural resort for lobsters and crabs.

---

16. Prof.Caroline Skeel, MA, DLitt: *The Cattle Trade Between Wales & England from the 15th-19th Centuries.*

The early methods of catching fish have survived particularly strongly in Wales – ways of fishing that have remained virtually unchanged for 2,000 years may still readily be seen, though it seems unlikely that they can persist much longer. . . already there is only one wade-net fisherman left, catching salmon by this method in the estuary of the river Tâf at Laugharne.

At low tide, lines of horn-shaped basket-work putcher weirs for catching salmon extending into the Severn estuary can just be seen from the suspension bridge, maintaining an idea developed in prehistoric times. The fish are trapped in them when the waters are full; when they recede, their keepers go out to claim the fish.

Caesar and Pliny wrote about the strange Welsh coracles; frail, almost circular craft of skin stretched over a willow frame, and though their once widespread use throughout Wales has now diminished, their descendants can still be seen on three Welsh rivers – all in Dyfed – the Teifi, the Tywi and the Tâf. Coracles fish in pairs, the two oarsmen holding a trawl net between them while with the other hand they skilfully keep their fragile craft steady in the strong currents and eddies. They are so successful that they are subject now to severe licensing restrictions in the interests of those who fish with rod and line.[17]

Fishing weirs of stone and wattle for catching salmon on the Conwy and other Welsh rivers were referred to in the *Laws of Hywel Dda*, as was the netting of fish, particularly salmon and sewin. The tradition of seine-netting is still carried out in the estuaries of the Teifi, Tywi, Nevern, Conwy and Dee, and these may have been the nets whose use in rivers was governed by the *Laws* and valued at twenty-four pence for a salmon net, sixteen pence for a grayling net and twelve pence for a sewin net. In the *Laws* a coracle was valued at eight pence. However, there is still an ancient fixed basket trap for salmon and sewin, working on the putcher-principle, in the river Conwy in north Wales. It is privately-owned and used twice a year only.

Improvements in the water quality of the erstwhile heavily

---

17. J.Geraint Jenkins gives very detailed descriptions of these old fishing methods in *Life and Traditions in Rural Wales*.

industrially-polluted rivers Taff and Afon in south Wales, the former flowing down the one-time coal valley from Merthyr Tydfil to exit at Cardiff, the latter joining the sea at Port Talbot, has led to salmon and sewin entering their waters once more. Here the Welsh Rivers Authority have intervened to circumvent the obstacles to the fish reaching their spawning grounds, raised in the past when all hope of these fish entering the rivers' murky waters ever again seemed gone – by building fish ladders up the weirs. The development of the hydro-electric scheme and its dam on the river Rheidol near Aberystwyth led to the provision of a fish ladder to help the fish up the waterfall, and a fish lift on the dam itself. A fish ladder bypasses the dam and consists of a series of pools and steps cut in to the rock at the side of the dam which the fish can easily jump and thus reach their spawning grounds in the higher waters. In the same way as a canal lock works, the 'Borland' fish lift here takes the fish to the top of the dam, automatically releasing them over the weir every four hours.

Preserving fish by wind-drying and smoking were early processes of preserving fish in glut, but it was with the availability of salt that herring fishing acquired its importance, which was to continue in Wales until the end of the 19th century.

Fish and shellfish were fashionable eating in Roman Wales, but lost their popularity after the Romans left. This situation did not change until Roman Catholicism came to Britain with the conversion of the Saxons to Christianity. But the Celtic church was a much older Christian influence and this early Christian teaching disapproved of sea fish because of their connection with the pagan goddess, Venus. Eventually the Roman practice prevailed and Wales along with the rest of Britain complied with the rule of fish-eating on Fridays.

By the Norman conquest, herring fishing was well established, not as an industry but as a part-time inshore occupation contributing to the self-sufficiency of rural communities, a characteristic of Welsh rural life until comparatively recently. Some off-shore fishing took place in the Autumn, but probably the only port to have a properly developed herring industry in the Middle Ages was Aberystwyth on Cardigan Bay. In 1206 the *Chronicle of the Princes* (*Brut y Tywysgion*) described the situation as: 'God provided more fish at Aberystwyth than ever before'.

Aberystwyth remained the busiest fishing harbour in Wales until the end of the 19th century. In his *New Description of Wales*, 1724, Herman Moll gives a clear picture '. . . the Herring Fishery here is so exceedingly abundant that a thousand barrels have been taken in one night. . . In addition to Herrings, they have such an abundance of Cod, Pollack, Whiting, Common Whiting, Ray and other fish that they set but little value on them. Bottlenoses (whales) and porpoises sometimes run on shore in shoals and blue sharks are frequently caught upon the coast, from all of which they make considerable quantities of Oil'.

The other Cardigan Bay ports – New Quay, Aberaeron, Aberporth, Fishguard and Cardigan – continued in importance as fishing ports until the coming of the railways. Many are still in use today for small-scale inshore fishing and lobster-catching, which has developed tremendously in recent times.

The 16th century was the era of the great herring fishing explosion all along the Welsh coast except the south. Swansea and Cardiff did not develop as important fishing ports until the late 18th century, when the great herring shoals in Cardigan Bay were declining. Later still, Milford Haven's deep-sea trawling industry based on rail communications developed.

George Owen described the coast of his native Pembrokeshire in 1603 'as if it were enclosed in with a hedge of herrings', while Tenby's Welsh name, *Dinbych y Pysgod* (Denbigh of the Fish) indicates its importance as a fishing port. Nefyn on the Llŷn peninsula, Caernarfon and Hoylake were important north Wales fishing ports, but nowhere in Wales was the industry ever as important as along Cardigan Bay. Yet everywhere it remained essentially a seasonal activity of the Autumn months, when the herring catch was at its best and men could be spared from their agricultural activities to become temporary fishermen, netting the fat herring in small open boats.

Whales which were grounded on the shores were a welcome windfall in prehistoric times, but came to be classed as Crown property by Welsh as well as English Law, although the bulk of the carcase was usually granted to the tenant upon whose shore it had been beached. The exception was the tongue, a great

41

delicacy, and sometimes the whole head. Whale meat was preserved by drying and smoking and later salting, and eaten for Lent. The whale was also a useful source of oil.

Welsh rivers are fast-flowing and this discourages their inhabitance by coarse fish like perch, pike, roach, carp, except in short reaches where the rivers stretch themselves lazily before gathering momentum for a last dash to the sea (as with the Usk between Abergavenny and Usk, and the Wye between Newtown and Welshpool). These same fish could of course be obtained from the slack waters of moats, canals and pools, but on a scale too limited to have created a tradition of cookery methods – on the whole they were simply fried.

So, along with mackerel and herring from the sea, the trout, salmon and sewin characteristic of fast-flowing rivers were the five fish which were a regular feature of the Welsh table.

Although the quality of Cardigan Bay lobsters, until recently much admired by French restaurateurs to the tune of £75,000 per annum, was reported by George Owen, in his description of Pembrokeshire in 1603, as 'very sweete and delicate meets and plentie taken', lobster catching on a large scale was not then a feature of Welsh seaboard life. The demand in the '60's and '70's all but had the lobsters fished-out, until drastic conservation and re-stocking measures were undertaken as part of general measures to protect the Cardigan Bay fishing industry. The Welsh fisherman traditionally prefers to eat crab, and lobsters were obtained for their local saleability. But on Bardsey Island and along the Llŷn coast both lobster and crab had been fished with a willow pot of local design for centuries and regularly exported to Liverpool. In all other parts of the Welsh coast small-scale lobster fishing was much a matter of keeping the local *plas* and coastal hotels supplied.

Cockles were popular with the Romans in Wales – excavated sites have revealed vast quantities of their shells – and they remained a common food for coastal dwellers throughout the centuries. They are still of some importance in Carmarthen Bay. For although the former beds at Laugharne, Llanstephan and Ferryside are now unpredictable, there is still an appreciable and growing cockle industry on the windswept Llanrhidian sands along the Burry Inlet, with another purpose-built cockle-shed on an industrial estate – a co-operative of five – about to come on stream. The activity is no longer centred on the village of Pen-clawdd as it was of old, but has spread to Crofty and to the tip of the Whiteford Burrows. The old laverbread place and its adjacent cockle shed in Pen-clawdd are now derelict. (With the wide sands behind them they always put me in mind of Peggotty's curious little dwelling on the shingle shore in 'David Copperfield' – but the shingle here is actually millions of discarded cockle shells.) No matter which part of the north Gower peninsula they come from, the cockles are collectively known as 'Pen-clawdd cockles'. The industry has survived everything EU regulations have thrown at it, though the high cost of complying with draconian hygiene regulations for what was a simple cottage industry has been punitive.

The cockles are boiled and shelled in sheds which may also process laverweed for sale in the shops and markets of south and south-west Wales, and for export, frozen or canned.

The Pen-clawdd women may only gather cockles in the old, traditional way, using no other equipment than a hand rake (*cram*), scraper (*scrap*), and a riddle which regulates the size of the cockles for collection – and they must be licensed.

These same women also gather mussels, usually by scraping with a knife.

Winkles and limpets were another source of free food for coastal dwellers, although it would take a long time and much effort to prise them off the rocks and collect enough of the latter to provide sufficient for a family meal. Winkles were brought to the boil in salt water, but limpets were often tossed in oatmeal and fried in bacon fat after boiling (the addition of nettle tips was advised to help tenderise the limpets) or fried in bacon fat and served with eggs and sliced onions, or put into a pie.

Winkles often had eggs scrambled into them, as did cockles (see pp 85-6). Custom prevented the eating of both these shellfish except in months with an 'r' in them.

There are also records of the collection of sand-eels, which were fried in bacon fat and eaten for the mid-day meal or for supper. Eels and congers were caught on the Caldicot Levels in the Severn estuary.

In the mid-19th century the oyster fishing industry of Mumbles and Port Einon on Gower was at its height. These notably large oysters obtained off the peninsula had been procured from Roman times, but like lobsters, the trade was essentially a livelihood and the catch was not commonly for local consumption. But the shells were employed as a primitive and not very efficient oil lamp before manufactured oil lamps came into general use in Wales in the last quarter of the 19th century.

6. Fruit, flowers and vegetables The progression from the consumption of wild fruits and berries to the cultivated variety began with the Romans, who introduced so many revolutionary eating habits into early Britain. By early-medieval times the practice of enclosing hazel groves and setting a value on wild fruiting trees was already established – the *Laws of Hywel Dda* valued a hazel grove at twenty-four pence and a crab apple tree at four pence – thirty pence when it had fruited, which suggests some system of ownership similar to that of the Irish Brehon laws. But in the Celtic west orchards and gardens were rare, except in lowland areas. Wild woodland fruits and nuts were usual fare, and it is thought that the Norman system of planting cherry, apple, pear, plum, quince and medlar trees on the edge of woodlands so the peasants could easily get at their fruits, while the open-field system of cultivation was in operation, was established in both Saxon England and Celtic Wales well before the Norman Conquest. It is due to this system that semi-wild fruit trees were so frequently found in the boundary hedges of later pasture or tillage. Welsh country reminiscences are full of references to plum, cherry, damson and medlar growing wild in the hedges.

The Welsh laws also saw to the protection of cabbages, leeks and other garden produce by decreeing that they should be fenced-in against wandering cattle. Since leeks and cabbages are the only two green vegetables specifically mentioned in the Welsh laws it would seem as though these were the only two to be cultivated, although there would be no limit to the use of wild plants. And it was at this stage that the garden leek was established in Wales as the commonest of all the onion types then in cultivation.

By later medieval times the feasts consumed in Welsh castles reflected the more sophisticated cookery which had departed with the Romans and been reintroduced by the Normans, and the increased variety of foods and culinary ideas. New varieties of fruits, imported dried fruits and nuts (most notably almonds, which were to play such a prominant role as a thickener in high-class British cookery for so long), were absorbed into the native diet.

Apart from the 'causs boby' (*caws pobi* is the later and correct spelling) this menu devised for an early 15th -century banquet in Pembroke castle given by the powerful Earl Marshal is typical of the feast of that late medieval period:

	Ballock broth	Caudle ferry	
Lampreys en galentine	Oysters in civey		Eels in sorré
	Baked trout		
Brawn with mustard	Numbles of a hart		Pigs y-farsed
	Cockyntryce		
Goose in hogepotte	Venison en frumenty		Hens in brewet
	Squirrels roasted		
Haggis of sheep	Pudding de capon-neck		Garbage
Trype de mouton	Blaundesorye		
Caboges	Buttered worts		
Apple muse	Gingerbread		Tart de fruit
	Quinces in comfit		
Essex cheese	Stilton cheese		
	Causs boby		
Ale, old	Port	Claret	Metheglyn
Ale, new	Clarée	Hock	Perreye
Mead	Sack	Beer	Hippocras
		Uisce Betha	

from Mediaeval Pageant *by John R Reinhard.*

Potatoes were not to become a staple of the ordinary people of Wales until the first half of the 18th century, and their popularity even then was only gained at the expense of grain crop failures. It was not until the second half of the century that they lost their curiosity and monetary value and became a field rather than a garden crop.[18]

In *Adam's Luxury And Eve's Cookery*, 1744, the Welsh are noted for 'baking potatoes with herrings, mixed with layers of pepper, vinegar, salt, sweet herbs and water' – the origin of the dish known throughout Wales as *Swper Sgadan* (herrings for supper) with the later addition of apple and cider sometimes substituting for vinegar.

The same book also describes the Welsh mutton and potato dish: 'they cut mutton slices, and lay them in a pan, and on them potatoes and spices, then another layer of all the same with half a pint of water; this they stew, covering all with cloths around the stewpan, and account it excellent'.

There is also a reference to the practice of boiling potatoes first, 'before laying them in the dripping pan under roasting meat', which also became a commonplace in Wales (see Recipe, Six).

Potatoes were absorbed into everyday diet, being added to *cawl*, the meat and vegetable broth of Wales, which in the harder times formed a meal in themselves, after acquiring some nourishment from being boiled in the bacon or mutton liquor of the previous day's *cawl*. This was known as *cawl eildwym* – second *cawl*. New potatoes were especially liked in the westernmost part of Wales, where the early potato industry was to become a major agricultural activity along the mild-climate coast of that region, which rivals Cornwall for its early Springs, to the extent that the race to capture the first of the market for early potatoes is in present times a fierce annual contest between the two areas.

Until as recently as 1939, and in some areas even later, the Welsh cottager continued the tradition established by the end of the 19th century, which allowed him to plant rows of potatoes in a neighbouring farmer's field, to enable him to feed his family and the pigs and hens he kept at the bottom of his garden. In return, he would give the farmer his labour in the harvest field. The system worked well for both parties: the usual number

---

18. C.Anne Wilson: *Food and Drink in Britain*, pp.197-9.

of rows of potatoes required by the cottager was between two and five; for each row of eighty yards the work required exactly matched the farmer's labour requirements in the harvest field.

In the hill farm areas, where kitchen gardens were, and still are, rare, the farmer often planted peas and beans and carrots in rows in his potato or swede field in the belief that they did better there – Mati Thomas mentions the practice with broad beans.

Flowers played a part in cookery in Wales, as elsewhere, as a source of flavour and colour before the arrival of chemical agents. Marigolds, violets, roses, tansies and elderflowers were the most commonly used: marigolds for their pungent flavour (in Wales they floated the flower-heads on top of the *cawl*) and their yellow colour (a few marigold petals would effectively colour a custard or a cheese or second-grade butter); violets went into creams and puddings to impart both flavour and colour (see Recipe, Seven). The scent and flavour of elderflowers is so powerful that a bunch of them drawn through any fine jam before bottling would flavour and scent it most deliciously, while the simply-made elderflower wine, which the bouquet of German white wines echo more delicately, was employed to flavour junkets, cakes and light puddings. Country women in Wales today recall these practices and many still employ them.

Home-made wines and home-brewed beer played a significant role in the social life of the Welsh countryside for longer than they did in England, because tea, which replaced buttermilk and the home-produced beverages, was slower to win acceptance in Wales than it was in England. The hedgerows and moorlands provided a useful harvest of wild fruits and berries – whinberries, wild raspberries, cranberries, blackberries, crab apples and medlars – which came to table in simple pies and puddings. The former were often made with considerable skill upon the ubiquitous bakestone. For special occasions fruits were dressed into custardy mixtures adorned or served with cream in the English tradition of 'conceits'.

Honey, as elsewhere, was the earliest sweetener. It survives in the Welsh recipe for Honey Cake (see pp 211-2). The Welsh had as lasting a love affair with spices as did the English, with, it seems to me, a persistent fondness for ginger. In the 15th century

47

Guto'r Glyn wrote in praise of:

Sinamwn, clows a chwmin
Siwgr, mas i wresogi'r min
Cinnamon, cloves and cumin
Sugar, mace to warm the lip[19]

indicating the availability of these spices in Wales in the later Middle Ages, but the words for them in Welsh indicating their novelty.

The use of apples in the traditional cooking must have been confined in earlier times to the eastern parts of Wales – the old counties of Breconshire, Radnorshire and Monmouthshire – for elsewhere the soil tended to be too acid to enable the apple tree to flourish to any degree. And it is the border area where cider-making was an important activity until quite recent times.

Herbal lore

No discourse which attempts to explain Welsh attitudes to food and drink can fail to mention the early Welsh involvement in the serious study of herbal medicine, for herbs played a much more significant part in doctoring in Wales than they did in the kitchen. Thyme, savoury and mint were the main culinary herbs, but the entire galaxy of herbs and flowers known to be of remedial value was employed in treating complaints and illnesses of all kinds. Although people everywhere in early times relied upon herbal medicine, in Wales there was a special reliance based on the herbal learning of the *Meddygon Myddfai* – the Physicians of Myddfai, virtually unknown outside Wales but greatly respected within the Principality.

Myddfai is a small village near Llangadog in Dyfed, a few miles east of the main A40 between Llandeilo and Llandovery. That the *Meddygon Myddfai* actually lived and practised herbal medicine, there is no doubt; they wrote 188 of their prescriptions into the *Red Book of Myddfai*. But how Rhiwallon, the first physician of Myddfai, acquired his herbal lore is lost in the mists of Celtic folk tales.

---

19. Quoted by Gwyn Williams in *The Land Remembers*.

According to the charming legend, the Physicians are reputed to be descended from the fairy Lady of the Lake (*Llŷn y Fan Fach*, near Myddfai) who married a local farmer but later returned to the lake. She reappeared one day at the lakeside to console her three grieving sons, telling the elder, Rhiwallon, that his mission in life henceforth was to heal the sick. She gave him instruction in the herbal remedies he was to employ.

Rhiwallon and his three sons – Cadwgan, Gruffudd and Einion – and their sons were for generations the *Meddygon Myddfai*, and there is at least one herbalist in Dyfed today who claims to be descended from the famous family.

The doctors of Myddfai were not only exponents of the practice of healing with herbs, they employed also the Hippocratic virtues in their treatment of the sick: skill in prognosis and knowledge of régimen. The latter featured large in the finale of the medical manuscript – in fact the whole of this section is devoted to diet, constitution, digestion, hygiene and exercise. This exposition shaped the pattern of Welsh domestic life for five or six hundred years. Its influence is clearly seen in Mati Thomas' description of Welsh farm-life in the mid-18th century, when the healthful properties of the food and routine of daily life were of paramount importance: 'Their lives were simple as indeed was the food they ate. There was a variety in their food list, indeed, each season having its particular meals. The usual practice was to have three meals a day, except during harvest time. During this time it was customary to sit in a circle and have what would be termed today a snack. They worked long hours before breakfast, very often during harvest their day in the field would commence at 4 am. This meant that the horses would have been prepared and fed before this time. Work often continuing until around 11 pm. Meals would be: Breakfast at 7 am, Dinner at 12 mid-day, Tea at 6 or 7 pm. . . even though long hours were worked a very healthy breed of men emerged on a diet of Barley Bread, *Cawl*, Two year-old Cheese, and Whey'.

A century later Lady Llanover took up the theme, expressing strong ideas on nutrition in *The First Principles of Good Cookery*, 1867, which is first and foremost an educative work, if eccentric in its presentation.

Welsh Food Today

Though Wales was the first part of Britain to experience the full effects of the Industrial Revolution, the urban Welsh have maintained far stronger links with the land than have English town-dwellers. The creation of urban communities around the new industries effectively diverted large sections of the Welsh population from the land, traditional source of their food, making them dependent for the first time upon food which could only be acquired with money. The rural poverty which many had left had been harsh enough, but there even the meanest cottage had its strip of garden and the hedgerow and woodland to keep starvation at bay; but urban poverty and its inescapable money-factor was something new and terrible.

The longing to return home has always been strong for the Welsh. Now, with the increase of car ownership, there's a regular weekend exodus of men and women who work in the industrial south and north-west to their family home in the country. And part of the pleasure of the visit will be the acquisition of some country produce to take back to town with them.

I feel it's a shame that there isn't greater awareness, both in and outside Wales, of the Welshness that still characterises Welsh food today, sometimes to the despair of the health promoters – the salty Welsh butter, the splendid honey and spicy cakes, the marvellous mountain lamb, the sea and river fish, and the superb shellfish, the good, wholesome toffee and the mysterious laverbread.

Although there is little conscious cooking evolved from the old traditions in Wales today (as with all regional British cookery, standardisation spread with improved road and rail communications) this is not to say that a certain Welshness has totally departed from the style of Welsh tables. In all but the homes of the trendy young, and middle class, tea will always be served in pretty, flowered china cups with gold about their rims; and with the tea will come a variety of freshly-baked cakes and scones with home-made rhubarb or gooseberry jam. In most Welsh homes, the Sunday rice pudding is still a feature, even if a more sophisticated dessert is offered as well for the traditional Sunday lunch. And if you look a little closer, simply at the ordinary commercial level you can observe a certain Welshness about food in Wales.

Food shops and supermarkets in Welsh towns and villages may at first glance appear to be much the same as elsewhere in Britain, but a closer look reveals the differences which cater for Welsh tastes. There's a great deal of good, crusty, oven-baked bread as well as the uniform British wrapped slices of flannel; in the cake shops Welsh Cakes, Seed cake and *bara brith* are regular items; small, independent butchers still make their own generous, coarse-cut sausages and haslet (or aislet) (see p.119); you can buy real old-fashioned Welsh peppermints and humbugs in the sweet shops, and out in west Wales the brisket in the butcher's windows may well be marked '*cawl* meat'.

In the supermarket, amongst the imported and English butters there will be salty *Shir Gâr* and *Ymenyn Cymru* made in Wales; the fish counter will have laverbread and fresh cockles; and with the chickens and ducks in the frozen food locker there'll usually be a few geese – most Welsh farms kept them in the old days and the Welsh are fond of them still, especially at Christmas.

The larger supermarkets now stock the 'exotica' needed for Indian, Chinese and Thai cookery, and the fruit, vegetable and salad counters have the currently fashionable produce – at last, for it was slow to arrive beyond Cardiff and Swansea, Wrexham, Llandudno and Colwyn Bay. Speciality food shops have burgeoned, offering Welsh and other fine quality foods. Wholefood shops, too, have proliferated until even the smallest country town or village has one.

Country markets are worth visiting for the chance of local produce and Welsh specialities like laverbread, aislet, and toffee and home-cured bacon. Be prepared for plenty of fat here; in the old days they fattened the pig as much as they could to obtain fat bacon, for fat keeps the cold out; those today who still prefer home-cured bacon do not want too much lean.

It is in the country that the real Wales is still to be found. In their spotless, shining homes the women are talkative, quick-moving and bright-eyed; even those in their seventies are nimble and amazing in their energetic bustling about to make you comfortable and fetch you a cup of tea. The older men are big and quiet, keeping to their corner, having their say in the end, mostly about the old days. Their sons, alas, are unlikely to be as happy working the land as they were a decade or so ago, for they are probably working single-handed and machine-aided, as bedevilled as their counterparts in the rest of Britain by the demands and restrictions of the EU, MM (Milk Marque) and the other regulatory bodies which have taken away their farming freedom and turned them into hard-pressed agri-businessmen. When they come in from the fields they must attack their computers, and when they get to bed, hope that the new day will not greet them with yet another agricultural catastrophe to wrestle with. Yet there are still those who make the time to write the complex Welsh poetry and literary offerings to the *eisteddfodau* adjudicators and win the coveted Crown and Chair – or even just verses to order for their friends and neighbours, as their forbears have done since medieval times.

It's encouraging to note that rural Wales is satisfying a large part of the growing market for 'real' food which is materialising out of the dominance of packaged foods. Often this is through the enthusiastic efforts of non-Welsh immigrants, opters-out from the rat races of advertising and marketing, who see more sense in being country flour-millers, vegetable-growers and fish-smokers than what they were. They use their sophisticated business techniques to make their bucolic enterprises viable, while the locals, who accepted the demise of the old rural industries as the result of the so-called march of progress with Celtic fatalism, are heartened, if surprised, to see them profitably revived.

On the eating-out front there have been dramatic strides forward, particularly in the upper echelons of restaurants, but there has also been a growth of small and imaginatively-run, inexpensive eating places and cafés (in the true sense of the word): no longer does the former 'gastronomic desert' tag apply. Pubs, too, have upgraded their food, though there is still too much reliance on the ubiquitous meals from the local frozen food locker – but in some areas where trade is spasmodic, this is under-standable.

The real stunner (in terms of contrast with the preferences of yesteryear) is the enthusiasm for Far Eastern food – Indian, Chinese, Thai, Indonesian, and Japanese (the latter reflecting the Japanese presence in industrial South Wales) – the spicier the better. Perhaps the ease of ordering by number and very late opening (after the pubs closed) had something to do with it, but expertise was surprisingly quickly acquired.

Many restaurants now do not hesitate to state their Welshness in the food – not often in the traditional sense, except for *cawl* – but in the clever use of Welsh ingredients. A last observation: how many years now is it since Elizabeth David kindly pointed out to me, when I was desperate for something from the Welsh tradition to put on my dinner menu, Lady Llanover's recipe for Welsh salt duck? Must be 30 years. For at least 25 years nobody took much notice, though I invariably featured it on the St David's Day dinners the Tourist Board asked me to devise; and now, suddenly, it is on menus everywhere, principally, I guess, since Franco Taruschio applied the hand of a skilled chef to its execution at his celebrated Walnut Tree Inn near Abergavenny. The Llanover recipe is in the section on the cookery of the *plas* here.

If there is a shortage of regular cookery books about Welsh cookery, I find that a great many Welsh people have written in loving praise of their old foods. It seems a good idea to let them tell a great deal of the Welsh culinary tale, with Richard Llewellyn doing most of the talking through quotations from *How Green Was My Valley*, in which he was remembering the good Welsh cooking of his Pembrokeshire grandmother. Thus this book is as much an anthology of what Welsh people have written about Welsh food as an attempt on my part to unravel its history.

Prince Owain Glyndŵr, who installed a brief parliament in Machynlleth around 1402 in defiance of English rule, was especially noted for the excellence of his hospitality; a peacock, arrayed again in all its plumage after roasting, would undoubtedly have taken pride of place at many of his lavish banquets. This is how it was done, according to *Bwyd Y Beirdd* (Food of the Bards) by Enid Roberts and is a reminder of the magnificent feasting which went on in the castles and great houses of the Welsh princes in medieval times, when they ruled Wales, bravely fought first the Norman invaders and then the English, until with Henry Tudor they finally put a Welsh king on the throne of England.

STUFFED PEACOCK (*PAUN WEDI EI ROSTIO*)

Flay or skin the peacock by making a hole in the head of the bird and then blowing (using a quill) between the meat and the skin, until the skin is freed from the meat. In this way the skin and feathers are kept together. After roasting and allowing the peacock to cool, vinegar and lombard powder (mustard) was sprinkled on it, and the skin and feathers replaced.

Croeso i fwydydd Cymreig! Welcome to Welsh food!

1. River and sea fish, lake fish, shellfish

1. Trout

And there is good fresh trout for supper. My mother used to put them on a hot stone over the fire, wrapped in breadcrumbs, butter, parsley, and lemon rind, all bound about with the fresh green leaves of leeks. If there is better food in heaven, I am in a hurry to be there. . .

HOW GREEN WAS MY VALLEY: Richard Llewellyn

Only the fisherman who can get his catch to its cooking within a very short space of time can hope for such superlative enjoyment of trout as this, for trout from the deep-freeze or fishmonger's slab in an inland city is unlikely to have retained the melting tenderness and delicate flavour of fresh-caught fish. The method of using a strong, centre-folding leaf to hold a fish occurs elsewhere – a palm leaf serves the same purpose.

Substantiation of the use of leek leaves comes from Dorothy Hartley, who says in *Food in England*: 'a single folded leek leaf holds a trout very neatly for grilling.' The flavour would be an added bonus. I would assume that cooking the fish on a hot stone came from riverbank fire cooking and that the method was eventually brought home, as it were, and taken over by an experienced cook, who made her own contribution – the stuffing mixture. Or the reference to the hot stone could simply have meant the bakestone.

The Welsh have three interesting traditional ways with trout other than the one just detailed, each designed to protect a fish with a tendency to dryness. Remember, they had no grills in the early days, and so could not solve the problem by liberally basting with butter as the fish cooked. Instead, in one dish they used their fatty bacon for lubrication, a jacket of oatmeal for insulation in another. In the third, bacon dripping and warm water keep

Fishmonger at Llanbedr. Photo by Keith Morris.

the fish from drying-out. All three are oven-cooked, which suggests they belong to the more recent period of Welsh cookery, when the oven was an integral part of the fireplace and in daily use. Otherwise, freshwater fish would simply be fried, in either butter or bacon fat.

BAKED TROUT WITH BACON (*BRITHYLL A CHIG MOCH*)

A breakfast dish in former days when miners and quarrymen used to tickle a few brown trout in the early morning. But the method of wrapping the fish in streaky bacon is good for the more easily obtainable rainbow trout as it adds lubrication and flavour. If you stuff the trout with lemon and parsley stuffing as Richard Llewellyn suggests, you will have a truly special dish – perhaps one of the best in the Welsh repertoire. I don't know about the wrapping in leek leaves, though – I use very thin bacon rashers, two to each fish, as binding to hold the stuffing firmly in the fish. It's best to take the bone out of the cleaned fish first. (Remove the head, slit the fish along its belly, turn it face down on a board and press all down the bone with your thumb to loosen the flesh. Turn it over and lift the bone at the head end with the point of a knife, then pull gently forward and up.) Lay the fish in a lightly-greased fireproof dish, sprinkle with a little salt and fresh-ground black pepper, bake 15-20 minutes in a medium to hot oven – 400° F, 195° C, gas 5. The bacon on top of the fish should be just lightly crisp.

LEMON AND PARSLEY STUFFING:

4 oz stale breadcrumbs	4 oz lightly salted butter
(white or light wholemeal)	or soft margarine
3 tbs chopped fresh parsley	1 large egg
1 large lemon	

pinch each marjoram, lemon thyme, salt and fresh-ground black pepper

Grate the lemon rind, then squeeze the juice. Soften the butter, if used. Combine all ingredients.

BAKED TROUT (WITH OATMEAL) (*BRITHYLLOD WEDI EI ROSTIO GYDA BLAWD CEIRCH*)
from Welsh Fare *by S Minwel Tibbott.*

three or four trout   oatmeal
salt   bacon dripping

Split and clean the trout and dry thoroughly. Remove the heads and tails, if desired. Melt a little bacon dripping in an earthenware dish, or roasting tin, in the oven. Roll the trout in salted oatmeal, place them side by side on the melted fat and cover with greaseproof paper or lid. Bake in a moderately hot oven for about half an hour, remove the covering and allow them a further ten minutes to brown.

three or four trout   a large onion or a few chives
bacon dripping   a little warm water

Split and clean the trout and dry thoroughly. Remove the heads and tails, if desired. Place the trout, side by side, head to tail in an earthenware dish or roasting tin and pour over them the bacon dripping dissolved in a little warm water. Slice the onion and place the rings on the trout. (Alternatively, use chopped chives.) Cover them with greaseproof paper or lid and bake in a moderately hot oven for about half an hour. Remove the covering and allow them another ten minutes to brown.

2. Sea trout *(sewin, gwyniedyn)* Sea trout is known throughout Wales as *sewin*, though nobody seems to know why, since the Welsh word is *gwyniedyn*. It is somewhere between a salmon and a trout, and yet is neither, but a separate species. Though the flesh is pink, it is a different, paler pink than salmon, and the taste is quite different, so delicate that I feel it needs only the simplest of cooking. I always followed what I was told was the local way, just grilled or baked gently with plenty of salty Welsh butter. We served it with no sauce at first, advising people to put plenty of butter on the hot flesh as they ate through the fish, as this again brought out the flavour.

We also suggested our customers ate it with the locally-baked brown bread whose rough texture contrasted nicely with the smooth sewin flesh – and this again I was told was a local way with this fish.

In time I found a cucumber and lettuce sauce delicate enough to enhance rather than overpower sewin's beautiful flavour. It was such a success and I have been asked for the recipe so often that I give it here, although it is in no way Welsh.

Sewin come in all sizes from the babies of less than a pound in weight to about 3 lbs, known as *shiglin* (the smallest), and *twlpin* (the larger) in late July and August, to fully grown fish known as *gwencin*, which equal a salmon in size and come in May or June or earlier, and again in September. (I have been offered a whopper in the dark of a December evening following a discreet knock at the back door. . . that's when I learned to distrust a big *sewin* for flavour, because that fish had quite grown out of its taste, and was completely flavourless.)

Large *sewin* is sometimes mistaken for salmon. They can be told apart by the tails (the *sewin* body is slimmer near the tail, and the 'v' in the tail is much more deeply indented and the colour (sewin is a browny-grey, salmon is a blue-grey.)

The way to tell how good the flavour of a large *sewin* will be, if you are going to buy it whole, is first to examine the colour of the flesh (if the fish is already in steaks you can see straight away). The vendor should let you make a tiny incision with the point of a knife in the middle of the back of the fish, and you can then peek in at the colour. If the flesh is a good, clear pink, all will be well, you can pay up and carry off the fish secure in the anticipation of joys to come. But if it has turned to a pale, fawny pink, it has been in the river too long and I wouldn't buy.

Welsh anglers claim that Welsh rivers are incomparably the best for large *sewin*, and that the Tywi, which flows through Carmarthen, yields more *sewin* of over 10 lbs than every sea-trout river in England and Scotland put together, and the Dyfi further up the coast almost equals it. Be that as it may – it's the little 'uns I like.

One solution to the flavour problem of a large sewin is to stuff it. I did this once and didn't like the result, but you may have a different opinion.

STUFFED SEWIN

from Welsh Fare *by S Minwel Tibbott*

one whole *sewin* (large)   bacon dripping
thyme and parsley stuffing

Clean the *sewin* in the usual way, and fill with thyme and parsley stuffing. Put it in an earthenware dish with a little bacon dripping and bake in a moderately hot oven (350° F, gas 4).

CUCUMBER SAUCE FOR SEWIN

1 small cucumber   ¼ pint single cream
1 onion   1 oz butter
outer leaves of 2 lettuce   *beurre manié*
  (an excellent way of using them up)   tarragon, salt, pepper
  or one small whole one
½ pint chicken stock, (made with a cube if necessary)

Peel the cucumber and cut into smallish dice. Finely chop the onion and soften with the cucumber in the butter. Add lettuce, finely shredded. Then add stock and a good pinch of tarragon, and simmer for about 20 minutes – until all is soft. Put through a fine sieve or liquidise. Return to pan, heat to boiling, then thicken with a little *beurre manié*. Add the cream, check seasoning, re-heat but do not boil. This sauce can be made in quantity and kept, covered, in the fridge until needed, even after adding the cream. And it can be frozen. But be careful not to boil when re-heating, otherwise the cream may curdle.
    A *beurre manié* is a mixture of slightly more flour than butter, worked together to form a smooth paste. Add it, bit by bit, to boiling liquids to thicken. It's a useful idea to keep a quantity ready made in the fridge as it will keep, sealed, for months.

In south Pembrokeshire they used to add chopped, blanched fennel leaves to a *béchamel* sauce to serve with *sewin*, salmon or mackerel. I find I prefer the older way with fennel (which grows wild along the west coast of Wales, especially Cardiganshire and Pembrokeshire), which is just to mix the blanched, feathery leaves with melted butter and pour over the fish.

3. Salmon *(Eog)*   It's hard to realise that apprentices in Britain once petitioned for special clauses in their indentures: that they should not be compelled to eat fresh salmon more than twice a week. The Welsh rivers were so plentiful with salmon that in Wales, too, it was once a food of the poor. In the great houses, where the English fashion for employing a veritable battalion of spices and aromatics for every dish grew to incredible proportions with the long success of the East India Company (granted a Charter in 1600 by Elizabeth I and operational until 1858), and the need to enliven the many compulsory fish days, salmon dishes were complicated. In addition to the spicing, oysters and shrimps were often added to the dish. In contrast, the Welsh cottagers' artless ways with salmon are a lesson in simple perfection. They cooked it in salty butter, sometimes with a feathery leaf of fennel, in a covered soup plate or between two saucers. The plate went over a pan of boiling water, in which new potatoes were economically cooking; the saucer method was for the oven – a simply-contrived *en papillote*. Both ways take about 30 minutes to cook the fish. Nowadays you would use foil instead of saucers.

Salmon are still relatively plentiful in Wales. When I was running the hotel in the mid-sixties, most of mine came from the river Teifi, and were sent down by bus from Cardigan, fresh-caught and packed in cool, fresh green bracken, 6 or 7 big fish to a box. The bus would pull up outside the hotel, less than a hundred yards from its scheduled stop on the town square, and the conductor himself would carry the salmon down our kitchen area steps. Service like this was part of a delightful way of life, now gone, though it is little more than 20 years ago.

Together, Pepita, my Spanish cook and I would carry the fish off to the pantry to gut and clean them, bloody to our armpits. We put an extra edge on our knives to cut the fish into steaks, calculating each to a nicety of weight. Good judgement was necessary with such an expensive item.

After the steaking, into the deep-freeze with the salmon, to keep it at that point of freshness. Later we would poach the tail pieces and bits to serve cold with mayonnaise, and grill the steaks with butter, serving them with the same cucumber sauce as we

Salmon fisherman. Photo by Stuart Ladd.

had for *sewin*. Meanwhile the cats feasted on one of the heads – the rest went for fish stock.

In The *First Principles of Good Cookery* Lady Llanover gives precise instructions for crimping fresh-caught salmon (see p.65). Crimping was a common practice in Victorian times. It was done to 'set' the flesh before the curd (the white substance which lies between the flakes of flesh) had melted and made the fish oily. The prepared salmon would then be sent up to table with a highly-flavoured sauce, such as the unusual Granville sauce Lady Llanover recommends in the same book, a sauce possibly of her own devising and named after a relative.

Smoked sewin and salmon in Wales

The village of Cenarth on the banks of the river Teifi by the famous falls, where the river shoots in a series of foaming rapids, is indelibly associated with salmon and sewin. At one time the Cenarth area was full of small fish smokeries, for this was not then a luxury trade but the only known method of preserving the abundant supply of both fish.

As S Minwel Tibbott's *Welsh Fare* has it:

'In the past experienced fishermen would smoke salmon during the winter months towards the beginning of the salmon season. This was the only method of preserving them at that time. The following method was practised by a fisherman from the Cenarth district, on the Carmarthenshire border.

Hang the salmon from its tail, split it open from the tail down to the head, remove the entrails and wash it thoroughly. Remove the bone found underneath the vent and fill that cavity with saltpetre. Keep the salmon open with a row of short skewers (approximately nine inches long). Treat about a dozen salmon in this way. Lay the salmon on their backs on a bed of salt in a stone or wooden trough, fill the open cavity with salt and keep all well covered with salt for a fortnight. Then remove them from the salt and wash them in fresh, running water (the old fishermen laid them in a shallow pool in the river for three days and three nights). When clean, hang them over a fire of withered oak leaves, allowing the smoke to whirl around them for three days and three nights. Usually, they would be hung by their tails from large nails driven into the open chimney stacks, with large branches of holly keeping them well away from the chimney wall. Store them in a convenient dry place, cut into steaks when needed and fry in butter.'

Gradually the small smokeries fell into disuse and were lost. But salmon and sewin are being smoked again near Cenarth, by a young couple who bought a farm in the early 1970's and discovered old slate salting slabs when they came to renovate some near-derelict outbuildings. Realising they had stumbled upon one of the old smokeries they decided to restore it. Now, as well as smoking salmon and sewin (which I think is even better than smoked salmon) they are also curing and smoking bacon, beef and hams in various ways, and their products are highly-valued in the speciality foods trade.

This recipe from Mary Pearson's manuscript cookery book of 1755 (Bourdillon collection: National Library of Wales) illustrates very well the tedious complications associated with the 18th-century preparation of salmon:

To BOYLE SAMON AND MAKE SAUCE FOR IT:

Take your samon and a bundle of sweete hearbs, and boyle it very well in fair water, then take a quart of oysters to a tayle of samon, and stew them in their licquor, with too or three anchoues, and a blade of mace, and three or four peper cornes, and when they are stewed take them, and lay the oysters on the samon in the dish, then take a good peice of butter and beate it with the licquor of the oysters, till it be thick then power it on the samon and send it up, with the dish garnished with the crust of manchet grated and strowed round the dish sides, and sliced lemon, you may if you please cover your samon with picked shrimps, being put into hot water, till they be hot, then power the water from them and put them into butter, being beaten thick with some of the water, that your shrimps were scalded in, or you may take some water and dissolve too or three anchoues in it, and so beate your butter with that water, if you put shrimps to your samon, you must not put any oysters to it.

And this, from Lady Llanover's *First Principles of Good Cookery*:

SOUTH WALES SALMON:

As soon as a salmon is killed it ought to be crimped, by making incisions between the head and the tail, two inches wide and one inch deep. It should then be put in cold water for one hour, then put in a fish-kettle with as much cold water as will cover it; one quarter of a pound of salt, and as much vinegar as will make the water slightly acid. As soon as the water is scalding hot (but *not to boil*), take it off and pour the water into a pan and put it away in a cold place, leaving the fish in the strainer, and placing the strainer with the fish upon it over the pan of hot fish-water to cool together, where it should remain till the next day, when the fish should be placed again in the fish-kettle with the same water in which it was scalded, and when it is again warmed it is done. *It must not boil.*

In Welsh cottage kitchens they poached salmon in milk. Sometimes a bay leaf was added to the milk and the salmon served hot with parsley sauce, or allowed to go cold and eaten prosaically with bread and butter. But salmon poached in milk and eaten cold *with cream* is surely an idea borrowed from the kitchens of Heaven!

SALMON IN MILK (*EOG WEDI'I FERWI MEWN LLAETH*)

salmon steak   milk
salt

Immerse the salmon steak in hot milk, add salt to taste and simmer gently, allowing about fifteen minutes for every pound in weight. Boiling it too briskly will cause the salmon to flake in the milk. When cooked, drain and slice as needed. Serve warm with potatoes baked in their jackets or cold with fresh cream.

BOILED SALMON WITH FENNEL (18th century) (*EOG WEDI EI FERWI GYDA FENIGL*)

fresh salmon steak (one or two pounds)   water
fennel   a little salt

Bring a saucepan of water to the boil, add the salt and a few fennel leaves and then immerse the salmon steak carefully in the water. Simmer gently, allowing fifteen minutes for every pound, and taking care not to boil it too briskly to prevent the salmon from flaking in the water. When cooked, drain well and slice, as needed. Serve warm with parsley sauce or cold with salad and bread and butter.

Both recipes from Cenarth, the village at the great salmon leap on the river Teifi in Carmarthenshire.

SALMON AND ONIONS (EOG A WINWNS)

salmon steak (medium-sized)   bacon fat
one onion, sliced

Boil the salmon steak in salt water for about two minutes only. Drain well and remove all bone and skin. Flake the salmon and fry in bacon fat with the sliced onion.

A recipe from Breconshire, and all three recipes from S Minwel Tibbott's Welsh Fare.

Sauces for salmon   The Teifi valley in west Wales (the river rises above Tregaron in north Ceredigion and runs through heavenly country to a leisurely exit to the sea at Cardigan, *Aberteifi*) is thick with mansions and former great houses. 'Teifi salmon sauce', which is to be found in almost evey collection of Welsh recipes, must surely be an escapee from the repertoire of these country houses. The enormous quantity of butter used to cook the salmon points to its 18th-century origin, when butter was a common medium for cooking almost everything.

TEIFI SALMON 'SAUCE'

Mix ¾ pint of melted butter with a glass of port, a little ketchup and one boned anchovy in a pan over a low heat. Pour this sauce over the prepared salmon steaks, cover and bake in a fairly hot oven (375 deg F, gas 5) for three-quarters of an hour.

Note: these quantities are for a whole fish – reduce as necessary.

Fennel, with its lovely aniseed flavour and feathery leaves which turn such a bright, attractive green when they are cooked, was widely used in sauces for fish, especially salmon and mackerel, in the 18th and 19th centuries. Fennel grows wild in parts of west Wales so it crops up often in Welsh cookery.

FENNEL SAUCE FOR SALMON (18th CENTURY)

Boil a bunch of fennel and parsley, chop them small, and put them into some good melted butter, send it to the table in a sauce-boat.

(See also Granville Sauce on p.307-8)

4. Mackerel (*Macrell*)   Mackerel is altogether the best and the worst of fish. Its flavour when eaten fresh-caught is incomparable, but is loses its freshness almost within the hour and thus displays badly – more than an hour from the water and the sweetness and melting texture have gone. Living by the sea and eating mackerel straight from the quay spoils you for it elsewhere – as Wyn Griffith says in the *Wooden Spoon*, 'a man of sense will fit his dinner-time to the mackerel'.

When fresh, mackerel are firm and stiff and the sea-green colours very brilliant and beautiful, and the eyes are bright. Mackerel which is dull and glazed about the eyes is never worth buying. Its season is summer – late June to early September. They used to bring them up to us from the Lower Town quay around midnight, a hundred or more at a time, as we were clearing the kitchens up for the night. We couldn't refuse them, and however tired we were, there was no help for it – into the pantry to gut and clean for an hour or more until they were all safely in the deep-freeze, their freshness caught and held. They never stayed down there in the cold for more than a few days after we made them popular by serving small, whole mackerel as a mid-course. In the early days I could find few takers for this marvellous fish as people were then so prejudiced against it – it was thought to be unclean because of a reputation as scavenger of the sea. Useless to point out that pigs occupy much the same position in the animal world and yet pork and bacon are acceptable.

In the area around Porthmadog on the Traeth Bach estuary mackerel were often cooked in olive oil – an unsurprising medium for coastal Wales once it is realised that Porthmadog was from very early times until the end of the last century an important port trading largely with the Mediterranean. Olive oil was readily available in and around the port – and the same applies to many of the little west coast Welsh ports.

COLD FILLETS OF MACKEREL FOR SUPPER

I am now speaking of pre-war days when mackerel were very plentiful indeed in Cardigan Bay, and friends would very often bring half a bucket because we were a large family. Now my grandmother was very fond of cold fillet of mackerel for supper and her way of preparing them was: not to open the mackerel through the back of the belly in the traditional way, but she would cut fillets right along the backbone and not touch the innards whatsoever, so as to have white fish in the inside. These would be fried in vegetable oil preferably – olive oil, it was cheap enough – and her method was to put olive oil in a little skillet with onion rings I remember, and not to boil too fiercely because they were never allowed to get black, just cooked to a golden brown, and then she would take this off and I had to go for spirit vinegar to the Italian Warehouseman (not malt vinegar, God forbid) and after it cooled down she would add two tablespoons of this vinegar. Back on the slow fire again, raise it to a simmer and it would thicken like a sauce. By this time the fillets would have been cooked and she would pour the sauce over (she always used to say: 'Don't you leave a morsel of that fish without being covered otherwise the fly will get at it and that won't do it any good') and the whole lot would be covered over. For some reason which I don't know she would never touch it for the first two days – I rather think there was something about the sauce that was too strong, it would probably give her indigestion or something – but it seemed to have been allowed to mature. I do know that she would guarantee that she could eat those mackerel fillets for a whole week even in the middle of August when it was very hot, having been kept in the ordinary sort of cool cupboard outside, and they were beautiful. Fillets of mackerel with this lovely sauce for supper – you try them – they're gorgeous!
According to Commander John Pendry Davies of Cricieth.

Fresh mackerel. Photo by Keith Morris.

Commander Davies' grandmother must have obtained this recipe from an 18th-century cookery book. Both Hannah Glasse, in *The Art of Cookery*, 1747, and Elizabeth Raffald in *The Experienced English Housekeeper*, 1769, give similar methods for pickling mackerel in oil and spice. The method was called then *to caveach*, an abbreviation of the Spanish *Escabeche*, which came to us from the West Indies. His recollection of his grandmother's admonition not to use malt vinegar echoes that of my own mother, and we also dealt with an 'Italian Warehouseman' rather than a plain 'grocer'. The test was to ask for 'allspice'. If you were given mixed spice, you took your custom elsewhere! The older name for allspice is Jamaica Pepper. The flavour is said to resemble cinnamon, nutmeg and cloves. Note the remark about the cheapness of olive oil. . .

Sauces for mackerel

One of the best sauces to serve with mackerel is gooseberry, which goes far back in English cookery. Although every cottage garden in Wales has a gooseberry bush, and there is a delicious gooseberry mint jelly to serve with lamb in Welsh recipes, I have not found any evidence of the English idea of using the sharpness of gooseberries to partner the richness of mackerel being adopted in Wales.

But there is this nice

GOOSEBERRY PICKLE

contributed to *Farmhouse Fare* by a lady from north Wales. It goes well with mackerel and is useful to have in the store cupboard for when time is short:

3 lb gooseberries	¼ oz ground cloves
1¼ lb sugar	½ pint vinegar (preferably wine vinegar)

Put the ingredients in an enamel pan and boil, stirring carefully until the mixture is the consistency of jam. Put into jam-pots and cover when cold.

---

5. Herring *(Ysgadenyn/Pennog)*   *Ysgadenyn* is the south Walian word, *pennog* the one most commonly used in the north. Note that the street cries quoted here are slang Welsh, and *sgadan* is more often used than *ysgadenyn* because it is easier to say.

> "We cured fish, in the sun, on the roof of our cottage, so that we should not die of starvation in the winter. For I was a child in the lean and hungry years after the Napoleonic Wars, when poor folk suffered helplessly, and, as it seemed to me, endlessly."
>
> *Life at Rhiw, on the Llŷn Peninsula, described by*
> *L Wyn Griffith in* The Wooden Spoon.

The humble herring was important to the people living along the west coast of Wales. Places like Fishguard, Aberporth, Aberystwyth, Aberdyfi, Nefyn and Aberdaron on Llŷn were noted for their herring catches, and the fishing, selling, salting and curing of herrings was a major industry and an important domestic occupation for the people of those parts. In the 17th century salt for the herrings was produced by boiling freshwater brine sent from Northwich with seawater in the north Wales river mouths, but if salt was in reasonably good supply, the tax upon it was a burden upon the herring industry for nearly 200 years from the early 17th century.

Fresh herrings were sold in the streets: *Sgadan Abergwaun*, they used to cry in Fishguard (*Abergwaun* is the town's proper Welsh name: Fishguard derives from the Norse 'Fiskrgardr'),[1] as they trundled gleaming barrowloads of herrings up the steep hill from the quay and through the streets of the little grey town.

Fishguard once had a red-herring industry – the old salting and smoking house down on the quay in Lower Town now accommodates the Yacht Club. In Aberporth, further up the coast, where the RAF rocket research station has occupied the cliff-top and holidaymakers crowd the curved beach, the cry was: "*Sgadan Aberporth, Dau fola ac un corff, Sgadan Aberporth, Dau enaid mewn un corff* – Aberporth herrings, two bellies in one body. Aberporth, herrings, two souls in one body'; and in Nefyn, using the north-Walian word for herrings – *penwaig* – they cried: '*Penwaig Nefyn, penwaig Nefyn, 'U cefna fel cefna hen ffarmwrs, A'u bolia fel bolia tafarnwrs – penwaig ffres!* – Nefyn herrings, backs like the backs

---

1. 'fiskr' = fish, 'gadr' = yard, enclosure (Dr B.G.Charles)

71

of old farmers, Bellies like the bellies of inn-keepers – fresh herrings!"[1]

Mati Thomas described how a family would salt their winter supply of herrings in her manuscript *A Collection of Welsh Recipes*, usually bought (for 1d each or seven for 6d*) in November, when the fish were at their best:

SALTING HERRINGS

It was the custom to buy around 500 fresh herrings during the Autumn. This was the method of salting them.

Take a barrel and put a layer of salt in the bottom. Then put in a layer of herrings (unwashed). Put another layer of salt, and another layer of herrings. Continue until the barrel is full. Place the top on the barrel, and store in a dark cool place for two months.

When required for use, remove from the barrel and wash in a tub of cold water many times. Then allow to stand in cold water overnight. Next day place about twenty washed herrings on a skewer which pierces each herring through the eyes. Hang in the chimney nook to dry.

She then goes on to describe an unusual way of cooking the fish:

ROAST HERRINGS (SGADAN WEDI'U RHOSTIO)

Folk of old usually boiled all their meat, but roasted herrings in a rather unique way. The fire tongs were used, as of course the frying pan was unknown.

Salted herrings prepared for use.
Place the tripod over a peat fire, and place a tongs over it. Place a row of herrings along the tongs to roast, today's term would be grill. Turn at intervals until well cooked.

They were eaten with *bwdran* (thin flummery) and potatoes in their jackets.

---

1. 'Welsh Fare', S.Minwel Tibbott.
* 2½ new pence

HERRINGS FOR SUPPER (SWPER SGADAN)

4 medium-size herrings
1 large apple
2 lb potatoes
1 large onion
1 heaped teaspoon made mustard

1 teaspoon chopped fresh sage
1 oz butter
3 tablespoons tarragon vinegar
salt and pepper
boiling water

Clean the fish; divide into fillets. Spread insides with mustard; season and roll up. Lightly grease an ovenproof dish, line with potatoes, then a layer of sliced onions, then apples. Sit the rolled fillets on top, sprinkle with chopped fresh sage, vinegar and salt and pepper. Cover with remaining potatoes. Half fill the dish with boiling water (or half water half cider if liked). (I prefer to use even less liquid or the dish becomes much too watery). Dot with butter, cover and bake in a moderate oven (350 deg F, Gas 4) for 45 minutes. Remove lid to let the top brown for a further half hour.
Serves 4 – 6

Writing in *The Accomplisht Cook*, 1660, Robert May advised mustard as an essential accompaniment to herrings. His advice was sound and is still followed. This recipe is from *Lloyd George's Favourite Dishes*, recipes from Cricieth W I, first published about 1920 and re-published by John Jones (Cardiff) Ltd.

GRILLED HERRINGS

2 medium-sized fresh herrings, or 3 small ones
a small piece of butter

parsley
mustard sauce

Scale and clean the fish, then wipe with a clean cloth. Upon each side of the herrings cut three incisions 1½ ins apart, cutting down to the backbone but not through it. Remove the heads. Now as the herrings contain their own cooking fat, grill quickly under a very hot grill till brown on each side. Dust lightly with salt, garnish with parsley and serve with mustard sauce.

BROWN MUSTARD SAUCE

1½ oz butter, 1½ oz flour, fried till a nice golden colour, then mix with pint stock. Stir till it boils, add the juice of a lemon, a little cayenne pepper, a teaspoonful of vinegar and a teaspoonful of mustard. Strain through a tammy and serve.

The following is a recipe from a farm account book 1786 – 92 of Mrs C Jones, wife of Revd H Jones, Vicar of Penmark, Cowbridge, in the Peniarth collection, NLW:

TO BROIL HERRINGS

Scale, gut and wash good herrings. Cut off the heads, dry them in a cloth, notch them across with a knife, flour and broil (grill) them, in the meantime take the heads you have cut off, mash them and boil them a quarter of an hour in Ale or beer with an onion and some whole pepper then strain this mixture and thicken it with butter mustard and flour – put this sauce in a boat and send up with the Herrings.

A recipe attributed to Mrs Todd, West Cross, Swansea, c 1880, from *A Taste of Wales* by Theodora Fitzgibbon:

POTTED HERRINGS

6 filleted herrings   ½ teaspoon anchovy essence or paste
1 bay leaf   pepper and grated nutmeg to taste
a pinch of mace   4 tablespoons melted butter
water or fish stock

Put the filleted herrings in an ovenproof dish with the bayleaf and a pinch of mace, all barely covered with water or stock. Cover with foil and bake in a moderate oven (350 deg F) for 20 minutes, then let them cool slightly. Lift out the fish, remove all skin and any small bones that may be adhering to the rib-cage. Pound them well, mixing in the anchovy essence, pepper and grated nutmeg to taste. Put into a jar or pot, pressing down very well, and when quite cold pour the melted butter over the top. Serve cold, with toast, or it is particularly delicious with yeasted oatcakes.

A dish still popular in many parts of Wales was suggested for inclusion by a Pembrokeshire friend, although no recipe has been located in any Welsh collections. This one is from *Fish Cookery* by Jane Grigson:

SOUSED HERRINGS

6 herrings or mackerel
salt, pepper
¼ pt (full ½ cup) each water and malt vinegar,
   or ½ pt (1¼ cups) dry cider

1 tablespoon pickling spice,
   including a chilli
3 bay leaves
1 medium onion, sliced

Behead, bone and clean the fish. Season them and roll up, skin side either all inwards or all outwards. Arrange closely together in an ovenproof dish. Add the rest of the ingredients. Cover with foil and bake in a cool oven (300 deg F, Gas 1) for about 1½ hours. Serve cold.

Lake Fish

1. Schelly/Powan (*Gwyniad*)   A lesser-known fish connected with Wales is the enigmatic *gwyniad*, herring-like in size and shape, but whitish in colour, hence its name in Welsh: *gwyn* (white) which the Ice Age in its retreat left behind in Lake Bala (*Llŷn Tegid*) in Wales; and in Loch Lomond and Loch Eck in Scotland, where it is known as powan; and in several of the English lakes, where they call it schelly. Because it feeds solely on plankton it is difficult to catch. They used to take it in nets, but these are now forbidden in order to preserve the species. It may perhaps be tempted by a patient fisherman to rise to a feather. Lord George Lyttleton, the 18th-century traveller and writer in Wales, is said to have found the flavour of the *gwyniad* 'so exquisitely delicate as to more than rival that of the lips of the fair maids of Bala'. One is inclined to wonder how a man with such a marked reputation for respectability and strong religious convictions could have been in a position to make this comparison!

2. Red char (*Torgoch*)   Another relatively rare fish which finds just the lifestyle it likes in the deep, cold, well-oxygenated waters of the upland lakes of north Wales, principally *Llŷn Padarn, Llŷn Peris,* and *Llŷn Bodlin.* It is also found in some of the English Lakes. Like the *gwyniad* it is difficult to catch but can sometimes

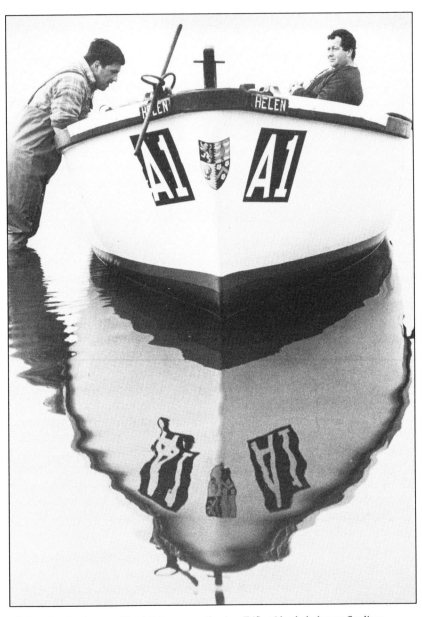

'Bois y Sarn', *salmon and trout fishermen on the river Teifi at Llandudoch near Cardigan.*
Photo by Stuart Ladd.

be taken with fake bait. Its rosily-blushing belly gives it its name (*tor* = belly, *goch* = red), but the flesh is quite white. When the Dinorwic hydro-electric power station was being built in the mountains of Snowdonia, the *torgoch* were transferred from *Llŷn Peris* to another lake whose waters would not be affected by the rise in temperature engendered by the construction works. Most of them were later returned to their original home. Char *(torgoch)* and powan *(gwyniad)* are now being farmed in north Wales. Char can be cooked like trout or salmon, but is most noted for its association with the once popular fish soup – *waterzootje*, or Water Souchy as it became known in England.

The fish soup, which depends upon the freshness of the fish for its thickening – hence its name, water soup – originated in the Low Countries and is similar to the *bouillabaisse* of Provence in that it is more a stew than a soup.

Water Souchy, with its characteristic, bright-green colour, became a customary prelude to the fashionable summer whitebait repasts to which Londoners flocked in the Nineties. In July and August at that time whitebait could be caught in vast quantities in the Thames, in great bag-nets secured to vessels moored off Greenwich and Blackwall. Taverns overlooking the river in that area made a speciality of quick-fried whitebait cooked straight from the nets, and Water Souchy was a logical starter to the meal since it could be made from the miscellaneous small fish which came up in the nets with the whitebait. It was served in a special wide dish which was created for it.

The same meal of Water Souchy and whitebait has much grander associations with the Greenwich area, though. It could well have been the whitebait dinners which were held up to 1895 to mark the end of the summer Parliament session that sparked off the fashion for these pleasant riverside repasts amongst less exalted folk. The Ministers of the Crown reputedly held their whitebait dinners in the Trafalgar in Greenwich, while Her Majesty's Opposition took theirs in the nearby Ship Tavern. Later in the year, on Trafalgar Day (21 October), whitebait dinners were held in the Royal Naval College (as Greenwich Palace had then become) presumably because of its connection with Lord Nelson. The much-prized red char was more or less obligatory for the traditional Water Souchy on these splendid occasions, presumably the 'small, white fish' in Eliza Acton's is the 'Greenwich Receipt' in *Modern Cookery for Private Familes:*

WATER SOUCHY (Greenwich Receipt)

This is a very simple and inexpensive dish, much served at the regular fish-dinners for which Greenwich is celebrated, as well as at private tables. It is excellent if well prepared; and as it may be made with fish of various kinds when they are too small to present a good appearance or to be palatable dressed in any other way, it is also very economical. Flounders, perch, tench, and eels, are said to answer best for water souchy; but very delicate soles, and several other varieties of small white fish are often used for it with good effect: it is often made also with slices of salmon, or of salmon-peel, freed from the skin.

Throw into rather more than sufficient water to just cover the quantity of fish required for table, from half to three quarters of an ounce of salt to the quart, a dozen corns of white pepper, a small bunch of green parsley, and two or three tender parsley roots, first cut into inch lengths, and then split to the size of straws. Simmer the mixture until these last are tender, which will be in from half to a whole hour; then lay in the fish delicately cleaned, cleared from every morsel of brown skin, and divided into equal portions of about two inches in width. Take off all the scum as it rises, and stew the fish softly from eight to twelve minutes, watching it that it may not break from being over-done.

Two minutes before it is dished, strew in a large tablespoonful or more of minced parsley, or some small branches of the herb boiled very green in a separate saucepan (we prefer the latter mode); lift out the fish carefully with a slice, and the parsley roots with it; pour over it the liquor in which it has been boiled, but leave out the peppercorns. For a superior water souchy, take all the bones out of the fish, and stew down the inferior portions of it to a strong broth; about an hour will be sufficient for this. Salt, parsley, and a little cayenne may be added to it. Strain it off clear through a sieve, and use it instead of water for the souchy. The juice of half a good lemon may be thrown into the stew before it is served. A deep dish will of course be required for it. The parsley-roots can be boiled apart when more convenient, but they give an agreeable flavour when added to the liquor at first. Slices of brown or white bread and butter must be sent to table always with water souchy: the first is usually preferred, but to suit all tastes some of each may be served with it.

The taste of char was described in the late-17th century by the traveller Celia Fiennes as 'very nice and fat when in season, though not so strong and clogging as lampreys are, but as fat and rich a food'.

Though it sounds rather churlish to say so, when I sampled some hatchery-raised char through the kindness of what was then the Gwynedd River authority I found the flavour of the fish disappointingly insipid.

Potted meats and fish were fashionable in the late 17th century. Preserved by their covering of spiced butter they were sent from the district of their origin to the tables of the rich in London and elsewhere, served among the lighter dishes of the second course. Recipes for potting fish are numerous, for the practice was continued with undiminished enthusiasm throughout the 18th century, and for that matter persists with some special varieties to the present day. Mrs Raffald gave precise instructions for potting char in *The Experienced English Housekeeper*, 1769:

> Cut off the fins and cheek part of each side of the head of your chars, rip them open, take out the guts, and the blood from the backbone, dry them well in a cloth, lay them on a board and throw on them a good deal of salt. Let them stand all night, then scrape it gently off them and wipe them exceedingly well with a cloth. Pound mace, cloves and nutmeg very fine, throw a little in the inside of them and a good deal of salt and pepper on the outside. Put them close down in a deep pot with their bellies up with plenty of clarified butter over them. Set them in the oven and let them stand for three hours. When they come out pour what butter you can off clear, lay a board over them and turn them upside down to let the gravy run from them. Scrape the salt and pepper very carefully off and season them exceedingly well both inside and out with the above seasoning, lay them close in broad thin pots for that purpose, with the backs up. Then cover them well with clarified butter. Keep them in a cool dry place.

Shellfish

The Romans made shellfish a popular delicacy in Britain, often transporting it up to fifty miles inland from the coast. In Wales, whelks, cockles, mussels, limpets and oysters were featured regularly on the menus at the Roman villa of Llantwit Major near the Glamorgan coast. But they lost popularity after the Roman departure, and during the Dark Ages there is little evidence of their being eaten at the prosperous settlement of that period at Dinas Powys, also near the Glamorgan coast. In later centuries the smaller shellfish became a useful food for the poor, troublesome to gather but eking out an impoverished diet. The larger crustaceans were caught for trading purposes and seldom enjoyed as a food by those who sold them.

1. Oysters (*Wystrys*)   In the 1830's Port Einon on Gower was the centre of the notably large oyster industry off south Gower. Oyster fishing dovetailed neatly with the limestone trade by providing local employment during the summer months when the oystermen would otherwise have been idle.

Famous from Roman times, the beds went on record in 1674 as being the best in Britain – at that time the fishery at Oystermouth on Swansea Bay was flourishing – hence its name. At the beginning of the 18th century, large-scale dredging operations began at Port Einon, where enormous daily catches of 7 to 8000 oysters were landed by each skiff, demanding large-scale storage space in inter-tidal perches pools. The lines of pitched stones which sectioned these off can still be seen on the foreshore near Salthouse. At a halfpenny a dozen at the beginning of the 19th century oysters were cheap food indeed; by the 1870's the price had escalated to a penny each, the supply had declined and the movement of oysters into the luxury food class had begun. The last haul of oysters at Port Einon was in 1879; now, a century later, the oyster beds are being re-planted and it is hoped to revive the industry again, albeit on a very much smaller scale than before.

During the last decade oysters have been grown on a commercial scale in various parts of Wales, notably on Anglesey, and at Carew in south Pembrokeshire.

Local dredgermen had a novel way of cooking their oysters. They wedged them between the bars of their kitchen fires, the bars kept the shells tightly closed while the molluscs cooked in their own juice on the pressure-cooker principle.

Enough mussels would usually come up with the oysters to make a supper for the dredgers' crews, and the dredgermen became fond of mussel stews and broths. The man who commanded the *Rising Sun*, the last of the dredgers, Captain Wil Davies, was noted for his curried mussel broth which he cooked for his crew himself. The area around Pen-clawdd on the north side of Gower, where the laverweed and cockle 'industries' are sited, was especially noted for mussels.

The rocky Gower coast was good for lobsters and crab, too, and there was no need for pots to catch them in – they could be taken at low tide with a hook, off the rocks – the same method was also successfully employed along the opposite north Devon coast. Crabs and lobsters were seldom eaten by the locals, for their commercial value was always too good.

OYSTER SOUP FROM GOWER

A recipe which belongs to the Victorian tradition of English cooking and not to the Welsh tradition at all. When oysters were coming in by the tens of thousands to Oystermouth and Port Einon it would very likely have been prepared in the homes of the wealthy, and in hotels of Oystermouth and Mumbles and Langland Bay:

> Melt 2 oz butter in a saucepan and work about 1½ oz flour into it. Gradually add some well-flavoured mutton broth (onions, mace and black pepper should have been in the broth to flavour it), bring to the boil and simmer for about 15 minutes. Strain and pour over the required quantity of oysters, ready-bearded. Tuck triangles of toast or fried bread around the edges of the dish to serve.

TO FRY OYSTERS

(from a farm account-book 1786 – 92, kept by Mrs C Jones, wife of the Revd J Jones, Vicar of Penmark, Cowbridge):

> Make a batter of milk, flour, eggs, mace and nutmeg. Wash your oysters clean, dip them in this batter, roll them in crumbs of bread and fry them a light brown in hog's lard or butter – they are a pretty garnish for any dish of Fish – or a side dish at supper.

Oyster Loaves

(from the manuscript book compiled by Merryell Williams, Ystumcolwyn, early 18th century, in the Peniarth collection, NLW):

Take a dozen of good oysters & Clean 'em as usual, y^n boyl 'em in their own liquor till they be enough to pickle, then take a fair sweetBreed of Veal and Boyle it in water till it be enough to be eaton, but rather under than overboyled, your oysters must be underdone. When the sweetBreeds and oysters be thus boyl'd shred the Sweetbreed into small squares about the bigness of a french bean, & take the finns from ye oysters and put em altogether, and grate over them half a Nutmeg or more and sprinkle also over them two pennyworth of Capers shreed as small as Dust, & a reasonable quantity of Peper and sault according to y^{re} Palat and let em stand by, Y^n take a Quarter of a Bint of Gravie y^t is good and stronge. And shred it into half a midling oyster and half an Anchovie & put it over a Gentle fire, till ye anchovie be disolved y^n strain ye gravie from ye onion into a Sauce-pan to wh^{ch} put a quarter of a pound of frsh butter & shack it about in ye pan till be melted thick & y^n put in your prepared Oysters and SweetBreeds and sturr-em Gently together till they be well mixt & put them by, till the loaves be fry'd as followeth. Take 4 new French Rowles, & cut a peice Neatly out of ye top of each, no bigger than that y^{re} finger and thumb will just go in, & carefully take out all ye crumbs as close as can, not to breake thro' ye sides, when you thus order'd y^{re} Loaves, Gett a narrow skellet barely wide enough for a loafe to goe Cleverly in, & be turned, & putt into it a pound of fresh butter without any watter and lett it boyle a little, scuming it clean from the Butter-Milk, into the Boyling butter, put first one Rowle, And lett it take one or two turns Round, turning it that Each side may be fry'd y^n take it up & lay it upon a plate to drain, ye hole downwards & then put in another, till the Loaves be all Fry'd, & att last putt in ye Bitts, t^t you cut out, and when they be Enough lay 'em to Drain, as the loaves, y^n take your Loaves and fill 'em wth your Oysters with a sweetmeat spoon taking care y^t every part be full & y^n Close 'em with ye piece, when y^u would Eat them y^u must put 'em in an oven Moderately hott for about a quarter of an hour or till y^u think they be thoroughly hott, Serve e'm on a plate Either by themselves Or with roasted fowles.

OYSTER SAUSAGES

From the same source

Take a quart of large Oysters & Parboule 'em and then let it be Cold y^n chop them with sage and sweet herbs very fine, y^n grate the yolks of hard Eaggs, and 4 or 5 Anchovies & a little grated bread, pepor, nutmeg, and a few Cloves beaten very small y^n work it up together, with 2 pounds of the best suet, Shreded very fine.

A common recipe of the period. What we aren't told is to roll the 'sausages' in breadcrumbs before frying. If you do feel like trying this, it's good idea to blend everything in an electric liquidiser.

TO MAKE A SAVOURY PYE

(From a late 17th-century manuscript cookery book found at Gogerddan, near Aberystwyth, National Library of Wales):

Parboyle your Oysters, and season them with nuttmeg, pepper, and salt, and putt them into your pye, with half a pound of butter, and so close it: when it is baked, Mince 2 Anchovies small, and putt them into some of your oyster liquor, and dissolve them; beat up a pound of butter in the same liquor, and putt the Juice of a good Lemon in it, putt this into your pye, serve it to the Table.

TO STUFF A SHOULDER OF MUTTON WITH OYSTERS

(From Mary Pearson's manuscript book, 1755, Bourdillon collection, National Library of Wales).

A typical 18th-century recipe reflecting the end of the demarcation between fish and meat meals after the era of compulsory meatless days. Oysters were especially popular as a stuffing for meat or fowl.

Split it and then cut it slanting and then stuff in the oysters and bast it with claret wine, and a sliced onyon and a little salt and when it is roasted take all the gravy that comes from it and the liquor of the oysters and more oysters and some capers and samphire and lemon cut small and boyle them together, then take up the mutton and pwre the sauce all over it, and serve it up hot, you must not put the lemon in the sauce till you go to serve it up.

2. Cockles (*Cocos*) The approach to the 'laverbread place' at Pen-clawdd was a scrunching pathway of cockle shells, for right next door was the 'cockle place' (I don't know what else to call these establishments, for they were neither factory nor plant and were more substantial than sheds). For a hundred years or more the foreshore had been covered with millions of discarded shells. Cockles are excellent eating if they are fresh – and unvinegared. Try this instead of scampi next time you're hard up – it's not an imitation of scampi by any means, but it's quick and tasty and shellfishy.

'COCKLES PEN-CLAWDD'

Cliff Roberts, one of the 'laverbread brothers' of Pen-clawdd on the Burry Estuary, north Gower gave me this dish – given to him by Mrs Williams of the next-door 'cockle place' – while I gave it the name.

Exact quantities don't matter – use commonsense. Melt some butter in a heavy pan and throw in some fresh breadcrumbs (white or brown, it doesn't matter, but a mixture of both does well) and chopped spring onions, with some of their green part. Turn this mixture around in the butter for a few minutes for it to acquire a little colour, then add some freshly-boiled cockles, plenty of fresh-ground black pepper, and salt. ("Clap a lid on tight for they cockles do skep!") Shake the pan vigorously to cook the cockles through for a few minutes (don't overcook). Serve with a generous sprinkling of chopped parsley.

COCKLE PIE (*PASTAI GOCOS*)

(a south Pembrokeshire recipe from Welsh Fare *by S Minwel Tibbott):*

cockles	salt and pepper
salt water	white sauce (unsweetened)
a little oatmeal	cheese or shortcrust pastry

Soak the cockles in salt water overnight, adding a little oatmeal to the water. (The oatmeal helps to clean the cockles.) Then boil the cockles in clean water until the shells open. Take out of their shells, put in a pie dish, season with salt and pepper and pour the white sauce over them. Cover the sauce with a thick layer of grated cheese or with shortcrust pastry. Bake in a hot oven until golden brown.

WELSH COCKLE PIE (PASTAI GOCOS)
(*from* English Recipes *by Sheila Hutchins*).

This pie is delicious served hot with new potatoes, or cold with mixed salad and a thick cream dressing. . .

Cook 1 quart of cockles in a cup of water only long enough for the shells to open. Line the sides only of the pie-dish with thickly rolled pastry. Put a layer of shelled cockles in the bottom of the dish. Sprinkle these with chopped spring onions, or chopped chives, then add a layer of diced fat bacon. Repeat these layers until the dish is full, then pour in the strained liquid in which the cockles were boiled, adding pepper. Cut fairly thin strips of pastry and with these make a criss-cross over the pie. Cook slowly until the pastry is done.

COCKLES & EGGS (COCOS AC WYAU)

No wonder this traditional combination was thought to be aphrodisiacal – shellfish and eggs. Cdr John Pendry Davies (Uncle Jack to his many friends) of Cricieth gave me the recipe and the verse – in Welsh only, of course. The indelicacy of an English translation was something he preferred not to tackle for a lady. . .

6 oz shelled cockles	bacon fat
2 beaten eggs	·black pepper

Fry cockles in a little bacon fat, turning well, then pour eggs over. Stir with a wooden spoon and season with black pepper.

The use of this latter in any Welsh recipe is an indication of its origin in the time before white pepper became the norm in most British households. Black pepper, which has a much warmer flavour than white, has come into its own again.

Cocos a wya	Cockles and eggs
Bara ceirch tena	And thin rye bread
Merched y Penrhyn	Penrhyn ladies
Yn ysgwyd 'u tina!	Shaking their bottoms!

Imagine my joy at finding a very early and much more complicated version of this dish entitled:

85

A PHRASE OF COCKLES
(phraise – prepared in a frying pan)

(from The Whole Body of Cookery Dissected *by William Rabisha.* London, 1671. *Master Cook to many honourable Families before and since the wars began, both in this my Native Countrey, and with Embassadors and other Nobles in certain forraign parts).*

Take your Cockles, boyl them and pick them out of the shells, wash them clean from gravel, then break a dozen eggs with a little Nutmeg, Cinamon and Ginger, and put your Cockles therein, and beat them together with a handful of grated bread, a quarter of a pint of cream, then put Butter in your Frying-pan and let it be hot, as for eggs, and put in the Phraise: supply it with Butter in the sides of the pan, and let the thin of the eggs run stiff into the middle, till it moves round; and when it is fryed on that side, butter your plate and turn it and put it into your Pan again and fry the other side brown: then take it forth and dish it, and scruise on the juice of Lemmons, and strow in Ginger and Cinamon, and send it up: you may green it with Spinnage, and cut it into quarters, and garnish your fish, or either sort; thus may you fry Pranes, Perriwinkles or other shell fish.

Wirt Sikes, US Consul in Cardiff a century ago, wrote *Rambles & Studies in Old South Wales* originally as a series of articles for American magazines popular at the time, such as *Harper's*, because he had been unable to find a single line of information on South Wales in American bookshops or libraries before leaving for Cardiff. Entranced by the area and its people, his observations make fascinating reading, and the book which was published in 1881 has recently been reprinted by Stewart Williams of Barry. This is his description of the 'cockle-wives':

A somewhat similar industry is that of the cockle-wives. These women – who, although thus generically dubbed wives, are often young girls, and handsome ones – are to be met with in great numbers at various points on the Welsh coast. At the little village of Pen-clawdd, in Glamorganshire, countless tons of cockles are gathered and despatched by rail to all parts of England. Women alone do this work; men are absent from the scene, and spectators are not wanted. But it is a unique spectacle when the sand-bank is lined with the cockle-wives, bent over with their heads near the ground and their bright-hued drapery flying in the fresh ocean breeze, "scraping" for cockles. The tide here recedes for as much as a mile, sometimes farther, leaving exposed acres upon acres of sand in which the cockles are embedded. The great day for this

Cockle harvesting at Pen-clawdd. Photo by Stuart Ladd.

business is Friday – the day when nothing is doing, Saturday; both facts accounted for by the potent influence of Saturday's market. The habits of the cockle are very similar to those of the American clam, and he is caught in much the same manner. The searcher for cockles finds the sand dotted with thousands of little holes about as large as if pierced with knitting-needles; the cockle is there, embedded a couple of inches below the surface. The cockle-wife is armed with a "scraper" made from an old reaping-hook, and a deft Pen-clawdd lassie will pick up the cockles as fast as a farmer can dig potatoes. Some of the women have little carts or pannier-laden donkeys, but the majority bear their baskets on their heads. They can earn in good times three or four shillings a day.*

Like laverbread, cockles were sold door-to-door in the villages around the estuaries where they were gathered. Boiled, shelled cockles went into wooden pails carried on the heads of cocklesellers; untreated cockles were sold from large baskets. Around Porthmadog, where the cockles and eggs recipe comes from, was also a notable cockle area, and here they liked to eat the rich fish and egg mixture between slices of barley bread or oatcakes as a special treat – to which the verse refers.

3. Limpets and winkles *(Llygaid meheryn a gwichiaid)* It was a common practice to scramble eggs with limpets and winkles after first frying them in bacon fat; sometimes limpets were boiled in nettle tips to help tenderise them before tossing in oatmeal and frying.

Limpets are the devil to gather, as any child knows who has tried to lever them off rocks. A sudden, surprise attack with a knife blade is recommended as the best tactic. Few bother to collect limpets now, but a hungry family in the past would have been glad of them and not minded how long it took to gather enough for a tasty supper.

---

* She also needed a small, short-handled rake, and a large sieve. The bent sickle blade was called a *cocses*.

LIMPET PIE (*TARTEN LYGAID*)

limpets   a large leek (white part only)
fatty bacon (diced)   shortcrust pastry

Boil the limpets for about half an hour, drain them and take them out
of their shells. Wash them well and cut into quarters. Line a deep dish
with a layer of pastry, cover with the limpets and place the diced bacon
and the leek, cut into one inch pieces, over them. Sprinkle with salt and
pepper and cover with a second layer of pastry. Seal the pie around the
edge of the dish and bake in a hot oven for the first half hour, but
reducing the heat for the second half hour. Chopped, hardboiled-eggs
were sometimes included.

The pie was served warm, generally for dinner or supper,
and is from Aberporth, Cardiganshire, as recorded in S Minwel
Tibbott's *Welsh Fare*.

Sand-eels (Llymriaid)

Minwel Tibbott also records a recipe for these little creatures –
long, silvery, small-scale eel-like – which can be dug up from the
sands if they are known to be hiding there. They are firm and
sweet to eat, but not at all like eel. They should be thoroughly
washed, their heads cut off and their innards squeezed out. Then
they used to be fried in bacon fat, sometimes with a sliced onion.

2. Bread, Oatcakes, Bara Brith

Good Jelly dripping and crusty, home-baked bread, with the
mealy savour of ripe wheat roundly in your mouth and under
your teeth, roasted sweet and crisp deep brown, and covered with
little pockets where the dripping will hide and melt and shine in
the light, deep down inside, ready to run when your teeth bite in.
Butter is good, too, mind. But I will have my butter with plain
bread and butter, cut in the long slice. . .
HOW GREEN WAS MY VALLEY, Richard Llewellyn

1. Wheat Bread (white and wholemeal) *(Bara gwenith)* The Welsh
were, and still are, good breadmakers and are making their own
bread again. Wholemeal flours of character, including some from
organic and Welsh-grown wheat, stone-ground in small Welsh
flour mills, are still available in all parts of Wales.

The old breads in Wales were mostly rough – coarse, even;
made from wholewheat flour, barley-meal and oatmeal and
rye flour, and it required great skill and ingenuity to produce
acceptable bread in quite primitive conditions. Sometimes
bread was baked in the wall-oven, specially heated for the
day, or in a bread-oven housed in a separate little building of
its own, across the yard from the house. Or, in areas where
peat was used for fuel, in the *ffwrn fach* – the little pot oven –
in reality a large cast-iron pot with a lid. It worked on the
principle of heat below and on top: the pot stood on a tripod
over the indoor fire of red hot peat, or over a similar fire built
out of doors in a sheltered spot. Either way, the inside of the
pot was greased, the bread dough placed inside, and glowing
peat coals heaped on top of the lid. The *ffwrn fach* was usually
employed to bake white bread – a great treat.

Lady Llanover employed this traditional utensil in many
individual ways of her own, described in her intriguing
cookery book, *Good Cookery* (1867), facsimile edition 1991
(Brefi Press).

The bakestone was used to make quick breads of all kinds, and in Anglesey and the Llŷn Peninsula made to work in a similar way to the *ffwrn fach*: the dough was placed on the heated bakestone, standing on a tripod over an indoor or outdoor fire of gorse or straw. The bakestone was then covered with an inverted cast-iron pan on to which glowing embers were heaped, a method which can be traced to a very early Celtic baking-contrivance*

BAKESTONE BREAD
(BARA PLANC, BARA CRAI, BARA CI, BARA TRW'R DŴR)

1 lb plain white flour   ½ pint buttermilk
½ teaspoon salt   1 teaspoon soda

Dissolve the soda in the buttermilk and pour it gradually into the flour, to which the salt has already been added, mixing well to form a soft dough. Knead lightly and turn on to a floured board. Shape into a round, flat loaf, flattening the top lightly with a rolling pin. Bake on a greased, not-too-hot bakestone until the surface begins to harden. Turn and bake the other side.

The bakestone was often pressed into service to make a quick loaf for tea on baking day, when a small piece of dough was regularly kept back for this purpose. Small batch loaves were made on the bottom of the oven, too. Another piece of dough was often kept back for making oven-baked currant loaf or small currant buns for the bakestone, and in this case lard, sugar and currants were worked into the basic white bread dough.

---

* also known as *planc, llechfaen, gradell*. S.Minwel Tibbott, *Welsh Fare*, p.47.

Slater's bakery, Aberystwyth. Photo by Keith Morris.

92

Planc Bread with Yeast

(an Anglesey receipe, from Farmhouse Fare*):*

2 lbs flour	1 teaspoonful salt
1 oz yeast	1 teaspoonful sugar
1 oz lard	1 breakfastcupful milk and water

Warm the flour and put into a large bowl, which should have been warmed. Rub the lard into the flour. Put the yeast into a jug with the sugar, and mix with the milk and water, which must be just tepid.

Make a well in the centre of the flour and pour in the liquid. Make into a soft dough, cover with a warm cloth and leave it to rise for 1 hour in a warm place, out of the draught. Mould into a large flat cake, kneading and pressing with the hands towards the sides. When shaped it should not be more than 1 in. or 1¼ ins. 2½-3 cm thick. Leave to rise for 15 minutes.

Place carefully on the *planc*, which should not be too hot. Bake for 20 minutes on one side, then turn and bake for another 20 minutes on the other side.

Pikelets (*Bara pyglyd*)

Breadcakes formed of a leavened batter of flour and milk and baked on the bakestone. Sometimes known as 'pitchy bread', they were taken to the West Midlands where they became very popular, and still are.

4 oz flour	3 oz butter or margarine
2 eggs	½ pint milk or buttermilk

Rub the butter into the flour, beat the eggs and mix into a batter , beating well with a wooden spoon. Leave to stand overnight if possible. Drop in tablespoons on a hot griddle and turn once when holes have formed in the surface. Eat hot and buttered.

Ordinary white bread in Wales was no different from white
bread elsewhere in Britain. As in other parts it was regarded as a
luxury, a mark of esteem until with the development of
commercial baking it became commonplace. Contemporary
home bread-makers in Wales are interested in the health aspect
of wholemeal or wholewheat bread.

When I began gathering material for the first edition, restored
watermills stone-grinding grain in the traditional way were a
rarity. Now there are at least ten Welsh cornmills (one, on
Anglesey, is a windmill) all grinding by the slow method which
retains the wheat germ in its entirety, the warm but not hot friction
generated between the stones gently releasing the wheat oil, thus
retaining all the nutrients. Seven of the water-powered mills are
in Dyfed: Y Felin, St Dogmaels near Cardigan, Cenarth Mill by
the famous falls on the River Teifi, Felin yr Aber in an organic
smallholding near Lampeter, Felin Newydd in a nature reserve
at Crugybar, Llanwrda, Melin Maesdulais, Porthyrhyd,
Carmarthen, and Felin Geri in the tranquil valley of the River
Ceri near Newcastle Emlyn.

In Powys there is Felin Crewi at Penegoes, Machynlleth, and
Bacheldre at Churchtown, Montgomery; and in Clwyd, Melin-
y-Foelas at Pentrefoelas (this mill once belonged to Mrs
Horsefield, pioneer of watermill restoration in Britain), and

Cochwillan Mill in Gwynedd. There is even one near Cardiff, Melin Bompren at the Welsh Folk Museum – and a Cardiff baker using their flour. All have their wholemeal, and often other flours, such as barley and herb, for sale, and many supply local bakers with their flour. One long-standing water-powered mill, Felin Gwyn at Whitemill, Nantgaredig, near Carmarthen, is still stone-grinding, but driven now by diesel engine due to the idiocy of the water authority, who put the price of the use (and refreshment!) of their water beyond the means of the mill's owners. The availability of these flours, and the pleasure of being able to visit the mills to obtain them, is one of the joys of living in Wales. And since most if not all are open to visitors, one of the attractions of a holiday in Wales.

STEAMED BROWN BREAD

An interesting idea from Caernarfonshire, especially in hot weather when perhaps it would be better not to use the oven.

The recipe appeared in *Farmhouse Fare* (1966 edition):

1 large cupful bran	1 tablespoon sugar
1 cupful wholemeal flour	½ teaspoonful salt
2 cupfuls plain flour	1 teaspoon bicarbonate of soda
1½ cupfuls thick sour milk	½ cupful sultanas or raisins
1 tablespoon black treacle	

Mix the dry ingredients; heat the sour milk and add the treacle, mixing well. Stir in the dry ingredients, and lastly the sultanas. Pour into greased tins two-thirds full and steam for 3 hours. Straight stone marmalade jars are excellent for making this, as they turn out nice shapes which can be cut into dainty rounds to be spread with butter for afternoon tea. Rye flour, oatmeal, Indian corn meal, or any coarse flour can be substituted for the bran.

The only other reference to baking bread in stone marmalade jars I have found is in connection with the Llanuwchllyn area by Bala in Merionethshire, where the little loaves of white bread were called 'dolly bread', and baked for the children. Perhaps this contributor to *Farmhouse Fare* came from that area, as I am told the method was exclusive to Llanuwchllyn.

2. Barley Bread *(Bara barlys)*

Better barley bread and peace than white bread and discord.

17th century Glamorgan ploughman's verse from
Tradition and Folk Life, Iorwerth C Peate

Mati Thomas says barley bread *(bara barlys)* was 'the prime bread in days of old, eaten with all meals'. There was a weekly baking and the large, finished loaves were kept on a bread rack – a kind of ladder, fixed to the wall, the bread fitting between the rungs. Stored in this way the bread must have become rather hard by the end of the week, and I think the custom of breaking it into broths and pouring tea or buttermilk over bread must initially have been devices to soften up this hard, old bread and so use it up, for there was no waste in the old days.

BARLEY BREAD *(BARA BARLYS)*

barley meal	salt
brewers' barm	lukewarm water

Wet sufficient barley meal, calculated on the size of the family. Sometimes it was the practice to mix the meal in a large shallow bowl the day prior to baking. Put salt into the lukewarm water and pour into the meal. Mix by hand. Then add a pint of brewers' barm to the mixture and mix well. Leave to rise overnight covered with a cloth.

The first operation the following morning was to obtain lukewarm water. Wet the hands, and remix the dough. It should attain a uniform tough consistency. Allow to stand whilst the wall oven was being heated. A culm fire was usually used for this baking. The oven was large enough to take four loaves at a time. Two in the lower section and two in the higher one. The barley bread was prepared on a bread board. A little barley meal was sprinkled over the board, and a bowlful of dough was lifted from the dish and worked on the board. This was called 'folding'. The loaf was shaped by hand, circular and about two inches thick. Barley meal was then sprinkled over the loaf. The surplus meal being whisked off with a goose wing . . . It was then ready to bake. After it had hardened in the oven, the loaf was turned over, when almost ready it was placed on the lower shelf of the oven.

A barley meal loaf took almost an hour to bake. When baked it was removed from the oven and placed on its edge on the floor. After it had cooled it was placed onto the bread rack.

There is little or no rise in barley flour, but the taste is attractive. These two adaptations appeared in my *Book of Welsh Bread* (1981), Y Lolfa: reprinted 1983, 1987, 1993. The first was a run-away success when I contributed it to an international buffet table at the 1981 Oxford Symposium.

1½ lbs barley meal	1 tablespoon vegetable oil
1 tablespoon salt	16 fl. oz tepid water
1 tablespoon dried yeast mixed with	
2 teaspoons molasses sugar or honey	
in warm water.	

An acceptable all-barley meal loaf is not easy to make unless you are prepared to use a lot of yeast. I find this loaf a pleasant change from wholemeal, for the scent and flavour of barley are very attractive.

You can also experiment with 1 lb barley meal and ½ lb plain white strong flour and the usual amount of yeast which will give a tight-textured loaf which is nice with cheese.

Mix the frothed yeast into the warmed meal, to which you have added the salt. Add the oil to the warm water and mix to a dough. Knead well and set to rise in a warmer place than usual – about 1½ – 2 hours, until doubled in size. Knock back, knead again, place in a large (3 pint) but not too deep tin and set to prove for up to an hour, covered, in a warm place. Make a deep cut along the top of the loaf and open it out with the side of your hand before putting in to bake in a fairly hot oven for approximately one hour. Sprinkle the top with sesame seeds if liked before baking.

BARLEY AND WHEATMEAL BREAD

1 lb wheatmeal	2 teaspoon sea salt
½ lb barley meal	1 pint tepid water
1 teaspoon dried yeast dissolved	
with one teaspoon honey or molasses	

An alternative barley meal recipe which gives a dark loaf with a nice nutty flavour and a good, close texture. Very good for toast, or as a base for open sandwiches.

Mix the frothed yeast into the flours. Knead very thoroughly (this is a lovely dough which leaves a slight film on the hands due to the wetness of the barley).

Put to rise for a longer time and in a warmer place than usual. Knock back, knead again, place in tins or bake as a round on a greased baking sheet, or as rolls, leave to rise until doubled in size – again this may take longer than usual. Sprinkle the tops lavishly with cracked wheat, sunflower or sesame seeds, or a mixture of seeds as you wish.

BARLEY BREAD ON THE BAKESTONE (*BARA CANCAR*)

a bowlful of barley meal   cold water
(I take this to be a *cawl* bowl
which holds about 1 lb weight)

Place the barley meal into an earthenware dish. Add cold water until you have a solid mass. Use the hands to mix well. Place the bakestone over the tripod on the fire. Whilst it is heating the bread is made on a bread board. A little dough is lifted, and with the hands it is spread to make a thin circular loaf. Only one at a time is placed on the bakestone. Bake both sides. It baked rather quickly.

Stale cheese was usually eaten with this bread.

In early times thin, round barley bread as described here was used as a plate to hold the meat and gravy, the bread being eaten last.

3. Rye and maslin bread *(Bara rhyg a bara cymysg)*

RYE BREAD (*BARA RHYG*)

The Welsh ate rye bread for its medicinal value as they didn't like either its taste or appearance. It was very dark, almost black, a thin loaf with little rise. Rye was sown in the Autumn, as farmers today sow winter wheat. Some was cut for forage, some retained and harvested as grain. It made a very strong bread, so less was baked than usual.

| rye meal | a little salt |
| brewers' barm | warm water |

Place the meal in the large bowl in the evening and moisten in readiness for next day. Pour lukewarm water over the meal and mix until fairly hard. It had a tendency to 'run' as meal had that was ground from sprouted corn. Place the brewers' barm into the mix, according to requirements, cover with a cloth and leave overnight.

First thing the following morning the dough was remixed. Then allow to rise until the oven was ready to receive the bread. It was then placed in the oven on the brick to bake. Baking took about an hour.

A 2 to 1 mixture rye with white flour and 2 teaspoons dried yeast and 1 tablespoon oil is worth trying – cut thin it is good with cheese. In the proportion of 5 to 1 white flour you get a good loaf for toasting, which is again good with cheese. Rye smells beautiful when baking, and has a lovely golden crust which contrasts attractively with the dark interior. The dough is tough, benefiting from the electric dough hook. But these mixtures will rise well – give them two rises if you can. Smaller loaves bake better than large. Make a long centre cut on the tops, sprinkle with rye meal, bake for 30 minutes in a hot oven, then 30 minutes in a moderate oven.

MASLIN BREAD (BARA CYMYSG)

Another of the old breads which used to be made in Wales. It was a mixture of grains – usually rye and wheat flour – deriving from early times when the sowing of mixed grain was an insurance against the failure of wheat on its own. At the medieval table maslin bread was for the lower orders. 'Maslin' derives from 'miscelin' of the French Merovingian and Carolingian domains. The Saxons later corrupted it to 'mancorn' or 'monkcorn'.

A 20th century version, from S. Minwel Tibbott's *Welsh Fare*:

3 lbs white flour   1 oz dried yeast *
1 lb barley meal   salt dissolved in warm water

Crumble the yeast into a little warm water to soften it. Mix together the
two kinds of flour in a large bowl, make a well in the centre and pour
in the yeasted water. Sprinkle a little flour over it, cover the bowl with
a clean cloth and leave to stand for about twenty minutes until the
yeast becomes frothy. Then, gradually add the warm, salted water to
make a soft dough. Knead thoroughly, for a longer period than is usual
for ordinary dough. Cover and allow to rise for approximately one
hour. Divide the dough and shape into loaves according to the size of
the tins. Put the loaves in greased tins and bake them in a hot oven.

Mati Thomas records a thin, round loaf baked quickly on
the bakestone from barley meal when supplies of ordinary
bread were short, or when yeast was unobtainable.

4. Oatcakes *(Bara ceirch)* Oatmeal was a valued staple in the old
days of Welsh cookery, much respected for its body-building
properties. In fact, it was the only reliable cereal crop in the wet,
cold, upland regions to which ultimately the bulk of the Celtic
population of the British Isles was driven.

Though the methods varied, all the Celtic peoples of Wales,
Scotland and Ireland made oatcakes (and in upland regions of
England, too, the use of oats and oatcakes was a common feature), and it was a skilled operation. In Wales there were two
basic types of oatcakes: one made with a little fat (deriving from
the incorporation of fat in the early grain pottages), and one without any fat at all – the latter, crumbled, was used as the base of
brŵes and *siot* (see pp 225-6).

Oatcakes were made on the bakestone. There was a special
instrument for turning them, a wooden slice called a *crafell,*and
a wooden rack, *diogyn,* for drying them. Some were only cooked
on one side and finished at the back of the fire. In North Wales
they tended to make their oatcakes by rolling small round shapes

---

* By dried yeast the author means bakers' yeast (as against brewers' yeast)
  not our present-day dried packet yeast – but this can equally well be
  used if the instructions on the packet are followed.

of the oatcake dough with a rolling pin; in South and West Wales they rolled the dough first into a long sausage shape which was then divided into small balls.

The oatcakes were then formed by a deft 'palming' method. The balls of oatmeal dough were first roughly flattened with the palm of a hand, piled on top of each other with plenty of oatmeal in between, then the whole pile was worked on with the palm of one hand while the other, cupped around the pile, kept the shape evenly round, until, miraculously, the oatcakes emerged about ten inches across, thin as wafers. This method corresponds with the 'clapbread' of Cumberland.

Mati Thomas gives a recipe using only skimmed milk – no water or fat:

OATCAKES (BARA CEIRCH)

oatmeal   skimmed milk

Place the oatmeal in a bowl. Moisten with milk. Mix with a wooden spoon. It is essential that the dough be soft. Make each loaf on the bread board. The first loaf fairly thick. Sprinkle a little oatmeal over it. Make a second loaf and place on top of the first, and sprinkle with oatmeal. Do similarly with the third and fourth, until the twentieth is made.

The bakestone should be heating on the peat fire and by now should be ready. The first loaf was placed on it and baked one side only. It is then placed standing up at the back of the fire with the unbaked side towards the fire. The same process repeated for each loaf. The size of each loaf was about dinner plate size and very thin. Indeed approaching transparency. The country folk would set aside a whole day for the making of bread, and it would keep for six months.

OATCAKES (made with a little bacon fat):

3 tablespoons hot water   4 tablespoons medium oatmeal
½ tablespoon bacon fat   pinch salt

The small quantities are explained by the advisability of mixing and rolling out only a few oatcakes at a time.

Melt the fat in the water. Sprinkle the oatmeal on to it, kneading well. Flour a board with oatmeal, roll the dough out very thinly to about 10 in. diameter. Bake for about 10 minutes on a moderately hot bakestone. Stand upright to harden in front of the fire.

SOUR OATMEAL BREAD (*BARA SURGEIRCH*)

This isn't at all easy to make, nor did I find it tasted particularly good, but it's interesting to try, to obtain the idea of the skill of former Welsh cooks, and the tastes the people enjoyed.

½ lb wholemeal flour
a little sugar and salt
a little fine oatmeal (make sure it is fresh)

½ teaspoon bicarbonate of soda
about ½ pint buttermilk

Put all the ingredients, except the oatmeal, in a large bowl and mix thoroughly. Sift the oatmeal over the top and gradually add the buttermilk to make a fairly soft batter which will drop off the spoon easily. Pour into a greased, hot heavy cast-iron frying pan and bake the loaf on both sides over a moderate heat. This is the difficult part, as the bread burns before the interior is cooked if the heat is not even and exactly right.

5. Speckled (fruit) bread *(Bara brith)* The famous Welsh tea-bread stands virtually without need of translation, being synonymous with the fruit loaf as we understand it in Britain. And many Welsh speakers accept the name without stopping to realise that in translation it means 'speckled bread', the speckling meaning the fruit. Like any other national dish, variations in Wales on the basic theme are legion, everyone claiming their very own family recipe. Originally it was a yeast cake, like all the other ancient cakes and breads, before the arrival of chemical raising agents like bicarbonate of soda which later versions adopt, along with the substitution of margarine for the earlier butter or lard.

This Welsh tea-bread is echoed in Brittany *(Morlaix Brioche)*, and in Ireland *(Barm Brack)*, and in Scotland *(Kerrie Loaf)*.

The best *bara brith* is firm with juicy dried fruits (soaked beforehand in cold tea to plump them), moist and spicy.

I was given an old and treasured family recipe by a relative of the Mortimer family, owners of Trehowell Farm at the time when it was commandeered for use as military HQ by the French when they landed in 1797 at Carreg Wastad Point on the massive bulk of Pencaer, behind Goodwick, during the Napoleonic Wars, only to be defeated three days later in what turned out to be the last time Britain was invaded.

All manner of versions of the event can be found, from the tale of heroism of Jemima Nicholas, who reputedly led the women of Fishguard, armed with scythes and staves, to battle with the invaders, to the authentic details held in the official records of the two armies. For my part, I'm inclined to agree with the late Rowe Griffiths, whose whimsical weekly column used to appear in the local Fishguard paper. In a piece deploring the shameful signposting of the myriad lanes which criss-cross Pencaer, he said he wasn't surprised the French invasion ended in a *débacle* on Goodwick beach because, like everybody else, the French got lost on Pencaer. . .

This recipe from *Croeso Cymreig* is a reduction to family size of the same recipe, yielding one large (3-pint capacity tin) loaf or two smaller ones. Good *bara brith* is always made with yeast, which is simple and satisfying to work with once the initial plunge into its use has been taken. The instructions here are for experienced breadmakers, so perhaps it should be noted that all the utensils used (mixing bowl, baking tins) are warm, and that the fruit is better added after the initial rise of the dough – it should be worked in, warmed, during the second kneading of the dough, which is then inserted in the tins and proved for a further hour and a half until the dough has risen to the top of the tin.

1 lb flour	3 oz sultanas or raisins
½ oz yeast	3 oz currants
4 oz brown sugar	2 oz candied peel
(reduce if you feel the	½ teaspoon salt
cake may be too sweet)	½ teaspoon pudding spice (mixed)
4 oz fat	warm milk

Mix all the dried ingredients into flour and rub in the lard; clean fruit and put in, leave in a sponge for 2 hours, then knead up with warm

Prize-winning bara brith. Photo by Keith Morris.

milk and water; let rise for 2 hours (do not make too stiff) then put into greased tins (just lifting the dough up into the tins without kneading up). Bake in a moderate oven 1 – 1½ hours. The secret is the baking in a brick oven.

When cold, cut into thin slices, butter liberally. *Bara brith* is best kept a day or two, sealed in a tin, before eating. When old and dry it is nice toasted and buttered.

BARA BRITH

(with buttermilk, from Montgomeryshire, as in Farmhouse Fare):

1 lb self-raising flour
½ lb brown sugar
¼ lb lard or butter
½ lb currants or sultanas
1 egg
1 lemon

1 teaspoonful caraway seeds, if liked
salt and spice to taste
1 teaspoonful bicarbonate of soda
1 large tablespoonful of treacle
½ pint buttermilk

Mix fat well into flour, add sugar, egg, grated rind of lemon, fruit, salt, spice and (last of all) juice of lemon and treacle. Mix all well together with the bicarbonate of soda in the buttermilk. Put into a bread-tin and bake for 1¾ to 2 hours.

---

3. Cawl, bacon, faggots, liver, savoury pies

1. Cawl

. . . and lovely it was, too, only the leeks were a bit old, and the
bacon was a little on the briny, and winter potatoes, of course,
but still, with Bron to smile across the table, lovely.
HOW GREEN WAS MY VALLEY, Richard Llewellyn

There is no translation for *cawl*. In its literal sense it means soup or broth. But as it is used here it conveys a dish which is a whole meal in itself, whether the broth is taken first, then the meat and vegetables, or all together in a bowl, eaten with a special wooden *cawl*-spoon (to avoid burning the mouth on the hot broth). It is pronounced 'cowl'.

Oatmeal dumplings and 'trollies' (see pp 190-1) were often boiled in the *cawl*, especially when potatoes were scarce.

One Welsh friend described cawl as 'an unspoken part of life so much so that nobody could say, consciously, how it was made. . . the joint was put in the pot and we ate bacon, cabbage, floury potatoes and parsley sauce on the first day. The jelly was saved in a stone crock. . . skimmed. . . and the white fat saved for cake-making or frying. The jelly, then, was returned to the saucepan. Leeks and anything else handy was added for the second day's dinner of soup. Cabbage made a variation.'

This friend said how she remembered the delicious flavour of the cabbage cooked in bacon liquor, a combination not overlooked by the peasant folk of other countries where cabbage and bacon were staples of everyday diet.

In his first book about Wales and the Welsh, Trevor Fishlock relates an incident during the making of the film of *Under Milk Wood* in Fishguard in the early part of 1971. Some visiting journalists were lunching on *cawl* with the film-makers, one of whom remarked: 'This food, it's soul food'.

In fact I have never yet encountered anyone who has not reacted with very special gusto to a bowl of well-made *cawl*.

The parsley sauce to which my friend refers was not made with milk in the usual English way, but with the potato water, thickened with a little flour mixed with cold water. A little milk would be added to the water. Because the same terms are often used to describe or name Welsh dishes, quite broad differences between Welsh and English cookery are often missed. No-one thinks to point the differences out because the familiar is taken for granted, and the shock of realisation that something is not quite as one had assumed can be disconcerting.

This sauce of course could be made in relatively primitive cookery conditions where the usual *béchamel*-based parsley sauce could not – and the potato water would be nutritious.

My friend's description of *cawl* as she remembered it I think conveys the essence of this 'intangible' soup. It's terribly hard to be precise; ways of making *cawl* varied from region to region of Wales and simply with what was to hand. More vegetables would be added to second and third and even further re-heatings – some say that the longer *cawl* goes on the better it gets! Sometimes the subsequent re-heatings were drunk for breakfast. Second-eating *cawl* was known as *cawl aildwym* or *cawl twymo* and many older folk say with relish that they prefer it. Again, when it had to be made quickly, everything was cut up quite small, meat and vegetables boiled rather rapidly together. This was the type of *cawl* my children had for school dinner when we lived in Fishguard.

The quick way was probably the most sensible method to adopt for school dinners, but the *cawl* it produces isn't nearly as good as that made by the longer method. Now, this quick *cawl* is made even more rapidly – in the food processor: 'Magimix' *cawl*?

Because there's no standard *cawl* recipe, I'm going to lead a selection of recipes off with the one I developed and used for years in the restaurant. The mixture of bacon and brisket was locally popular and I felt it gave the best flavour.

Eating *cawl* with cheese is a Brecon custom, I'm told, and to eat the whole mixture of meat, bacon, vegetables and broth together in one bowl (as we offered it in the restaurant) is more precisely *lobscouse*, though this dish in its original northern English form bears no resemblance to a true *cawl*, other than that it is essentially a meal of meat and potatoes and liquid taken all together. Nor does it contain the necessary Welsh ingredient – leeks.

As the quotation from Richard Llewellyn implies, *cawl* is at its best in the spring, when the early potatoes are just in. Best of all are the tiny, marble-sized ones.

Note for purists: the prior browning of meat and vegetables which I recommend is not in the Welsh tradition, though Welsh friends are ready to agree that it gives better results, and that they also do it. Obviously it would have been impossible to carry out this procedure in the old tradition as there was quite simply no means by which they could effect it. The meal was essentially one cooked in water all in the one pot.

MY FISHGUARD CAWL

about 2 – 3 lbs combined weight
  of brisket of beef and
  smoked ham or bacon
  (a hock-end will do very well)
2 onions
2 or 3 each carrots and parsnips
1 medium swede or turnip
  (these quantities can be varied to taste)
2 stalks celery

about 1 lb new potatoes
a small white cabbage (optional)
a fistful of small leeks
bouquet garni – use plenty of
  thyme, fresh if available
beef dripping or bacon fat
sea-salt and fresh-ground
  black pepper

Melt the fat in a large, heavy saucepan, and brown the beef and bacon, lift out, and brown the rough-cut root vegetables. Add the celery, chopped, and when the vegetables are nicely browned, place the meats on top. Fill with cold water to cover, leaving room at the top of the pan for the later addition of the potatoes. Bring gently to the boil, skim off the scum, adding salt and a dash of cold water to assist this process. Do not over-salt at this stage because of the bacon. Add the herbs and black pepper, lower the heat to a mere simmer, leave for 4 – 5 hours – overnight if the heat is gentle enough. Add the potatoes half an hour before cooking is completed, and the chopped cabbage if included about 10 minutes before serving time. Adjust seasoning.

To serve: put a chunk of bacon and beef in each bowl, fill up with vegetables and liquor, strew with finely-chopped leeks (green part and white), and chopped fresh parsley. Eat with rough brown bread and a hunk of cheese.

> There's only one house near the place
> and that hides in the arm-pit of Garn Fawr,
> Dolgaer it is called, an old barn of a house
> but a place for a welcome and a cup of tea
> or a bowl of *cawl*, and that's a better feed,
> with leeks and potatoes and stars on its face.
> You'll see the cauldron on the tripod there
> and the gorse blazing gaily beneath it.
> You shall have the ladle full, and filled again,
> and that lovelier than any mixture;
> you shall have a wooden spoon in the bowl as well
> and a great hunk of a fine old cheese.

This poem in praise of *cawl* by the Welsh poet Dewi Emrys was translated for me from the Pencaer dialect by Dillwyn Miles, the Herald Bard of Wales. Good *cawl* should have plenty of 'stars on its face'; it is the first thing a Welshman looks for when you hand him a bowlful.

Mati Thomas' recipe recalls the old conditions under which *cawl* was prepared:

salted bacon or beef	leeks.
peeled potatoes	carrots
cabbage	parsley
swedes	oatmeal
parsnips	a little savory and water

Put four gallons of water into a three legged cauldron, place on the fire and bring to the boil. Put in a large piece of salted bacon or beef. Boil for an hour and a half. Lift the meat from the cauldron and place on a large wooden dish. Put in the vegetables and herbs as listed. Mix two tablespoonsful of oatmeal to a paste in cold water, and add to the cawl. When it is well cooked remove from the fire. Fill a bowl with cawl for each person. Each person then helping himself to meat from the large wooden dish on the table.

This was a dinner on the first day of cooking and a breakfast on the following three days.

In south Wales, *cawl* is usually made with lamb and nearly always with a piece of shin beef as well. There is no doubt that the addition of beef to either bacon or lamb *cawl* greatly improves the flavour. When using shin it is sensible to give it more cooking time than the lamb, which can be added with the vegetables an hour after the beef.

The selection of root vegetables in south Wales tends to omit the parsnips, and the carrots are cut lengthways. The leek content is often great enough to make onions superfluous – note that the white part is used for the cooking, the green being saved for a final garnish with the parsley.

Minwel Tibbott quotes a recipe in *Welsh Fare* from Dowlais above Merthyr Tydfil in Mid-Glamorgan called, strangely, 'Leek and Parsley Broth' (*Cawl cennin a phersli*), the mixed green garnish giving it its name. In *Croeso Cymreig* a similar recipe is called 'Granny's Broth' (*Cawl Mam-gu*). Both are thickened with flour and water but I think it is a mistake to do this.

The following is a combination of both recipes:

2 lbs best end of neck lamb	2 large leeks
1 lb shin beef	bayleaf
1 small swede (cut in large chunks or slices)	parsley
½ lb carrots (cut lengthways)	salt and black pepper
1 lb potatoes	

Put the beef into a large pan, cover with cold water, bring slowly to the boil, add a little salt and skim. Simmer gently for 1 hour. Add lamb, carrots, swedes and the white of leeks, chopped fine, salt and pepper, bayleaf. Simmer gently for two hours. Add potatoes cut in chunks and simmer a further half hour. Lastly add finely-chopped green leeks and plenty of fresh, chopped parsley. Simmer a few minutes further and serve in basins.

The broth can be served separately with bread, and the meat and vegetables as a second course. This was a commonplace for miners' supper in south Wales.

Note: The leeks can be added raw to the hot broth just before serving, and the parsley sprinkled on at the last minute.

CAWL AT HAY HARVEST TIME

One of the problems for the caterer who wants to serve *cawl* to tourists is that it can't always be made during the summer because the vegetables are not always available. I was therefore most surprised when my friend from a winter spent in a fold of the Preseli hills, Mrs Mair Edwards, gave me this recipe, I asked her how did you get leeks at that time of year? She looked at me, surprised, then said: "Well, we cut the tops off the new leeks coming through the soil. It helped to make them grow thicker too."

This was a 'luxury' *cawl*, made with a piece of best gammon and without root vegetables to please and reward the harvesters.

piece of best ham (gammon)	parsley
new potatoes	tops of shallots
savoury (similar to thyme)	tops of leeks
a whole white cabbage cut in half or quarters.	

Simmer the gammon for about an hour and a half. Then add the rest of the ingredients and cook until tender, about half an hour more. Reheated for supper, this would be *cawl twymo*.

Another harvest *cawl*, this one for the later corn harvest of August and September, is given by Mati Thomas: there was in former days a *cawl* eminently suitable for summer. In fact it was made on the first day of August, once a year, as a special feast primarily for sailors on the beach at Newquay on the Cardiganshire coast. It was a co-operative affair – one woman supervising the making in a large cauldron, while the families concerned would contribute their portion – a piece of beef, and the season's fresh garden vegetables. Because of the wide variety of vegetables it contained it was held to be the best *cawl* of the year. It was called, appropriately, *cawl Awst*.

This information appears in *Welsh Fare* by Minwel Tibbott.

BROAD BEAN SOUP (CAWL FFA)

It was customary to plant quite a large amount of broad beans in the potato field. The surplus to immediate requirements being dried for winter use. *Cawl* was made during August and September. It was accepted as an appetizing and nourishing meal.

broad beans	salt bacon
potatoes	oatmeal
swedes	salt
parsley	cold water
leeks	

Place a cooker full of water on the fire with a chunk of salt bacon in it. Bring to the boil and add a paste of oatmeal, one tablespoonful in water. Then add potatoes, swedes. Later add salt to taste, then add the broad beans, parsley and leeks. Boil until the contents are cooked. It was a thick cawl and dark green in colour.

When cooked the meat was lifted out and shared onto wooden plates. The cawl served into wooden bowls. This was usually a harvest meal.

And a spring soup, associated with the yearly pigeon shoot:

WOODPIGEON CAWL (CAWL YSGUTHAN)

When *cawl* is used as here it simply signifies 'soup' as the English would use the word.

Many woodpigeons were killed during the spring, as it was very easy to shoot them as they were eating the shoots of the growing corn.

three woodpigeons	a little salt
parsley	water
oatmeal	

Boil the three woodpigeons in a cooker with enough water to cover them. As it breaks to the boil add the oatmeal, which has been prepared to a paste in cold water. Chop the parsley and add to the cawl. Add salt to taste. Sometimes potatoes were added to the cawl. It was necessary to boil the cawl for quite a long time as the meat was hard. The flavour of this cawl could be classified as superb. It was often prepared for sick people.

This was served as a spring dinner.

Leek Soup (*Cawl Cennin*)

You'll see a lot of recipes under this title in collections of traditional Welsh dishes, and they are based on the early *cawl* recipe I've quoted from Mati Thomas. Usually, bacon is specified, and parsley rather than thyme as seasoning, and the broth is thickened with oatmeal. But there is another recipe which one comes across now and again; after I'd found it I used to tease the English who scoffed at Welsh food by serving *vichyssoise* under the title 'Chilled Cawl Cennin'. The joke was double-edged of course, because, elegant as it is, *vichyssoise* is nothing more than a country soup – *potage à la bonne femme* – chilled. (Far away from his home in the country, a chef working in Vichy recalled his mother's homely soup with affection, and with a touch of whimsy transformed it into a restaurant offering. . . perhaps he too enjoyed the occasional bemusing of his customers.)

3 potatoes	2 pints milk
pepper and salt, chopped parsley	butter
white parts of six leeks	1 pint of white stock

Slice the potatoes and leeks thinly and simmer in a shallow pan of water with a small lump of butter. When the mixture is soft, press through a sieve and add the milk, stock, pepper and salt. Heat, but do not boil or the milk will curdle. Add the parsley when serving.

Broth Mawr

Iris Price-Jones gave this recipe for St David's Day 1976 on BBC Radio Wales. I had not heard of a *cawl* as big and hearty as this one and I was anxious to know its origin. Iris Price-Jones said it was a family recipe which could have come from Pembrokeshire – her mother's home. I feel sure there is a connection here between this dish and the Brandy Broth described so eloquently if a bit 'over the top' by Richard Llewellyn in *How Green Was My Valley,* writing about the food he knew as a child in Pembrokeshire, and not that of the mining valleys.

113

piece of lean beef *or*
piece of lean bacon to weigh 1½ to 2 lbs
1 small chicken to weigh about 2 lbs
½ lb carrots
1lb leeks

½ lb parsnips
small piece of swede
parsley
salt and pepper for seasoning

Cut the carrots in half, slice the swede, parsnip and the white of the leeks.

Cover the meat and vegetables with water and simmer slowly for as long as you like – about 2½ to 3 hours is enough. Then add the chopped parsley and the chopped green of the leeks, and simmer for a further 10 minutes. Test for seasoning. Serve the liquid as the first course – the broth – and very tasty and nourishing it is.

Then serve the chicken and the bacon or beef, garnished with the vegetables as the second course, with the rest of the liquid thickened a little with flour as gravy – and with separately boiled potatoes, or better still with *Stwnsh Rwdan* – that is with potatoes and swedes boiled together and then mashed.

BRANDY BROTH

HOW GREEN WAS MY VALLEY: Richard Llewellyn:

O, Brandy Broth is the King of Broth and royal in the rooms of the mouth. A good chicken and a noble piece of ham, with a little shoulder of lamb, small to have the least of grease, and then a paste of the roes of trout with cream, a bit of butter, and the yolk of egg, whipped tight and poured in when the chicken, proud with a stuffing of sage and thyme, has been elbowing the lamb and the ham in the earthenware pot until all three are tender as the heart of a mother. In with the carrots and turnips and the goodness of marrow bones, and in with a mixing of milk and potatoes. Now watch the clock and every fifteen minutes pour in a noggin of brandy, and with the first a pint of home-brewed ale. Two noggins in and with the third, throw in the chopped bottoms of leeks, but save the green leaves until ten minutes from the time you sit to eat, for then you shall find them still a lovely green.

Drink down the liquor and raise your eyes to give praise for a mouth and a belly, and then start upon the chicken.

2. Bacon *(Cig moch)* – and pigs

Bacon, sliced thick, and potatoes.
HOW GREEN WAS MY VALLEY: Richard Llewellyn

Collections of Welsh recipes always include several based on the bacon-plus-potatoes theme: the self-explanatory *Ffest y cybydd* (The Miser's Feast) popular in Carmarthenshire 100 years ago and a number of 'potato' titled dishes, such as *Tato Rhost* (Roast Potatoes) which combines potatoes, bacon, onions in a one-pot dish.

Always the poor man's animal, because they could so easily be put out to feed on waste ground and in the woodlands, pigs were important in Wales from early medieval times, as can be seen from their value in the *Laws of Hywel Dda*.

Anyone old enough to remember the days in Wales when almost every country household kept a pig or two will tell you about the great excitement of the day the pig-sticker came to do his grisly work. . . the preface to bulging larders and satisfied stomachs.

In *Give me Yesterday,* James Williams gives a very detailed description of what he claims was the 'ritual' rather than task of pig-killing, which he insists should be carried out during a waxing, never a waning moon which was certain to prevent the bacon curing properly. It was traditional to preface the proceedings with a glass of brandy for the butcher and the pig-owner. This custom could sometimes be carried too far, as this recollection by Beryl and Anne Jane Jones of Llangrannog on the Cardiganshire coast reveals.

In the days when they kept pigs, they also had the local pub, so it was easy to be generous with liquid hospitality for the visiting butcher, and as well as the opening drink they got into the way of giving the butcher a drink between pigs, as it were. . . until one disastrous occasion when he was too affected by drink to satisfactorily complete the killing of the third pig, which escaped, bleeding but still alive, to lead them all a macabre chase through the village. After that, the butcher was given nothing at all to drink until all three pigs were safely strung up!

These two sisters have some very comic piggy tales to tell. They say bad pigs are born that way and remain so all their lives, and they relate the story of two of the naughtiest of their pigs, 'hunters' who repeatedly escaped from their quarters and often used their freedom to go swimming in the bay. . . an innocent enough pastime for a pig one might think, especially in hot weather, but as any pig-keeper will instantly tell you, too much swimming causes cuts to develop in the pigs' necks. Not content with a cooling splash in the main bay, these two porcine natators struck out for the adjoining bay, where, upon rounding the rocks they were encountered by some very surprised holidaymakers. Once they had recovered from the initial shock, these good people sensibly herded the pigs back to base, but the pigs' return happened to coincide with opening time at the pub; the bar was busy, and so the pigs were quickly shut in the coal shed until time could be found to return them to their sty. . . which wasn't until after dark, when, two pairs of eyes whitely and wickedly gleaming in the fitful light of a lantern, what predictably emerged from the blackness of the coal shed were a couple of *moch du* (black pigs). [1]

As the summer wore on, these two pig escapologists became more and more difficult to contain, until escape and capture became a daily ritual, so nearby campers had to be warned. One family of campers, however, foolishly allowed the pigs to fraternise, cementing the relationship with tit-bits of food and other demonstrations of welcome. Came the day when the campers went off on a day-long outing, leaving their tents tied back and open to the fresh sea-breeze. . . the pigs, when they arrived, sure of their welcome if puzzled by finding no-one at home, investigated the contents of the tents with commendable thoroughness. The insides of the sleeping bags proved to be especially interesting. . . When they returned, the campers found their friendly neighbours comfortably asleep, each in a cosy cocoon of feathers, a loose feather dancing gently in the snores above each porker's dreaming snout.

---

[1]. The famous Welsh comic lament 'Y Mochyn Du' tells the tale of a black pig who died from over-eating barley.

Pig farming. Photo by Keith Morris.

Pig-killing time was a major social occasion because all the parts of the animal which couldn't be salted or eaten at once were given away to neighbours who would, in turn, reciprocate with gifts in kind from their pig-killing, and neighbours would in fact arrange their pigs' demises on a sensibly-spaced rota basis. Meanwhile, as James Williams describes, there was tremendous activity in the kitchen over the making of faggots, sausages, puddings, brawn and haslet:

First the head was cut off close behind the ears, the back-bone removed with the tail attached, and a side at a time placed on an old table which had been scrubbed. The flare fat, kidneys, and ribs were removed and the whole side cut in three – ham, middle, and fore-leg. There were no sub-divisions into loin, belly, etc. Several dishes were heaped with choice fillet steaks which were not left to be cured as the strong salt would make them too salty. The pig's tail was chopped off, and put aside with the trotters, ears, pluck, tongue, brain, caul (we called it shawl), kidneys, all of which were used to make faggots, brawn, sausage and delectable puddings. The one part of a pig's offal which was always thrown away was the spleen *poten ludw* and I seem to remember that it was rejected also by both cat and dog – why I could not tell. The intestines, altogether about sixty feet of them, were turned inside out and scraped, after which they were cut into lengths and cleansed in warm salt water. Some were chopped, mixed with pieces of stomach, and fried with onions. I never cared for the bitter taste of this dish. But there would be lots of roast ribs and fried steaks – which were delicious hot or cold. There was also the pleasing custom of taking a few choice pieces to our neighbours, who in their turn, would reciprocate, when they had killed their pig. The house smelled for days of roasting, frying, and baking, and the atmosphere was greasy from the never-ending rendering down into lard of the flare fat. We never used the bladder to contain lard, though many did, the hot liquid being poured into a tundish inserted in the neck of the bladder, a tricky domestic operation, as spilt molten lard inflicted nasty burns. So on each pig-killing occasion the bladder became a veritable treasure for us boys. It was blown up – the tube tied and then its length shortened, and it was proudly taken to school and used as a football. Its flight after being kicked was wholly unpredictable, thus adding to the interest of the game. It was incredibly tough, as of course it had to be, to withstand the constant lambasting from metal-tipped clogs. Disaster usually met it when after being kicked over the wall, it would land on a thorn bush and be punctured. We never learnt of a way to mend a punctured pig's bladder.

Meanwhile a reception was being prepared for the 6 main pieces of pig to which was added the chin, or jowl. A wooden vat called *noe* was lined with salt which we bought in 'bars' weighing 14 lbs each, which we had to render into powder. The salt was well rubbed into the sides and hams which were placed skin downwards on the prepared bed of salt. After a day or two saltpetre was rubbed on the flesh – but not on the skin. Adding salt was continued for about 7 or 8 days, after which the vat contained a good deal of brine and the absorption of salt was now slow. The pieces were moved daily, but left for a total of about a month before they were lifted out, and hung to dry for a few days before being taken indoors to the big old-fashioned farm-house chimney, where they were strung up in serried ranks, being kept separate by bunches of holly. Mother claimed she could forecast the weather by examining the salt moisture on the sides of bacon.

PIG'S HARSLET (HASLET)

Haslet, a mix of pig's liver, sweetbreads and lean pork bits is still universally popular in Wales, though it is a British rather than a Welsh speciality. It is often found in Welsh cookery collections, copied word for word from Mrs Rundell's *New System of Domestic Cookery* as was the fashion in the 19th century, to be eventually assumed as 'mother's own' recipe. Mrs Togers of Wrexham, a prolific contributor to *Farmhouse Fare*, sent Mrs Rundell's recipe in as though it were her mother's:

Wash and dry some liver, sweetbreads and fat and lean bits of pork, beating the latter with a rolling pin to make it tender; season with pepper, salt, sage and a little onion shredded fine; when mixed put all into a caul and fasten it up tight with a needle and thread. Roast it on a hanging jack or by a string. Serve it in slices with parsley for a fry, or with a sauce or port-wine, water and mustard, just boiled up and put into a dish.

Local market versions of haslet in Wales are generally very good. They are often sold as 'aislet' or 'islet' and are much superior to the commercial products offered on the cooked meat counters of shops or supermarkets.

A Carmarthenshire Recipe for Brawn
from Farmhouse Fare:

The day we cut up the pig, I bring together all the pig's head which has been cut up and the trotters. I have ready by my side a good-sized crock and a good supply of crushed salt. Then I rub each piece well with salt and fit them as neatly as possible into the crock. I leave it like this for 2 or 3 days. I then wash all the pieces in cold water and place in a big boiler, covering them with water. Bring to the boil and simmer gently for 3 to 4 hours until the meat leaves the bone.

Lift all the pieces on to a large tray (a crock will do) and leave liquor to cool. Mince all the meat in a large bowl and add to this 8 medium-sized onions, minced; 2 tablespoonfuls dried sage and pepper. Add salt according to taste.

Remove fat from the surface of the liquor. Strain liquor into a crock and have boiler free from all tiny bones. Then replace 4 quarts of the liquor into the boiler and add to this all the mixture in the bowl. Place over fire and simmer for about 15 minutes, turning frequently. Have ready about a dozen good-sized basins and pie-dishes; fill them with the mixture. Leave till cold. When turned out it looks a lovely glossy jelly and tastes delicious with apple sauce.

Granny Morgan's Brawn
A Shropshire recipe, from the same source:

Clean a pig's head and soak in brine for a few days. Before using, wash in clean cold water. Boil until the meat drops from the bone. In a separate saucepan cook the liver, heart and tongue, until very tender. Strain the stock in which the head was cooked, then turn this stock into that in which the remainder of the meat was cooked; add to it 6 black peppercorns, and an equal number of whole cloves, and boil until it is reduced to 1 pint. Strain again, add 1 cupful of good vinegar and re-heat.

In the meantime, chop the meat or put it through the mincer, add seasoning of chopped onions or sage if desired. Add salt and pepper if needed. Pack into stone crocks, pour the stock over it, cover with a plate, weight well, cover with a cloth and set aside for a week before using.

Lloyd George's Favourite Brawn

Recipe from Mrs Blodwen Evans who worked for the family for many years, from *Lloyd George's Favourite Dishes:*

a pig's head	cloves
1 lb beef	bunch of herbs
blade mace	salt and pepper

Thoroughly cleanse the head and put to soak all night. Rinse well and put in a saucepan with the beef, cover with water and bring to the boil. When at boiling point, remove scum. Add a blade of mace, 3 or 4 cloves, and a bunch of herbs. Simmer gently for about 2½ hours.

Strain the stock from the meat, reserve and allow to get cold. Remove fat from the jellied stock. Turn out the tongue and skin, then cut into small pieces. Also cut all the meat from the head and the beef. Put into a bowl and add a little of the jellied stock. Add salt and pepper to your taste.

Black Pudding (Pwdin Gwaed)

from *S.Minwel Tibbott's* Welsh Fare

the pig's blood on day of killing	mixed herbs
one pint cold water	a little oatmeal
a little salt	pig's small intestine
onions	a little fat off the small intestine

Pour the blood into a large bowl while warm and stir constantly until cold to avoid clotting. Then dilute with a pint of water, add a little salt and allow to stand overnight.

Wash the intestine thoroughly, inside and out, and put in salt water overnight.

Chop the onions, coat them and the pieces of fat with oatmeal, season with herbs and stir into the blood. Work the mixture into the small intestine, secure with string at both ends, allowing for expansion during boiling. Boil the pudding in water for about half an hour and then hang to dry in a suitable place. Slice, when needed, and fry with bacon.

SCRUGGINS CAKE

A Welsh border speciality, made from the 'scruggins' or 'scratchings' – the crisp little pieces of fat or crackling left after the pig's flair has been melted down for lard or dripping.

Sheila Hutchins, who gives this recipe in her *Daily Express Cookery Book*, says that if they are made crisp in the oven and rolled in salt they go well with an *apéritif*. When I had my Aga I used to put a dish of bacon rinds in the slow oven for an hour or so, and when they were nice and crisp, crumble them up with salt for bar tasties, and they were good, too:

> For scruggins cake put 400g (1 lb) of self-raising flour in the mixing bowl with 200g (8 oz) of granulated sugar and 300g (12 oz) of scruggins, or scratchings, chopped up in small pieces. Stir and make it into a soft dough with milk and water then roll it out about 2.5cm (1 inch) thick and press it into a square tin well greased with lard. Sprinkle the top of your cake with a little caster sugar, and mark it into squares.
>
> Bake it for 30 minutes in a moderate oven (350 deg.F., Gas 4).

TRIPE (BOLA MOCHYN)
from Welsh Fare *again:*

The pig's tripe was washed and left to stand in salt water and lime for nine days after killing. Then it was washed and boiled until tender, when it was put on to a large dish and pressed. When set, it was cut into slices and fried in bacon fat with onions.

HAMS TO CURE

For this process Lady Llanover gives characteristically precise instructions in *The First Principles of Good Cookery:*

> Beat or roll the ham well with a rolling-pin on the fleshy side, rub in one ounce of saltpetre and three ounces of salt, well mixed, finely powdered, and warm; take one pound of pounded common salt, and one pound of treacle, mix together and make thoroughly hot in a double saucepan, then rub into the ham well by degrees (one spoonful at a time) till the whole is absorbed – it will take an hour to do it properly; let it lie one night, the next day rub in half a pound more of common salt pounded fine, rub it in evenly all over the ham, let it lie

till brine runs from it; then turn the ham in its own pickle, and rub it well every day till it begins to shrink, and it may then be hung up in an airy place and dried very gradually. Three weeks or a month is the ordinary time to cure a ham.

N.B. – After the first rubbing with saltpetre the ham must be placed in a long pan, out of which it can be taken, and put upon the stone to rub in the treacle and salt, but it must be kept in the pan or the pickle will be lost. Hams cured in this way, as in all others, should be used before they are old and rusty, but when used in the above manner they are particularly good dressed very fresh, and small hams from porkers should be cured in this way when required for eating cold.

ROAST POTATOES AND BACON (TATO RHOST A BACWN)
From Mrs Havard, Llandysul, South Cardiganshire:

new potatoes (all the same size) a bunch of spring onions
slices of bacon or ham (preferably home-cured)

Use a thick, heavy saucepan. Put a layer of bacon or ham on the bottom, fill the pan with layers of potatoes, cover with more bacon, then add the spring onions – whole. Add a very little water (one-third of a cupful) and cook over a low heat for about 1½ to 2 hours until the potatoes have absorbed the water and browned in the bacon fat.

Sometimes the potatoes were par-boiled for this dish, while other versions layer the onions in between the bacon and potato layers. Again, another version fries the bacon, sliced potatoes and onions first before cooking them in layers in the same deep frying pan. They are all good, simple dishes for busy days.

Yet another version is:

THE MISER'S FEAST (FFEST Y CYBYDD)

Cover the bottom of a saucepan with peeled potatoes (whole) and a sliced onion, with a little salt. Cover with water and bring to the boil. When the water is boiling, place on top of the potatoes and onion a few slices of bacon or a piece of ham, replace the lid and allow to simmer till the potatoes are cooked, when most of the water will be absorbed.

The miser was supposed to eat the potatoes one day, mashed up in the liquid, keeping the slices of bacon to be eaten the next day with plain boiled potatoes. The same idea of obtaining nourishment for two meals from an initial cooking was employed with *cawl*, as explained at the beginning of this section.

BOILED HAM (*CIG MOCHYN WEDI'I FERWI*)
From Welsh Fare.

Cover a ham joint with water and boil gently, allowing 15 minutes for every pound plus fifteen minutes. When tender, remove from the liquor and with a sharp knife remove the rind, coat the joint with demerara sugar and melt it over the meat.

Rolling a clean red-hot poker over the sugared joint was a common practice at one time, but nowadays the joint could be placed under the grill or in a hot oven for a few minutes.

3. Faggots

At a stall near the great entrance a buxom Welsh dame in her forties presided over a display of eatables. In pursuit at once of information, experience , and luncheon, I sat on the wooden settle behind the bench on which the viands were spread, and surveyed the board. A bouquet of flowers in a pot-bellied pitcher, with blue rings around it, stood surrounded by pies and tarts of various sorts; a huge rice pudding in a deep dish, a bowl of eggs, square cuts of German-looking pastry, and certain round boulders of black plum pudding. A pile of what I took to be sausages were steaming furiously over a brazier of burning coals on one end of the bench, with a teapot leaning lazily against it and thinking aloud. Choosing what seemed the least formidable specimen of the food before me, I pointed to the brazier and said, but in a tone so low I was not heard, "I will take a sausage." Obeying my gesture, the woman served me a saucer-full of the black balls, swimming in hot gravy, and gave me a pewter spoon with which to eat it, instead of the knife and fork which might have been expected with meat. The balls proved to be not unpalateable eating, and were, according to my best judgment, made of liver. What they were actually made of, however, is a question upon which I subsequently learned to entertain doubts; they are a savoury compound locally called "faggits" or fagots (Query, fag-ends?).

Wirt Sikes, the aforementioned American Consul in Cardiff in the 1880's, describing his luncheon at Merthyr Tydfil market, which with a portion of rice pudding (he was given an iron-pronged fork to eat it with – both the fork and the solidity of the pudding surprised him!) cost 6*d*., 1881.

The inquisitive Consul, eager to know more about the unexpectedly foreign country to which he had been sent, and puzzled over the word and the dish – faggots – wasn't too far off the mark with his explanation. The word *fagot*, originates from Old French, and means, simply, a bundle, to bundle. Thus faggots, or Savoury Ducks as they are sometimes more appetisingly called, are a very old British way of using up the bits and pieces after a pig-killing. (Faggots are unknown in America, and the word there means a rather unsavoury old tramp. . .)

Faggots are still popular in Wales, and many housewives make their own. Those sold in Welsh markets are often so good they are passed off as home-made *pâté* by hostesses in a hurry.

Commercially-made faggots usually contain the lights, heart and melt instead of the belly pork given in one of my household recipes. Pig's caul or fleed, or apron as it is sometimes called (the fine membrane, marbled with fat, from the inside of the pig) is essential for proper faggots as it keeps them nice and moist, particularly on top where they might otherwise dry out. It needs to be soaked a little in tepid water to soften it before using. Ask for it at a proper butchers – the supermarket may be baffled.

PEMBROKESHIRE FAGGOTS (*FFAGOTS SIR BENFRO*)

1½ lbs pig's liver	1 or 2 teaspoonfuls sage (chopped)
4 oz breadcrumbs	2 teaspoonfuls salt
3 oz suet	¼ teaspoonful pepper
2 large onions	

Mince raw liver and onions into bowl. Mix with breadcrumbs, suet, salt and pepper and sage thoroughly. Form into small balls. Wrap each in a piece of caul.

Bake in a moderate oven for about 30 minutes; pour boiling water into tin to form gravy.

FAGGOTS – MRS ELIZABETH EVANS' WAY *(for the freezer)*

Mrs Evans' daughter says there's something magical about her mother's way with this recipe which is quite inimitable however carefully she follows it. (But that's the alchemy of cooking!)

2 lb belly pork
1 lb pig's liver
1½ lb breadcrumbs
1½ lb onions or shallots

teaspoon chopped sage
salt and pepper
pig's caul

Mince the pork and liver (an obliging butcher may do this for you). Mince the onions, add breadcrumbs, salt, pepper and sage. If you are using pig's caul, cut it up into 5in. squares and wrap each one around about 2oz of the mixture. If there is no caul, roll balls of the mixture (about a tablespoon) in flour. Either way, place the faggots in rows in a baking tin. Dissolve one or two Oxo cubes in boiling water to make a stock and pour this over the faggots. Bake for 2 hours in a slow oven, adding more water if necessary to keep the faggots nearly covered. When the faggots are cooked the stock with have become a lovely gravy which can be thickened if liked to serve with the faggots.

When freezing, Mrs Evans adds the gravy to the faggots, packed in sealed containers.

4. Liver (Iau)

LIVER AND ONIONS (*IAU A NIONOD*)

Popular in north Wales with *stwnsh* (swede, turnips and potatoes mashed together). The tradition of cooking with liver is a survival of the later medieval times, when offal for eating included the lung, spleen and gut, whose flavours could be strong – even rank – powerful seasonings were needed to counteract them.

Cut liver into slices and roll in seasoned flour, then fry lightly till brown all over. Fry some sliced onions until golden, then place with the liver in a covered pan or casserole, season and cover with water, simmer slowly for 2-3 hours.

LIVER, BACON AND ONIONS (*CIG MOCH, IAU A NIONOD*)

A memory of childhood. My mother, whose family were from north Wales, where this recipe is from, gave identical instructions, especially the light frying of the bacon, which she pointed out would draw enough fat in which to cook the liver and onions – one of those little points of economy which are beginning to come back.

½lb bacon rashers   salt and pepper
1lb liver   a little plain flour
onions

Slice the liver and toss in seasoned flour. Fry the bacon rashers lightly (I often use streaky bacon or 'pieces' for this, for economy) and lift out on to a warm dish. Fry the chopped onion in the bacon fat and then (briefly) the liver, then place with the bacon. Make gravy by mixing a tablespoonful of plain flour into the fat in the pan, adding a little boiling water and stir well. Boil for a few minutes. Serve with boiled potatoes.

This dish was served at suppertime to the quarrymen of north Wales (*swper chwarel*), and is from *Welsh Fare*.

PIG'S LIVER SOUP (*CAWL HASLET*)
from Croeso Cymreig

1lb pig's liver   1lb potatoes
1lb onions   pepper and salt to taste

Cut liver in small pieces, slice onions and prepare potatoes. Allow the liver and onions to simmer in three pints of water for 1½ to 2 hours. Add potatoes, simmer for another half-hour, season with salt and pepper. Strain and serve very hot.

5. Savoury Pies (other than those associated with markets and fairs, for which see pp 238-40)

Although black puddings made with pigs' blood were common to all parts of Wales, goose-blood used for a similar purpose was a relatively rare practice, usually carried out when a fair number of geese were killed at the same time for the Christmas market. The following is from *Welsh Fare:*

GOOSE-BLOOD PUDDING (PWDIN GWAED GWYDDAU)

blood from a number of geese
one or two tablespoonfuls oatmeal
plain flour

salt and pepper
sugar
onion, chopped finely

Keep the blood from a number of geese (when killing them for the Christmas market) and beat well with a fork until cold, to avoid lumps forming. Mix the oatmeal and flour with a small quantity of the blood and add to the remainder. Season with pepper, salt and sugar and fold in the chopped onion. Remove the skin from a goose's neck and sew to form a long bag. Pour the blood mixture into it and secure tightly at both ends. Immerse in boiling water and boil for two or three hours. Slice when cold and fry in bacon fat.
This pudding was served with potatoes or with bread and butter.

Another use for goose-blood in cooking is recorded by Minwel Tibbott. It seems to be unknown outside Montgomeryshire. Mrs Dylis Blodwen Ellis, who talked to me about Goose-blood Tart, is now living near Tywyn, on the Merionethshire coast, but she learned the dish in her Montgomeryshire family home. For using in this way, the goose blood is cooked over water to make it solid. When it is cool and set, it is rubbed between the fingers to make fine crumbs. In this state it is mixed with the dried fruit, syrup and sugar for the tart filling, and is thus being used in exactly the same way as beef once was for mincemeat. In the cooking, both the meat, and in this case the blood all but disappear; eventually the beef was left out of mincemeat altogether, and what we have today is just the fruits, sugar and spices and beef suet mixture. Precisely the same thing happened with the mutton pies when lamb or mutton was cooked with currants or raisins (see p.239).

GOOSE BLOOD TART (CACEN GWAED GWYDDAU)
also from Welsh Fare:

short crust pastry	½lb shredded suet
½lb solidified goose blood	3 teaspoonfuls mixed spice
1lb currants	4 wooden spoonfuls golden syrup
1lb soft brown sugar	a little salt

Put the blood of about three geese into a basin and place this in a saucepan of boiling water. Boil for about three hours, keeping the water topped up, then leave the blood to cool and set. Rub into crumbs and add to the other ingredients. Mix thoroughly and spread between two layers of shortcrust pastry, as in a mincemeat tart. Bake in a hot oven for about half and hour. A Christmas dish.

CHICKEN AND LEEK PIE (PASTAI CYW IAR A CHENNIN)

This is an adaptation from Lady Llanover's instructions for 'Hermit's Chicken and Leek Pie' in *Good Cookery*. I do not think it is in the very old tradition of Welsh cookery, but might well have been made by certain well-to-do yeomen farmers' wives. Lady Llanover was inclined to add her own embellishments which is why I use a simpler version:

a chicken (a boiling fowl will do)	a stick of celery
3 or 4 slices of cold boiled tongue	mixed herbs, parsley, salt
a bunch of small leeks	3 tablespoons cream
a large onion	

FOR THE PASTRY:

6 oz flour	1 gill water
3 tablespoons mutton dripping (but I would use shortcrust)	

Put the chicken in a large saucepan and cover with water. Bring to the boil and skim. Then add the onion, quartered, the celery and herbs and season with salt. Simmer for 1½-2 hours according to the size and age of the bird. When tender, remove the chicken from the saucepan and strain the stock into a basin. Stand in a cool place until the chicken stock has set in a jelly. Remove green part of the leeks, scald the white part with boiling water. Split and cut in 1 in. lengths. Carve the chicken in neat joints and lay in a pie dish with the slices of cold tongue, the leeks, a little chopped parsley, and moisten with some of the chicken jelly. Cover with pastry, leaving a small opening in the centre. Bake in a quick oven until the pastry is a light golden brown. Through hole in the pastry pour in the cream, previously warmed. Cover the hole with a little piece of pastry cut in a fancy shape and baked alongside the pie. Serve warm.

To serve cold, omit the cream.

WELSH CHICKEN

This is a dish for a boiling fowl. I prefer to thicken the sauce at the end of the cooking time, and not to add the cabbage until the chicken is nearly cooked, otherwise it is flabby and unattractive. This recipe comes from *Croeso Cymreig:*

chicken (one or two)
½ lb bacon
½ lb carrots
1 oz butter
1 oz flour
1 small cabbage

2 large leeks
bunch of mixed herbs
pepper and salt
stock
dripping

Young birds need not be used for this dish. Truss them as for boiling. Cut the bacon, leeks, and carrots into dice. Put them into a casserole with the butter and fry for a few minutes, stir in the flour until it thickens and browns. Place the chicken in the thickened sauce. Wash and cut up a small cabbage and put it into the casserole with the chicken, add a bunch of herbs, leeks and sprinkle in pepper and salt. Add ½ pint of stock, put some small lumps of dripping or butter on the bird, cover, and simmer for 2 or 3 hours. When serving, make a bed of the cooked cabbage on a dish and place the bird on it. Garnish with the carrots and pour the liquor over the cabbage.

6. Welsh Salt Duck

Lady Llanover recorded this dish, which seems to have been confined to the Marcher counties. Whether the bird was salted to preserve it for a few days, or to tenderise it is a matter for conjecture: in Lady Llanover's meticulous hands the cooking of the bird becomes a matter for the employment of one of her culinary hobbyhorses – what she called a 'double', that is to say: one pan inside another with water in between; a *bain marie* in fact. The same principle was used for the accompanying Onion Sauce.

The method produces excellent results and her remarks in praise of salt boiled duck worth noting, for this is a delicious dish very little understood. One of its virtues is that all the fat is carried off in the water (the stock makes an excellent base for soup, such as lentil) leaving only lean, tender, delicately salted meat.

Laver Sauce is an alternative accompaniment, or laver with orange zest (see p.170), or *Suryn Cyffaith Poeth*. Salt duck is also good eaten cold with a plain green salad, or orange and watercress salad.

SALT DUCK

For a common-sized duck a quarter of a pound of salt, to be well-rubbed in and re-rubbed, and turned on a dish every day for three days, then wash all the salt off clean, put it into a double with half a pint of cold water to the pound, and let it simmer steadily for two hours. Salt boiled duck, with white onion sauce, is much better than roast duck.

I usually add an onion, a *bouquet garni* and a few black peppercorns.

ONION SAUCE

Cut up four onions and stew in a double with a little water until tender: then pour off the water and mix half an ounce of flour with it; then add half a pint of milk, and stir well until of a proper consistency, then pass through a wire sieve and return into the double saucepan; stir well, and when quite hot it is ready to pour over.

Suryn Cyffaith Poeth

A rough translation of this would be: 'hot, sour pickle confection', and that is just what it is – one of the many recipes for this kind of sauce which has its roots in the very earliest condiment, the *liquamen* of the Romans, made from the salted putrified remains of fish and their entrails, which took the place of salt in most of their dishes. The Romans had adopted it from the Greeks (*garum*) and used it throughout their western Empire. British MS cookery books contain similar recipes, together with a number of catsups or ketchups of various kinds. Eventually the preparation of these condiments was taken over by commercial firms and are with us today under their famous brand-names. This particular sauce is remarkably like H.P. sauce. The recipe undoubtedly found its way into *Croeso Cymreig* from an MS book in a Welsh *plas:*

6 lemons	¼ oz mace
2 oz horseradish	¼ oz nutmeg
1 lb salt	¼ oz cayenne
6 cloves of garlic	2 oz mustard
¼ oz cloves	2 quarts of malt vinegar

Cut the lemons into eighths and cover with salt, cut the horseradish very finely, then place with the rest of the ingredients in a big jar that has a lid. Place the jar in a boiler of water (with the water coming to within two inches of the rim of the jar). Bring to the boil and boil for 15 minutes. Stir the mixture every day for six weeks, and keep the lid on. At the end of six weeks strain into small bottles and cork tightly. This will keep for years, and a little will go far. Serve with veal, or Salt Duck.

4. Mutton, Lamb, Goat

The woman next door was very civil, and gave me a shoulder of lamb, with a lesson in cooking, as though I had watched my mother and Bron for more than two years for nothing.
HOW GREEN WAS MY VALLEY: *Richard Llewellyn*

Welsh lamb is justly prized, its fame resting on the sweetness of Welsh mountain lamb, which is a distinct breed, much smaller than other breeds, so more of the meat is nearer the bone.

The once equally famed Welsh mutton, on the other hand, is with us no longer, its disappearance due to changes in demand and the economics of present-day sheep farming. Mutton, for younger cooks, who may find the term a puzzle, was grown-up ewe, or mummy sheep. The real old Welsh mutton of which George Borrow and others wrote so enthusiastically, from Elizabethan times on, when Welsh mutton began to find its way on to English tables, was until thirty or forty years ago obtained from ewes kept for three or four years for their wool. Nowadays the high cost of feed outweighs the price paid for wool, so the economics of producing real mutton do not make farming sense.

What you might get now under the label of mutton is old lamb, i.e., fattened wether (castrated ram), which is exceedingly dull in comparison with the old lean and well-flavoured mutton. But to get this your butcher will have had to get in to the market before the ethnic buyers, who want it for their curry and kebab houses, and they will have had to get there ahead of the food manufacturers who want it to keep their profits up on tinned Irish stew, 'beef' sausages, 'pies' and so forth which are turned out on a largely uncritical eating public in the questionable name of British 'manufactured' food products. They, in turn, will have had to be ahead of the pet food boys.

Lamb in any case is now finished younger, as the trade has it, because of better hill pastures. A visit to some bleak upland, such as *Mynydd Bach* behind the Cardiganshire coast will give an idea of what this bog-riddden land, no good for anything, once offered. No wonder its inhabitants emigrated.

Wales now produces three groups of lamb. The most lucrative is the heaviest – 17 kilos in weight. This is the lamb most liked by the French. Next comes what is known as 'supermarket lamb' – 16+ kilos and very lean. Lastly, the lightest weight – 14 kilos, very popular in Italy and Spain. The French also like it, but for the legs only which they want for their *gigots*, which means a lot of lamb to dispose of elsewhere. So when you see a pile of bargain shoulder cuts on offer in the supermarket, you might be right in deducing that they are the result of a big order of legs for France.

Anything specifically labelled 'Welsh Lamb' should have come from the breed known as 'Welsh Mountain Sheep' – a smaller breed valued for the extra amount of meat nearer the bone.

How much of the information I have given here on Welsh lamb will be applicable in the future I cannot say. As I write at the end of 1995, the turmoil of the EU makes stability impossible and prediction equally so, and it is not sensible to go into too much detail except to say that the current experimental introduction of the Merino breed to Welsh sheep is likely to result in an extremely marketable fleece. Mutton again?

The Welsh lamb industry now benefits from the promotional activities of 'Welsh Lamb Enterprise', an organisation which enlightens butchers and encourages caterers in Wales to make as much use of Welsh lamb as possible in their hotels and restaurants. They have devised new and wondrous cuts with suggestions as to how to use them in novel ways designed to appeal to their clientèle. Their efforts tend to make me smile when I recall my first hotel guests' relief when they did not encounter the ubiquitous 'roast lamb' on my early 1960's menus. . . their first chance, they said, to avoid it during a week or more in Wales. Nothing had changed, apparently, since Wirt Sikes recorded in the 1880's the over-reliance of Welsh hotels and inns on the native product in his delightful *Rambles and Studies in Old South Wales*:

The Beaufort Arms in Monmouth was the same as all the

other hostelries he had sampled:

> It is quite in vain to give a *carte blanche* order for dinner in a British hotel; on no account will such an order be accepted, although the preposterous and crafty maid or butler knows perfectly well that the resources of the inn, when tested to their utmost, will produce at the last, and inevitably, chops – neither more nor less.
>
> "What can you give me inside half an hour?" I ask. "Anything you like, sir" the woman answers with unblushing effrontery, and a respectful cordiality delightful to see in such a connexion. I am tempted to ask for buckwheat cakes, prairie chicken, roast saddlerocks, and watermelons, but compromise with "How about a fowl?" "Fowl, sir? – take about an hour to cook a fowl, sir." But it is idle to defer the climax of this thrilling – or grilling – tale. I had chops for dinner.

In an earlier chapter, while his enthusiasm for the ubiquitous lamb chops was still undimmed by over-familiarity, he described them as 'done to a turn. . . juicy and tender with the true Welsh tenderness and juice. . .' This was at the Gold Croft Inn at Caerleon.

The Welsh shepherd of long ago, eking out a bare living by tending flocks in rugged conditions would not be familiar with the delights of tender Welsh lamb. Unless it dies on you, one does not eat the source of one's income. Mutton now and again, maybe, but not very often lamb. Hence there are few recipes in the Welsh tradition for dealing with succulent little joints and tiny, tender chops.

The old mutton recipes from Wales and elsewhere tend to make one's mouth water and one's spirits fray with frustration. However, some of them are worthwhile adapting to present-day lamb, and they would certainly be worth trying if you have been landed with some of that ram mutton which even the Asians and the food and pet food manufacturers didn't want. Even a reasonably good leg of lamb could be boiled for a change, thus reverting to an old habit much in favour in Victorian times. Lady Llanover makes this suggestion in *Good Cookery:*

Sheep-shearing at the Royal Welsh Show. Photo by Keith Morris.

Boiled Shoulder of Mutton

Weighed three pounds; onions, half a pound; celery, half a pound chopped fine; marjory and a small sprig of orange thyme. Put in a double with one pint and a half of water, and water boiling round for two hours and a half. Produced one quart of good broth, the meat being tender and juicy.

To Stew a Neck of Mutton
from an 18th century MS cookery book, NLW:

Cut your neck of mutton in stakes beat very flatt, lay it in a stew Pan, and put into it a pint of strong broth, a bunch of sweet Herbs one onion or two, stew it over a gently fire, till most of the liquor be wasted, turn it over the stew Pan, have ready a handfull of Sorrell grossly cut, put them into the stew Pan, with a pennyworth of Capers shread Season it with Nutmeg and Salt to your taste putting in a small Glass of White Wine a good piece of Butter worked with Flower toss it up with two or three spoonfulls of Cream then dish it and lay it upon the Melt heaps of Spinnage boil'd green, garnish your dish with horse Reddish Capers, Barberics and Spinnage. The 'butter and flour' is equivalent to *beurre manié* and Barberics were yellow berries valued for their colour and flavour.

Forced Leg of Mutton

Another very common 18th century recipe found in most of the old books goes something like this:

Raise the skin and take out the lean part of the mutton, chop exceedingly fine; shred a bundle of sweet herbs, grate a penny loaf, and half a lemon, take nutmeg, pepper and salt to taste, make them into a forcemeat, but leave the bone and shank in their places, so that it appears like a whole leg; lay it on an earthen dish, with a pint of red wine under it, and put it in the oven. After two hours and a half, when it comes out, take off all the fat, strain the gravy over the mutton, lay round it hard yolks of eggs and pickled mushrooms. Garnish with pickles and serve up.

Salting or 'powdering' mutton meat was carried out from medieval times and continued until Victorian times when 'Welsh Mutton Hams' were a regular feature of daily fare. The idea could be worth reviving for Christmas-time. The following is from the *Art and Mystery of Curing, Preserving and Potting*, 1864:

WELSH MUTTON HAMS

Take a couple of legs of prime Welsh mutton, rub them well with treacle made hot, and put them away in a deep pan until the next day. Make a pickle of a handful of thyme, and same of marjoram, then of bay leaves, with 1 oz salt petre, 2 oz black pepper, 2 lb bay salt, 5 pints water boiled together for an hour and well skimmed. When cold to be poured over the meat which is rubbed every day and turned for three weeks. Then take the legs out of the pickle, rub them well in all parts with strong vinegar for one hour. Then wipe them dry and hang them up in a current of air until well dry. Then give them a thorough coat of bran or oatmeal and smoke them with 2 parts oak sawdust, 1 part peat, 2 parts beech, 1 part turfs or fern for three weeks or more. Store them in malt cooms of pulverised charcoal, and in three months they will be very good.

Sometimes mutton was spiced in the curing; this recipe is from Mrs. Beeton:

SPICED MUTTON

A boned leg or shoulder of mutton, 8 oz common salt, 1 oz bay salt, ¾ oz saltpetre, 4 oz moist sugar, 1 teaspoonful pepper, 1 dessertspoonful finely chopped shallot or onion, 1 saltspoonful powdered allspice, 1 saltspoonful powdered chives.

Mix the ingredients together, rub the preparation well into the meat, and repeat daily for a fortnight. When ready rinse in warm water and bind into a good shape with strong tape. Cook very gently for 5 or 6 hours in good stock, or water flavoured with vegetables, press between two dishes until cold, glaze, and use as required.

Time to cook 5 – 6 hours.

Ways of treating mutton to taste like venison occur frequently in the old cookery books. The same treatment was given to goat meat – which lingered longer in Wales than in the rest of Britain as a table-meat. Goat hams were known in Wales as 'hung venison' and were probably being prepared in Wales and on the borders in early medieval times, where they were eaten in place of bacon. It was still an accepted meat-animal at the end of the Middle Ages; roast and soused kid, popular in England until the mid-17th century, stayed in fashion in Wales longer. Thomas Pennant in 1776 reported that kids in Wales were 'a cheap and plentiful provision in the winter months'. He went on:

The meat of a spayed goat of six or seven years is reckoned the best; being generally very sweet and fat. This makes as excellent pasty; goes under the name of rock venison, and is little inferior to that of the deer. Thus nature provides even on the tops of high and craggy mountains, not only necessaries, but delicacies for the inhabitants.

WELSH VENISON

from Good Things in England, *edited by Florence White.*

INGREDIENTS:

A loin of mutton; sweet herbs; pepper and salt; vegetables and a brown braise, port wine 2 glasses; red currant jelly.
Time: to braise, 2½ hours.

METHOD:

1. Bone the loin of mutton.
2. Season it with powdered sweet herbs, pepper and salt.
3. Skewer it and tie it up tight.
4. Braise it in a brown braise for 2½ hours.
5. Lift out and keep hot; and
6. Reduce the braise to a half glaze, add 2 glasses of port wine.
7. Glaze your mutton, and send to table with hot red currant jelly.

Mutton pies, or tin-meat as they were known on Gower, were a traditional dish at a Gower wedding feast. Large pies were baked beforehand by the bride's womenfolk and portions were sold to guests at the wedding feast – the money went to the young couple to help them set up home. The wedding *beader* or bidder, who had been given the function of inviting or 'bidding' guests to the wedding, kept a tally of all the money taken in this way. The custom of *beading* weddings continued until about the end of the last century, and the following is from *Gower Gleanings:*

On the eve of the wedding day, relatives and friends visited the wedding house bringing gifts of currant loaves, always referred to as *present*. These were cut into slices and sold at the wedding supper. The eager purchasers were young men who presented them surreptitiously to the maidens of their choice. Later in the evening the girls displayed

their collection of slices of *present*, and the possessor of the largest
number was declared the belle of the ball.

The morning of the wedding day saw the *brides* leaving the wedding
house for the church accompanied by their guests. The fiddler, who
was specially engaged for the whole of the proceedings, led the
procession. After the ceremony, they re-formed and marched to the
local inn, where the *brides* officially thanked the innkeeper for his
generosity in allowing them to"steal his trade". The company partook
of his hospitality and danced in his tap-room. After leaving the inn, the
procession was greeted by gunshots,and was several times brought to
a halt by a rope stretched across the road. The "chaining of the brides"
was accompanied by a demand for a money toll, which was gladly
paid. The rope was then lowered, and the merry company proceeded
on their way to the wedding house, where dinner awaited
them. . . After supper the guests repaired to the barn where the
fiddler tuned up in preparation for the ball, which continued into the
small hours. The dancers rang the changes on the horn-pipe and the
four-handed reel, and for once in a while, the old threshing floor,
accustomed to the slow and heavy rythm of swinging flails, resounded
to the quick beat of dancing feet. The proceedings sometimes ended
with a fight, which may have been the climax of a long-nursed
grievance, or the outcome of an incident arising during the evening.

BIDDING PIE (*PASTAI NEITHIOR*)

From Welsh Fare *by S. Minwel Tibbott.*

twelve ounces plain flour	one teaspoonful mixed herbs
five ounces lard	a little water
half a pound mutton, boiled, boned and diced	a little mutton stock
one teaspoonful salt	

Sift the flour and salt into a large bowl. Melt the lard slowly in a little
water, bring to the boil and immediately pour into the flour. Work the
melted lard into the flour and knead well to a soft dough. Turn out on
to a floured board and roll out fairly thinly. Grease a pie dish and line it
with the pastry. Fill with the mutton and onion, add the seasoning and
stock. Cover with a second layer of pastry, pressing the edges of both
layers together to seal. Cut a slit in the centre and cook in a moderately
hot oven for about an hour.

LOBSCOUSE (*LOBSCOWS*)

Not a Welsh dish, despite its often-seen Welsh spelling 'lobsgows', but this in itself indicates how deeply it has been absorbed into the Welsh cookery tradition. Lobscouse (lob – sheep, scouse – broth) originated in the north of England, from where it eventually reached north Wales where it became extremely popular, though it is virtually unknown in south Wales. Some Welsh recipes specify beef rather than lamb or mutton.

Dorothy Hartley gives detailed instructions in *Food in England:*

> The neck portions are best made into lobscouse. Chop the joint neatly and, bending it, rub pepper and powdered thyme into the slits, and cover all with a dusting of seasoned flour. Put a lump of fat at the bottom of an iron saucepan and fry the meat in this till lightly browned. Meanwhile, cut up carrots, turnips, a little swede or parsnip, some onions, or if you are using leeks they will be found to make a very delicate dish and should be sliced across and across. Add a sprinkling of barley. (On no account put either onions or leeks *uncut*; or they will stew to a soft stringly lump, instead of permeating evenly.) Add these to the meat and then cover the whole with a layer of sliced potatoes followed by a layer of whole potatoes. (The idea of the cut layer is that they will simmer down in the cooking to a creamy mass and thicken the gravy.) Add a good sprinkling of mountain herbs and fill up just to the level of the *whole potatoes. (Note.* The whole potatoes should not cook in the broth, but in the steam above the water level.) Put on the lid closely, and simmer gently *without stirring*, till the top potatoes are cooked through(by which time the smaller vegetables, lower and nearer the heat, will be done, and the meat just leaving the bone). This dish is best served direct from the pot. If it is taken out, lift the potatoes and arrange them round the dish, and put the meat and vegetables in the centre.

2. Lamb *(Oen)*

Roast potatoes with best end of neck (*Tatws popty*)
A north Wales recipe:

Place a layer of peeled potatoes in a meat tin or casserole. Large potatoes should be cut in half. Slice a large onion over the potatoes and season. Then add water to almost cover the potatoes. Place a joint of best end of neck on top of the potatoes and onion; cook in a fairly hot oven for 1½ or 2 hours. If the meat cooks before the water is all taken up by the potatoes, take it off, turn up the oven and finish the potatoes until they are nice and brown.

Welsh lamb pie
From Croeso Cymreig

This is an adaptation of an old dish, very similar to the mutton pie Lady Llanover quotes in *Good Cookery*. But she had cooked the meat, bones and vegetables together first; next day, when cooked, she put them all in the pastry – and the jelly was melted and poured in after baking:

1½ lb neck lamb	pepper and salt
teaspoonful finely chopped parsley	shortcrust
small bunch young carrots	

Bone the meat and cut into small pieces, clean and cut carrots into thin rounds, put layer in bottom of dish, then meat, parsley and pepper and salt. Repeat until all is used; cover with water, 2 in. from top. Cover with pastry and brush over with milk. Bake two hours in a moderate oven. Boil the bones, one onion, pepper and salt 1½ hours, and when pie is ready strain and pour into pie. Serve hot or cold.

Judging at Tal-y-bont Agricultural Show. Photo by Keith Morris.

3. Accompaniments to mutton and lamb

Redcurrant jelly has been served with mutton since the earliest times. Rowan Jelly, with its more subtle flavour is better. Rowans grow prolifically in parts of West Wales and hang like scarlet curtains along the deep, narrow lanes. The recipe here is from Pamela Westland's *A Taste of The Country*.

ROWANBERRY JELLY

3 pounds rowanberries (mountain ash)   juice of 1 lemon
½ pint water   1 pound sugar to each pint juice

Wash berries and pick from stalks. Simmer in a pan with the water until tender. Strain overnight through a jelly bag. Measure juice and return to pan with the lemon juice and sugar, allowing 1 pound sugar to 1 pint juice. Bring slowly to the boil, stirring until sugar has dissolved, and then fast boil until setting point is reached. Pour into warm jars, cover and seal.
Makes about 2½ pounds.

A lovely deep, scarlet red jelly.

BITTER ROWAN JELLY
From Farmhouse Fare.

Pick the rowanberries clean from the stalks and stew them down to as near a pulp as you can, with enough water to cover them, and a tiny pinch of ginger. Crush and strain the pulp and boil it up again for ½ hour, with only (two thirds) of its weight in sugar. Put into small jars. It will become firm as it cools.

MINT SAUCE

Make this if possible with wild mint, which is very strong, and the best for drying (I have some a year old now which is still sharply minty). Apple mint is also good for mint sauce and the wide, soft, downy leaves look pretty growing up in the garden. Always make mint sauce with wine, not malt, vinegar, or lemon juice, and with just a little demerara sugar chopped in with the mint.

GOOSEBERRY MINT JELLY

A useful addition to the store cupboard, and an accompaniment which gives a good Welsh air to roast lamb. The jelly is an attractive pink colour, in the same colour range as Tavel *rosé* – which you could do worse than drink with tender Welsh spring lamb:

2 lb gooseberries (green)	sugar
about six stalks of fresh mint	

Place gooseberries in a preserving pan, just cover with cold water and cook until soft. Strain carefully and to each pint of liquid add 1 lb of sugar. Replace in the preserving pan, together with the mint tied up in a bundle. Heat gently till the sugar is melted, then boil until it "jells." Remove the mint, pour into glass jars and seal.

I have made this jelly successfully with tinned gooseberries when fresh were out of season and I had to have it for catering purposes.

Three 20 oz tins of slightly sweetened gooseberries equal 2 lbs of fresh berries. You will need about 2 lbs of sugar and perhaps a little water. *The yield will be about 5 lbs.*

RHUBARB MINT JELLY

A favourite of Lloyd George. This may have originated in Wales, where both rhubarb and mint are much used, but it has strayed to many other parts of Britain by now. Both this and the gooseberry mint jelly are very good accompaniments to roast lamb, and useful to have in the store cupboard for the times when fresh mint is unavailable. If you know where wild mint grows on hilly sheep pastures, gather some and dry it. The flavour is exceedingly pungent and long-lasting. The recipe came from Miss May Evans of Bwlch-y-groes in the Pembrokeshire/ Cardiganshire border-land, who has kept the next-door chapel spick and span for fifty years:

Wipe some early rhubarb and cut into pieces. Stew until soft and pulpy, then strain through a fine sieve. To each pint of juice allow 1 lb

of loaf sugar. Put juice and sugar into a preserving-pan with some fresh
clean mint tied into bundles.
  Boil until the jelly thickens when tested on a cold plate, stirring often.
Remove mint before pouring into small pots.

Many of the traditional accompaniments to meats tend to be
logical in that they accentuate the taste of what the animal has
grazed or fed upon. Thus mint sauce with mountain lamb from
hill pastures where there is wild mint growing amongst the short,
sweet grass; thyme with lamb in Provence where that herb grows
wild – a component of the *garrigue* which covers the Provençal
hills; apple sauce with pork, where pig has been fed on windfalls
in the orchard; and laver sauce with lamb which has fed on salt
marsh sea pastures.

LAVER SAUCE

Add a spoonful or two of prepared laver to a *béchamel* sauce, according
to taste (see page 171).

5. Cheese

1. Welsh Farmhouse Cheeses

Then Angharad called to me to open the door, and came in with tea, and laverbread, and butter and milk cheese, and lettuce and cresses.

HOW GREEN WAS MY VALLEY: Richard Llewellyn

Early Welsh cheeses were subject to immersion in brine solution; in the arrangements for divorce in the *Laws of Hywel Dda* the 'cheese in the brine' went to the wife, but 'the cheese which was hung up' went to the husband, while the 'cheese in cut' again went to the wife.

The production of cheese from cows' milk in Wales was very much a part of the system of transhumance, both butter and cheese being part of the activity of the *hafod*, the upper summer dwelling-place in the higher hill pastures. In areas where the stock was chiefly sheep and goats, ewes' and goats' milk were used for cheese-making, and sometimes on their own, sometimes mixed with cows' milk.

Cheese-making in Wales remained a farmhouse activity much longer than elsewhere in Britain. Welsh girls would be accomplished cheese and butter makers before they left home to undertake the responsibility of a household of their own. Mati Thomas writes:

> Farmers in the olden days would milk the ewes after selling the lambs. It was a common occurrence to see the dairy maids milking the ewes in their pens very early in the mornings, often finishing this task before attending to the cows. The ewes' milk was then brought into the house and placed with the skimmed cows' milk in the dairy.

She gives directions for making this cheese:

Caws Llaeth Defaid a Gwartheg

This cheese is made from sheep and cows milk, which Lady Llanover was familiar with – she refers to it in *Good Cookery* as real Welsh cheese, used for *caws pobi* – toasted cheese.

a gallon of ewes' milk
four gallons of cows' milk

two tablespoonfuls of rennet
a handful of salt

Mix the two quantities of milk together in the cooker. Heat on a slow fire until of blood heat. Remove from the fire and add two tablespoonsful of rennet. Cover with a cloth, and leave for a while. Then stir vigorously with a bowl. Allow to settle and clear. Pour off the whey and squeeze the curds dry with the hands. Break up the curds into small crumbs. Add a handful of salt and mix thoroughly. Place in a pan in the dairy until sufficient has accumulated to make a cheese.

In three mornings' processing sufficient curd was usually available. Then all the curd was well mixed together and placed in a muslin cloth in the mould. This was then placed into the cheese press and well squeezed. It was necessary to turn the cheese three times a day. On the first two days the cheese is punctured with a wooden skewer at regular intervals. This enabled the surplus whey to drain away. At the end of the second day the cheese was ready to be taken from the press and placed on the storage rack. It was usual to store the cheese for up to two years before using it.

In the lean times the farmhouse cheeses were reduced to poor, thin cheeses, made only with skim milk – typically Caerphilly – originally made for farm workers and miners. World War Two put an end to the old skim-milk Caerphilly, when under a wartime regulation only hard-pressed cheeses using full-cream milk could be made. Afterwards, increasingly stringent hygiene regulations led to the end of small-scale on-farm cheese-making and to large-scale 'creamery' (factory) production, in Wales and elsewhere. In 1955 the then Milk Marketing Board introduced the familiar 'farmhouse' cheese grading all with 45% butter-fat content. Today's Caerphilly is thus more like the old, richer Welsh cheese. The more quickly it is matured, the sharper the flavour and whiter the appearance: a good cheese-maker will give it at least three weeks.

Forty years on measures originally designed to protect the consumer had, as so often happens, worked in reverse, resulting

A selection of Welsh cheeses. Photo by Keith Morris.

in factory cheese so unlike the real thing that a steady revolt against mass production methods got under way, until real cheeses made from unpasturised milk began to be made once more on Welsh farms.

These 'poor, thin' Welsh farmhouse cheeses were not without value or counterparts produced elsewhere in Britain – Essex and Suffolk especially were notorious for their poor quality cheese produced in vast quantities to feed the labouring and working classes of London and the south-east. They were not disliked, either; the Welsh themselves appreciated them, and Caerphilly is recorded as being on sale in London long before other regional cheeses became available outside the area of their origin.

Not all Welsh cheeses were made to the Caerphilly method. These instructions for making a rich cream cheese in the Normandy-style appeared in 18th-century books:

NEWPORT CHEESE

To make the thick square cream cheese as at Newport (Monmouth) you must get a vat made a quartern and a half high, the bottom nor the top must be fastened in and it must be four-square with holes all over. This cheese must be made in May.

SAGE CHEESE

This cheese was expected to be colourfully green – if it were not green enough from the sage itself then spinach juice was added to it. There were other coloured and flavoured cream cheeses – marigolds were much used for their yellow colour and pungent flavour. Popular in Tudor and Stuart times, these cheeses remained in favour throughout the 18th century as a special summer treat rather than a substitute for the mature cheeses which were eaten all the year round.

The juice of the spinach and sage, pounded and put into the cheese, and sage pressed into it. Press, mound, and it will eat very agreeably in six months.

Lady Llanover maintained a liking for a sage cheese made at Pontllanfraith, then a village in the valley below Ebbw Vale, in the mid-19th century before coal-mining swallowed up all the Valley's farms. It was sent regularly to Llanover Court near Abergavenny. It was known as *Mynydd Islwyn* cheese. Although it is still remembered in Pontllanfraith I have been unable to find any record of its manufacture.

The above quotation prompted me to make some by mixing in chopped fresh sage with commercial cream cheese. This does work, and is a pleasant change, though I am not myself overfond of the slightly stuffy taste of sage as encountered in the cheese, and I'm not too sure about the wisdom of keeping it for six months.

RESURRECTION CHEESE

This cheese, with its macabre name, is associated with Llanfihangel Abercowin, Carmarthenshire. The attractive church now graces the Carmarthen by-pass near St. Clears. It was named, not for its flavour, but for the manner of its pressing – between fallen gravestones of a ruined church. The epitaphs, of course, were often impressed upon the cheese. I am indebted to Maxwell Fraser for this interesting information.

GLAMORGAN 'SAUSAGES'

George Borrow referred to them in *Wild Wales:* 'The breakfast was delicious, consisting of excellent tea, buttered toast and Glamorgan sausages, which I really think are not a whit inferior to those of Epping'. These 'sausages' made from cheese were erroneously assumed for many years to be a war-time expedient. Sausages in Borrow's day were very much regional specialities; Epping sausages were made with pork, but like those of Glamorgan, were rolled in white of egg and breadcrumbs rather than encased in skins.

The following from Croeso Cymreig:

1 egg
a little very finely chopped onion
a pinch of mixed herbs
a pinch of mustard

pepper and salt
5 oz breadcrumbs
3 oz grated cheese

Divide egg yolk from white, mix all dry ingredients and bind with yolk of egg. Divide into small sausages and roll in flour. Dip each into white of egg, then roll in breadcrumbs and fry in pork fat. Serve with creamed potatoes or chips.

I like to make Glamorgan sausages with half white and half brown breadcrumbs. I also find the onions need to be chopped very fine, otherwise the mixture is difficult to hold together. And perhaps today we would prefer to fry in vegetable oil. A good tomato sauce goes well with these sausages, which have become a favourite with vegetarians of late.

At the 'Walnut Tree Inn', Llanddewi Skirrid near Abergavenny, Franco Taruschio makes his own version of these sausages – very mustardy, very tiny – which he offers as appertisers.

It is reasonable to assume that Glamorgan sausages were so named after the especially fine, hard white cheese made from the milk of a rare breed of cattle – 'Glamorgans' – long thought to be extinct. Some years ago a herd was discovered in the south of England and successfully secured for Wales, where it remains, much increased, contentedly grazing in Margam Park, the splendid West Glamorgan estate behind Port Talbot once owned by the steelworks magnate.

Even more interesting. . . these chestnut-coloured cattle have identical counterparts in Austria in a breed known as *Pinzgauer*. It is thought that the Austrian cattle were brought over to Wales 500 years ago by the early Celts. Recently some of them were introduced into the Margam herd to improve fertility.

There is no milking parlour as yet at Margam, but there may yet be one, in which case Glamorgan cheese will be made again, from a 1780 recipe acquired in readiness by the Park manager.

The Glamorgans have now been registered with the Rare Breed Protection Society.

CAERPHILLY SCONES

Though I don't feel they are strictly in the Welsh tradition, these scones are a nice idea, possibly from one of the old country house cookery collections. The recipe was sent in to the *Western Mail* when they ran the competition for traditional Welsh dishes which resulted in the publication of the recipes by Wales Gas under the title *Croeso Cymreig*.

Parmesan cheese had been popular in Britain since the 16th century and was produced in Britain as a regularity – in Wales I believe in the Gower region.

Make sure the scones are made thick enough to be soft and moist. Made quite tiny, they are good for buffets or cheese and wine parties:

1½ oz butter	3 oz Caerphilly cheese
¾ lb plain flour	1 oz grated Parmesan cheese
¼ teaspoon salt	½ pint milk
3 teaspoons baking powder	freshly ground black pepper or a pinch of cayenne

Sift the flour, baking powder and salt and rub in the butter. Add the grated cheeses with the pepper and mix to a soft dough with the milk (you may not need all of it, just enough to make a soft dough). Roll out at least half an inch thick, stamp out with the largest cutter and bake for 15-20 minutes in a hot oven on a greased baking sheet. Serve hot with butter.

2. Welsh Rarebit *(Caws pobi)*

The Welsh loved the hard English cheeses which they could not easily produce themselves because of the soft, acid soil which covered such a large part of Wales. Those who lived in east Wales, in the old counties of Monmouth and Glamorgan, and perhaps parts of Breconshire and Radnorshire, too, drove their flocks of sheep to barter for the Cheddar cheese they wanted above all for their *caws pobi* (literally toasted or roasted cheese) for which they had had a passion since at least medieval times.

In areas of Wales where Cheddar cheese was unavailable,

ewes' milk cheese was used for *caws pobi*, as it had been from earliest times. Eventually this Welsh speciality became known as 'Welsh Rabbit'; finally, about the end of the 18th century we find the term 'rare-bit' coming into use.

Nearly all the southern and western English counties had a 'rabbit', and all were on the same lines – either toasted or melted cheese, or a cheese sauce with the addition of beer and mustard, and sometimes onion.

I think *caws pobi* was a part of Welsh fare much too early on, and the term rabbit too commonplace throughout Britain to give credence to the popular tradition that the dish was meant to replace the rabbits English landlords forbade their Welsh tenants to catch. But it is a fact that there are few recipes in Welsh collections for rabbit dishes, though rabbits must have been taken to supplement an impoverished diet.

Lady Llanover gave precise instructions for *caws pobi* in her *Good Cookery:*

> Welsh toasted cheese, and the melted cheese of England, called 'toasted cheese', are as different in the mode of preparation as is the cheese itself. . . Cut a slice of the real Welsh cheese made of sheep and cow's milk, toast it at the fire on both sides, but not so much as to drop; toast a piece of bread, less than a quarter of an inch thick, to be quite crisp, and spread it very thinly with fresh cold butter on one side (it must not be saturated with butter), then lay the toasted cheese upon the bread and serve immediately on a very hot plate; the butter on the toast can, of course, be omitted if not liked, and it is more frequently eaten without butter.

Mati Thomas gives us this more rustic version of the Welsh classic:

> Cheese made from sheep and cows' milk.* A slice of barley bread at least an inch thick. Cut a thick slice of cheese and toast both sides in front of the fire. It should not be allowed to drip. At the same time toast the barley-bread well on both sides. Place the toasted cheese on the toasted bread. This was eaten for supper during the winter.

But perhaps the most interesting feature about Welsh Rarebit is the way in which it was ultimately taken far beyond its rural

---

* She means mixed

Welsh origin, and embellished and enriched to a quite remarkable degree. This recipe, from *Cassell's Dictionary of Cookery*, 1885 illustrates the point very well:

> **Rare-bit, Welsh**. – Brillat Savarin, the famous French *Gourmet*,gives the following recipe taken from the papers of M. Trollet, bailiff in Meudon, in the Canton of Berne:-
>
> Take as many eggs as you wish, according to the number of guests, and weigh them; then take a piece of cheese weighing a third of the weight of the eggs, and a slice of butter weighing a sixth; beat the eggs well up in a saucepan, after which put in the butter and cheese, the latter either grated or chopped up very small; place the saucepan on a good fire, and stir it with a flat spoon until the mixture becomes sufficiently thick and soft; add a little salt and a large portion of pepper, and serve it up in a hot dish. Bring out the best wine, and let it go round freely, and wonders will be done.

A nice mid-way version of Welsh Rarebit, halfway between the original roasted cheese and the richer mixtures, is included in a MS cookery book attributed to Mrs. John Llewellyn, century 1854, NLW.

BOILED CHEESE

4 oz single Gloucester or Cheshire cheese, 4 oz fresh Butter, a tablespoonful of Cream, cut the cheese into little bits put all into a small pan Set on a low fire Keep stirring it till it boils and is quite smooth. Take off the pan, and break an egg into it both yolk and white. Stir it quickly put it into a dish and brown it before the fire in a tin (dutch) oven.

It was customary to drink ale with Welsh Rarebit; ultimately, towards the end of the 19th century, the ale went *into* the dish. So, for Queen Victoria, did the champagne.

Mrs Adams of Caws Cenarth. Photo by Keith Morris.

WELSH CHEESE PUDDING (*PWDIN CAWS POBI CYMREIG*)

The final development of *caws pobi* – into an interesting and unusual supper or lunch dish. Good with a green salad.

4 thick slices bread without the crusts	1 pint milk, or half milk and half cream
8 oz cheddar cheese	½ teaspoon dry mustard
butter	pepper and cayenne pepper, pinch of
One egg	nutmeg

Toast the bread on one side and butter the untoasted side. Place two toast slices, toasted side down, on the bottom of a round, greased, ovenproof dish. On top put half the cheese, grated, and half the seasonings. Then repeat the layer with the toast, toasted side down, and the rest of the cheese on top.

Bring the milk to the boil, add the remaining seasonings, beat the egg and pour the hot milk over it. Pour this over the cheese pudding and let it rest for at least half-an-hour, to let the bread soak up the liquid.

Place in a moderate oven (350 deg. F.) until it has risen and is light brown on top. Serve quickly.

Serves 2 to 4 people.

6. Vegetables

1. Potatoes and Root vegetables *(Tatws a llysiau)*

Out to the back to mix the potch, then. All the vegetables were boiled slowly in their jackets, never allowed to bubble in boiling, for then the goodness is from them, and they are full of water, and a squash tasteless to the mouth, without good smell, an offence to the eye, and an insult to the belly. Firm in the hand, skin them clean, and put them in a dish and mash with a heavy fork, with melted butter and the bruising of mint, potatoes, swedes, carrots, parsnips, turnips and their tops, then chop small purple onions very fine, with a little head of parsley, and pick the leaves of small watercress from the stems, and mix together. The potch will be a creamy colour with something of pink, having a smell to tempt you to eat there and then, but wait until it has been in the hot oven for five minutes with a cover, so that the vegetables can mix in warm comfort together and become friendly, and the mint can go about his work, and for the cress to show his cunning, and for the goodness all about to soften the raw, ungentle nature of the onion.

HOW GREEN WAS MY VALLEY: Richard Llewellyn

Such a detailed description of this old Pembrokeshire dish (in Welsh: *potsh*) is fortunate, for I can find no other written record of it anywhere, only verbal confirmation of its existence. The Welsh were good with simpler vegetables mixtures, too, combining perhaps only two root vegetables, as in *stwnsh rwdan,*a mash of swede turnip and potato popular in north Wales, commonly accompanying a casserole of liver and onions. *Stwnsh pys* was a variation – potatoes and dried peas – and so was *stwnsh ffa* – potatoes and broad beans – and *stwnsh moron* (carrots). In the old days buttermilk would be poured over a *stwnsh*.

Punch-nep, the white turnip and potato mash equivalent of *stwnsh rwdan*, has been declared a Welsh dish, but I am inclined to think, from the use of 'nep', a derivation of the old English and Scottish term 'neeps' for turnips and parsnips, that the dish belongs elsewhere. However, it's another good and simple idea: potatoes and white turnips in equal quantities, boiled separately and then mashed together and beaten well with plenty of butter. Season and transfer to a baking dish, prod holes over the top of the mash and into these pour warm cream or melted butter. The dish has a resemblance to the *stelk* of Ireland, in which spring onions and potatoes are cooked in milk, then mashed together and a pool of melted butter created in a well in the centre of the mounded mash. All these simple, quick mashes are good for busy days.

Potatoes were as much a staple in Wales as in Ireland, and whereas the Irish were said by Mrs. Beeton to have understood the cooking of potatoes better than in any other country, the Welsh, though perhaps not so finicky about the ordinary, plain preparation of boiled potatoes, developed some interesting ways of cooking and using them. The idea of cooking bacon and potatoes together I find particularly appealing, as the mealiness and blandness of the one is such a perfect recipient for the saltiness and fat of the other (as in the recipe for layered potatoes, onions and bacon *(tatw rhost a bacwn)* I quoted earlier, a dish which required little attention and in the old days would have been accommodated by the *ffwrn fach* (pot oven) hanging over the fire and it recurs again and again with infinite variations in Welsh cookery.

The other dish of roast potatoes *(tatws popty)*, which seems to belong more to north Wales and again crops up repeatedly in collections of old Welsh recipes, recommends cooking first par-boiled potatoes underneath a joint of meat, or around the joint, with the addition of water and a cover over the entire dish.

The first reference to this dish and its association with Wales is in *Adam's Luxury and Eve's Cookery*, 1744.

Potato harvesting on Llwynpiod Farm near Cardigan. Photo by Stuart Ladd.

TATWS POPTY

From Welsh Fare, *by S. Minwel Tibbott.*

After roasting a joint of meat, lift it out of the tin, and pour away all excess fat. Fill the tin with potatoes, sliced thickly, lengthways, and cover with a layer of finely chopped onion. Sprinkle with a little salt, pepper and flour and cover with boiling water. Roast in a hot oven until the potatoes are golden brown.

ONION CAKE (*TEISEN NIONOD*)

This is one of my favourite Welsh dishes. Except for the fact that Welsh recipes give instructions for it to be made in a cake tin, it it the same dish as the French *pommes boulangère*. It is immensely useful in that it lends a Welsh flavour to almost any meal: a roast of Welsh lamb with fresh mint sauce and *teisen nionod* is immediately lifted into a Welsh class of its own with very little effort. *Teisen nionod* cooks best in one of those thick, heavy earthenware oval baking dishes, which will also help to keep it hot until you are ready for seconds.

This is my own personal recipe for *teisen nionod*. In the Welsh kitchen the first process of soaking the slices of potato would not take place. Made in a cake-tin, with new potatoes, and turned out when cooked, the 'cake' would hold its shape very well.

2 lb potatoes	pepper and salt
1 or 2 onions	beef stock (optional)
butter	

Butter the inside of a thick baking dish generously. Peel and thinly slice potatoes, soak them for a few minutes in cold water to draw out the starch. Drain and dry in a clean cloth.

Layer some potatoes along the bottom of the dish, cover with a layer of finely chopped onions, season and dot with butter. Cover with another layer of potatoes and so on until the dish is full, finishing with a layer of potatoes and dotting the top with extra butter. Cover with foil, making sure the layers of potato and onion are firmly pressed down, and bake in a hot oven for about an hour. Ten minutes before the end of cooking time, uncover the dish to brown and crisp the top. I sometimes add a little good beefstock, which reduces the amount of seasoning needed.

POTATOES WITH BUTTERMILK (*TATWS LLAETH*)

A simple and well-loved dish using new or old potatoes, a commonplace, too, in north-west Spain, also a Celtic area. My Spanish cook, from Orense, was very familiar with it.

Boil potatoes in their jackets, skin and serve in individual bowls. Pour buttermilk over and eat while warm.

2. Leeks *(Cennin)* and Cabbage *(Cabaits)*

One of the extraordinary facts about Welsh cookery is that although leeks are by repute inextricably linked with it, very few recipes exist for their individual use. In early times they were employed for their onion properties as the only member of the onion family to grow extensively enough in Wales to be mentioned, along with the cabbages, the only other green vegetable, in the *Laws of Hywel Dda*.

LEEK PASTY (*PASTAI CENNIN*)

Simple and good:

8 oz shortcrust
2 or 3 medium leeks,
   green and white parts

4 rashers fat streaky bacon

Line a baking sheet with shortcrust, cover with finely-chopped washed leeks. On top of these lay some strips of fat bacon; season and add an egg-cupful of water before covering with a pastry lid. Make slits in the pastry and bake in a hot oven (400 deg. F./Gas 6) for ½ to ¾ hour. Serve hot. I like to add a little chopped, fresh sage to the filling, and sometimes enrich the dish by adding a couple of beaten eggs.

ANGLESEY EGGS (*WYAU YNYS MÔN*)

Though I feel this good little dish is too sophisticated to have originated in the old Welsh 'cottage' tradition it has been around in Welsh recipe collections long enough to have acquired a Welsh name.

6 medium sized leeks	1 lb hot mashed potatoes
2 oz butter	1 tablespoon flour
2 oz plus 2 tablespoons grated cheese	½ pint milk
8 hard-boiled eggs	salt and pepper

Clean leeks, slit down the length and hold under running cold water, then chop roughly. Cook in boiling salted water for 10 mins. Prepare 8 hard boiled eggs and about 1 lb mashed potatoes. Strain leeks, pressing out surplus water, combine with the potato; add half the butter, season, then beat vigorously until the mixture is light and fluffy and a delicate pale green. Arrange round the edge of a fireproof dish and keep warm.

Make a cheese sauce with 1 oz butter, warm milk, 1 oz flour and 2 oz grated cheese. Fill the interior of the potato and leek mixture with quartered hard-boiled eggs; cover with cheese sauce; sprinkle the remaining cheese over the top, fork a decorative finish to the potato mixture and bake in a hot oven (400 deg. F., Gas 6) until golden brown.
Serves 4 – 5
This dish can accompany slices of cold boiled ham.

BACON & CABBAGE (*CIG MOCH A CHABAITS*)

The practice of cooking cabbage in the liquor from boiling bacon or ham and the especially good flavour of cabbage cooked this way were recalled earlier in the section on *cawl*. In Minwel Tibbott's *Welsh Fare* it rates as a dish in itself:

Boil a bacon or ham joint until tender, keeping the stock. Cook the cabbage in the stock. Boil potatoes separately, again reserving the water. Use this to make a parsley sauce by adding a little milk, butter and chopped parsley and thickening with a little flour mixed to a cream with cold water. Serve this with sliced bacon, the cabbage and potatoes.

(I am inclined to think this is a south Wales dish.)

PARSLEY PIE (*PASTAI PERSLI*)

An interesting little idea from Gower: quoted from *Welsh Fare* again.

shortcrust pastry
two eggs
half a pint milk
one dessertspoonful plain flour

a little salt
two tablespoons sugar
one dessertspoonful chopped parsley
one and a half ounces fat bacon, diced

Line a deep pie dish thinly with the prepared pastry. Mix the flour with a little of the milk. Beat the eggs in a large basin, pour in the remainder of the milk and add the blended milk and flour, salt, sugar and parsley. Mix well and pour onto the pastry. Finally, add the bacon and bake in a fairly hot oven for half an hour or until the mixture has set.

3. Pumpkin and Marrow *(Pwmpen)*

Although it was early colonists who took it to America, eventually to become part of the traditional Thanksgiving Day feast, pumpkin is relatively little used in modern Britain. There are those who claim it was the Gower folk who took pumpkin across the Atlantic – certainly they grew extensively all over that little peninsula which was once virtually self-contained, developing in language, custom and culinary ways markedly different from the rest of Wales. There is no evidence to show that they were common in other parts of Wales.

Up to about 1920 every backgarden on Gower would have at least one pumpkin, ripening effortlessly through the summer days in rubicund splendour, to be made into pies and pickles in the Autumn. One old Gower eccentric is reputed to have grown them on the roof of his house simply as decoration!

Marrows, on the other hand, are still a familiar sight in vegetable gardens all over Wales. The Welsh for marrow is *pwmpen, bwmpen* when the 'p' is mutated, so do not be confused by recipes under this name – they are unlikely to be for pumpkin.

PUMPKIN PIE

An American recipe, quoted by Dorothy Hartley in *Food in England*, from a book of 1870. The Gower recipe is said to be almost identical:

> Cook the pumpkin till soft enough to beat to a pulp, then beat in (to a quart of pulp) 1 teacupful sugar, the rind of a lemon, a grate of nutmeg, and (if liked) a pinch of ginger, bake in a pie-crust. This is a standard 'plain filling' but melted butter and eggs and spice may be added to the pumpkin mash, and there is no question that the pumpkin is a very worthy vegetable: but the Marrow takes its place in English gardens.

PUMPKIN SOUP

This was also known to Gower. The recipe is another from the American book of 1870:

> Steam the seeded and peeled pumpkin slabs till soft, rub through a coarse sieve, and reheat with pepper, salt and enough milk to make a thick soup, butter and egg yolk are added to make a richer soup.

PUMPKIN PICKLE

Contributed by Mrs. Violet Morgan of Llanrhidian, N. Gower, to *Unusual Recipes*.

1 pumpkin of 4 – 5 lbs	2 pieces white ginger root
3 pints wine vinegar	2 sticks cinnamon
3 lbs sugar	1 dessertspoon white mustard seed
½ oz celery salt	10 whole cloves

Cut the pumpkin into small pieces. Boil sugar and vinegar together and pour over the pumpkin. Leave overnight. Next morning drain off the liquid, add all the spices and bring to the boil. Put the pumpkin in the syrup and simmer for 3 hours. Put into warm jars and seal in the usual way. Keep for a month before using. For a pale-coloured pickle use white wine vinegar and white sugar; otherwise red wine vinegar and demerara sugar.

PUMPKIN WINE (GWIN PWMPEN)
From Croeso Cymreig

Take a large pumpkin, extract the seeds and pulp and place the pumpkin in a large jar or suitable vessel. Fill the cavity with granulated sugar, cover with a cloth and stand in a warm place. Each day add more sugar until the pumpkin has completely dissolved. Then strain the liquor, add the juice of two lemons and for each quart of liquid add ¼ pint rum. Pour into bottles immediately and cork tightly. Keep this beverage for six months before using.

MARROW PIE (TARTEN BWMPEN)
From Mrs. Nellie James of Newport, Pembrokeshire, Dyfed.

Most Welsh recipes feature marrow in a pie, often it is mixed with a little apple. The usual injunction is to add no water, for the marrow will supply more than enough moisture. This one is typical:

1 marrow	a few cloves
cupful sugar	shortcrust pastry
cupful currants	a little vinegar
sprinkle of ginger	

Peel and slice the marrow, discarding seeds. Line a deep pie dish with shortcrust, then put in the slices of marrow. Add sugar, currants, vinegar and spices, cover with a pastry lid. Bake in a moderate oven until the marrow is cooked – take care the oven is not too hot or the pastry will burn before the marrow is cooked. Serve hot or cold.

4. Laverbread *(Bara lawr)*

Ah! Call us not weeds, but flowers of the sea.
Anon

Laverbread – the great Welsh mystery. What is it? A loaf?

At first sight it is very off-putting. . . a greenish-black gelatinous mass. . . heaven knows what it tastes like. Shall we dare?

Well, people were afraid of lobsters when they first beheld them; some East Africans still are, for the same reason – because they look so frightening. So it can be with laverbread but less so now, since chefs in Wales, and beyond, have taken it up with enthusiasm as the one culinary speciality identifiable as exclusively Welsh. It wasn't always so. In the 18th and early 19th centuries, laver was a popular feature of London tables. Potted laver was mentioned in the Bath Guide of 1766, along with oysters and pies. Even as late as 1894, the Daily News of 1st December gave the well-founded advice that laver was in 'full season and is best imported straight from Ireland'. Florence White wrote that in 1932 it was again available in London, though neglected for years, although it had always been served in a few clubs and private families.

But laver was eaten by coastal dwellers from north to south of Britain, and was probably a part of Welsh diet from prehistoric times. Pliny referred to it as a 'water plant'. I have not been able to trace when it was found to be edible – a remarkable discovery considering how it is found and the long boiling it requires. Some food buffs, without ever having tasted it, assert it to taste 'fishy', presumably because it comes from the sea. It doesn't taste of spinach, either, to dispel another misconception. Nor is it 'sea spinach' as sometimes claimed. It is a seaweed, and that is what it tastes like. It's a fairly innocuous taste with a little pungency from its potassium iodine content, not at all the strange, alien flavour which is said to be an acquired taste.

On the other hand, its flavour does depend to a certain extent upon how it is prepared for the table. The most usual Welsh way, mixed with a little medium oatmeal and fried in bacon or sausage fat, if the oatmeal is stale the taste can be a bit bitter.

It was suggested that laverbread was eaten by Welsh miners to rectify deficiencies caused by their life underground, and this is why it became popular in south Wales. Laverbread is so rich in minerals and vitamins that it must have compensated the miners for the lack of sunshine and fresh air in their lives. For decades, mothers spurned it, dismissing it as a Welsh oddity.

Writing to The Times in the 1870's, Mr Aeneas Dallas castigated the English for not according due recognition to laver as a speciality food: 'The French know it not. . . if we had had their business acumen we should have made it as famous as the truffles of Périgeux. There is a charm about it which ought to have kept it in the front as one of the distinctions of English cookery! Quoted in Good Things in England, edited by Florence White. One up for Wales then.

Laver is found on the beaches of south and west Wales, though not nowadays in large enough quantities to meet commercial demand. Local people gather and process their own as they have done for centuries – it's easy enough to do nowadays with a pressure cooker. Laverweed requires at least 6 hours' boiling.

Strangers to the weed may imagine they have eaten stewed and chopped ordinary seawrack, the kind they know as hard and dried or wet and shiny, with blisters to pop. The fine, silky laverweed is easy to miss – if exposed on a rock at low tide it simply looks messy, while in the water it tends to grow under the other weeds, looking like fronds of silky hair as it is swept by the sea.

Laverweed makes a distinct 'plucking' noise as it is pulled off the rocks. It grows where it will and all attempts to 'plant' it have failed. There will be plenty on a beach one year, none the next. Then it will come back. Heavy swells smother it under sand, needing a storm or sea-movement to expose it again. Laver is often confused with its sister plant, sea lettuce, *Ulva latissima*. What concerns us is *Porphyra laciniata* – purple laver, which actually looks brown.

When I first wrote about laverbread its production along the shore of the Burry estuary at Pen-clawdd was a mystery. Because

I couldn't get anyone to talk to me about it where I lived in north Pembrokeshire, I went down to Pen-clawdd to find out for myself. When I ventured into the strange little domain of the laverbread and cockle people, there was no reticence on the part of the Roberts brothers, Cliff and Doug, (alas no longer with us) only a little shyness of the eagerly questioning Englishwoman. We were soon getting on famously, our friendly relationship finally blossoming into a business one, for from then on they sent us our laverbread, and cockles from their next-door neighbours, in sacks, putting them on the train at Burry Port for us to collect at Fishguard Harbour.

I never knew how to describe this shoreline 'industry', housed in simple, breeze-block, corrugated iron-roofed buildings. The laverbread construction was unadorned, though it had a little entrance porch, but the 'cockle place' sported a crude attempt at a cockle shell motif, sculptured in cement, above its doorway. These strange little buildings, set against the wide, sandy shore, reached by crunching over an expanse of discarded cockle shells, always put me in mind of Peggotty's curious little hut on the shingle shore in 'David Copperfield'.

In those days the laverweed came down, dried, from Scotland, as it had done for a hundred years – and still does, by train. Then it is soaked, washed clear of sand with hosepipes. In the old days the streams which run down the Welsh beaches were used for washing the weed, which was dried in tent-like constructions on the beach. After boiling, the weed is strained and then put through a giant mincer to obtain an even texture.

Commercially-produced laverbread tends to be rather loose and wet. This,they say, is the way customers prefer it, and it also helps the freezing. But a local acquaintance does his own from weed collected from the shore here in in Newport Bay: his is very firm and fairly coarse in texture, due to being well-drained, and is much preferred locally.

In the early 1960's I was trying to make Pembrokeshire as much like a foreign country as possible. Laverbread went on the menu at breakfast-time but was not liked. Then I came across one of the old suggestions for serving laverbread: mixed with a few drops of olive oil and lemon juice and black pepper, eaten with fingers of dry toast. The similarity with caviare struck me, the alliteration appealed, and tongue in cheek, immediately dubbed it 'Caviare Cymreig'. Success with laverbread at last – but it was disastrous, really, as over the years the name 'Welsh Caviare' has stuck and even been attributed to Richard Burton! But a lot of interest in laverbread was aroused. We went on to use it in a *béchamel*, and with orange juice as a sauce for lobster, and in the gravy, again with orange juice, to accompany Welsh lamb. Finally I adopted Jane Grigson's suggestion of adding it to a vegetable soup made with chicken or lamb broth. After whizzing in the liquidiser this turns the weed a lovely sludge green colour. The flavour is so good I'm surprised it has never been taken up by anyone else.

Mrs Maria Rundell, who finished her famous, best-selling *New System of Domestic Cookery* in Swansea in 1808, where she must have encountered the Welsh speciality, had this to say:

TO MAKE LAVER 'BREAD'

After the laver has been very well washed first in seawater, then in fresh, and wrung quite dry, it should be put in a pan with seawater, and if liked a little vinegar, and then simmered for several hours. The drained pulp can be kept for weeks, and it is in that state that it is sold as Laver 'Bread'. After roasting, Welsh mutton used to be dished with the piping hot laver 'bread' mixed with Seville orange juice.

LAVER SAUCE

Set some of it *(laver bread)* in a dish with a lamp, with a bit of butter and the squeeze of a Seville orange, stir it till hot. It is eaten with roast meat, and is a great cleanser of the blood. It is seldom liked at first but people become extremely fond of it by habit.

(This is particularly good with lobster and with salt duck.)

Laver Sauce

This is another old recipe for using laver, on the principle of accompanying meat with a sauce composed of the same food-stuff upon which the animal had grazed. Hence mint sauce with lamb from hill pastures where mint grows wild, apple sauce with pork from orchard-grazed pigs, laver with lamb grazed on sea-shore pastures.

a lump of butter the size of a walnut	½ pint milk
flour to thicken	2 cupfuls prepared laver

Melt the butter and stir in the flour to make a *roux*. Add the milk gradually, and when the sauce is smooth and creamy, beat in the laver. Serve with lamb.

Laver 'Salad'

Dress some prepared laver with a little olive oil and lemon juice or wine vinegar, and a grind or two of black pepper. Serve with fingers of dry toast.

I believe this way of eating laver may date from medieval times. It was in serving laver this way, as a starter to a meal, that we popularised it in my restaurant. I called it 'Caviare Cymreig' for menu purposes – a nonsense of course in terms of traditional Welsh food.

5. Pulses

Pulses are notably absent from the general run of traditional Welsh cookery, in contrast to the peasant cooking of other countries which use these useful, cheap, store-cupboard standbys so extensively. The explanation I think lies in the essential self-sufficiency of Welsh cooking; pulses were simply not available. Broad beans, which were commonly grown in Wales, were sometimes dried for winter use, but did not produce any recipes for their specific use.

Gower, however with its tendency to be different, reveals two recipes using pulses; a rabbit dish with lentils, and pease pudding. Both would seem to have come from across the Bristol channel, and both recipes are from *Welsh Fare.*

RABBIT IN LENTILS (*CWNINGEN MEWN CORBYS*)

a rabbit
one cupful stock
a little parsley, thyme
  and bay leaf

a little bacon, diced
bacon dripping
cooked lentils

Wash the skinned rabbit thoroughly, joint and fry in a little dripping. When lightly browned, add the bacon and stock, and season with the parsley, thyme and bay leaf. Cover the frying pan and simmer slowly until cooked. Meanwhile, pass the cooked lentils and the liquid in which they were boiled through a sieve into a saucepan. Add to this purée any liquid that remains in the frying pan after removing the meat, etc. Boil the purée briskly until it is reduced to a thick gravy. Pour over the rabbit joints and serve with potatoes and swede.

PEASE PUDDING (*PWDIN PYS*)

half a pound of split peas
one egg, well beaten

a little butter and sugar
salt and pepper

Wash the peas thoroughly and soak in cold water overnight. Put the peas in a muslin bag, tie securely, but allow for expansion. Put the bag in a saucepan, cover with boiling water, and add a little salt. Boil briskly for about two hours or until the peas are soft. Lift the bag out of the water and drain. Take the peas out of the bag and work them through a fine sieve or colander into a large dish. Add the butter, the egg, salt pepper and sugar. Beat well for a few minutes until thoroughly mixed. Place the mixture on a floured cloth, roll up and tie both ends securely. Boil the pudding for another half an hour. Turn out on to a hot dish, slice and serve with salt beef or pork.

7. Puddings, Pies, Pancakes

1. Fruit bakes, fools and trifle, curd cake and cheesecake.

I often think of apple and ginger fool, and plum pie and medlar trifle.

HOW GREEN WAS MY VALLEY: *Richard Llewellyn*

Apple, plum, damson and medlar trees grew in their place behind farm or cottage wherever the soil was receptive, but these fruits have never been grown commercially in Wales. In much of upland Wales apple trees were a rarity because of the inhospitable acid soil. Recent years have seen the rapid development of a thriving soft-fruit industry in the more favoured areas.

James Williams, in *Give Me Yesterday*, writes lovingly of these fruits in his memories of his childhood on a farm on the Pembroke/Cardiganshire border. And apples, he says, of many varieties were stored under his bed. . . he wonders if he slept slightly doped by the powerful and potent apple scent.

In the quotation from *How Green Was My Valley*, Richard Llewellyn is probably recalling his Pembrokeshire childhood. His is a description of party fare, or the regular treats on a fairly well-to-do farm where there was always plenty of cream from their own cows – and a mother who cooked well.

How the Welsh loved ginger, perhaps because it was the cheapest they used it most of all the spices to enliven the often frugal fare.

Medlar trees were common enough in the south and south-west of Britain at one time, where they grew with other fruit trees in orchards. But as elsewhere, medlars have fallen out of use in Wales and it is unlikely that they would be recognised as an edible fruit today. They are rather like a small brown apple; a sharp, acid fruit, to be eaten essentially when very ripe – when they appear to be almost withered, i.e., 'bletted'.

The popularity of trifle endures in Wales to the present day. In west Wales at least it is more or less the obligatory *finale* to a special occasion feast.

Fruit tarts in Wales were traditionally made on the bakestone, without a plate or dish. The fruit was not sugared when it was put into its pastry case, but was added afterwards, when the fruit was cooked. The pastry lid was skilfully lifted off by running a knife around the edge, then the sugar was worked into the fruit and the pastry lid replaced. This would help to keep the pastry on the underside of the lid from becoming soggy.

Full, round fruit or jam tarts were also made in this way on the bakestone and those who remember them speak of their construction with awe, for they were as big as dinner-plates. The trick must have been in ensuring a perfect seal to the edges so that no juice could escape – but even so, to turn them over must have required consummate skill, even with the special wooden slice. Here is a recipe from Caernarfonshire, from *Farmhouse Fare,* for a jam tart made in the oven.

BAKESTONE TURNOVER (*TEISEN AR Y MAEN*)

8 oz flour	1 egg
2 oz sugar	½ teaspoon salt
2 oz lard	raspberry jam
2 oz butter	

Mix the dry ingredients, rub in the lard and butter lightly and mix into a stiff paste with the beaten egg and a little milk if necessary. Divide into two parts and roll out thinly (both the same size). Cover one with raspberry jam. Place the other on top and nip together. Place on a greased baking-sheet and bake in a moderate oven for 15 to 20 minutes. When cool cut into dainty shapes.

Turnover fruit tarts were also made on the bakestone. In these, too, the sugar was not added until after the turnover had been cooked. Shortcrust pastry was rolled out to the size of a dinner-plate, then the fruit was laid on one half; any fruit – apples, blackberries, gooseberries, rhubarb – and the other half folded over and the edges sealed. The turnover was baked on a moderate bakestone until golden on both sides – it would be turned with a wooden slice. Again, the top layer of pastry would be taken off and a little sugar, and sometimes a nugget of butter, too would be worked into the hot, cooked fruit before replacing the pastry.

Sometimes the turnovers were made as small, individual tarts (*teisennau ar y maen*), and in this form are absolutely scrumptious. (See p.201)

TINKER'S CAKE (*TEISEN DINCA*)

The travelling tinker was a familiar and welcome visitor to farms and cottages a century or more ago. Pans and kettles and other metal articles in need of minor repair were collected against his visit, and in executing these small repairs he made a valuable contribution to the well-being of the families he served. I don't know whether these cakes were made in his honour (for no visiting craftsman in Wales ever went away without being offered generous hospitality), or whether he contrived them himself as a quick camp-fire bake. They are quick and easy, rich and good. Don't economise on the brown sugar:

1 lb plain flour	½ lb grated cooking apple
½ lb butter	a little milk or beaten egg
6 oz demerara sugar	pinch salt

Rub the butter into the flour and mix in the apple, sugar and salt. Bind with a little milk, or, to make a richer, softer cake, a beaten egg and some milk (but in this case you must bake the cake in the oven) and knead to a fairly stiff dough. Roll out on a floured board into large rounds a third-of-an-inch thick. Bake on a moderately hot bakestone three or four minutes each side; when done, cut into squares and sprinkle with sugar before serving hot.

If making the richer, oven-baked version, put the mixture in a greased, shallow baking-dish and bake about half an hour in a hot oven. Serve with lots of thick cream.

APPLE CAKES (TEISENNAU AFAL)

These are very similar to Tinker's Cake, but contain a higher proportion of apple to flour – equal quantities, in fact:

½ lb self-raising flour
½ lb cooking apples,
    cut up very small
¼ lb buttter

¼ lb lard
1 egg + a little milk
5 oz sugar
pinch salt

Be sure the apples are cut up really small – almost but not quite as fine as grated. The texture of little chunks of apple in the rich shortcrust mixture is unexpectedly good, but spoiled if the apple pieces do not quite cook because they are too big.

To make: rub the fats into the flour, add the salt and sugar. Mix in the apple. Bind with egg and milk to make a fairly stiff dough. Roll out thinly and cut into small squares before baking on a moderately hot bakestone. Sprinkle with sugar before serving.

All the available wild fruits were employed by the Welsh: blackberries *(mwyar)*; whinberries *(llus)*; wild raspberries *(afan)*; and where they were available, wild cranberries.

The latter are now largely forgotten, eclipsed by their larger, cultivated American cousins which arrive here at Christmas-time. Wild cranberries grow, creeper-like, underneath other plants on wet, boggy uplands, especially amongst sphagnum moss. They grow in Wales in a broad sweep across the country, roughly from Radnorshire across neighbouring Montgomeryshire and Merionethshire up the coast to the Llŷn peninsula. They are also found on the wet, upland areas of the old counties of Pembrokeshire, Cardiganshire, Breconshire, Caernarfonshire, Denbighshire and Glamorganshire. But as Radnorshire has produced the only mention of their use, one has to assume that only there did they grow near enough to habitation to enable them to be gathered. The following comes from Maxwell Fraser's *Wales*:

CRANBERRY TART FROM RADNORSHIRE

In Radnorshire a delicious cranberry tart is made with a pound of cranberries, half a pound of raisins, and an ounce of sugar, put into a basin in layers, and left overnight. The next day the mixture is turned into a saucepan, brought just to the boil, and left to simmer for five minutes. Half a teaspoonful of vanilla essence is then added, and the mixture is left to cool. A plate is lined with good rich pastry, spread thickly with the fruit, covered with more pastry, and the whole baked in a hot oven. It can be eaten hot or cold, but cheese is always served with it.

I think every garden in Wales must have its rhubarb patch, and there must be more rhubarb jam eaten in country districts then any other preserve. Spiced rhubarb tart is still popular, though today's hands-down favourite in rural Wales is rhubarb crumble.

SPICED RHUBARB CRUMBLE

Peel and cut 1 lb rhubarb into ½ in pieces. Sprinkle with sugar and mixed spices – ginger, cinnamon and allspice (Jamaica pepper) – and the juice of half a lemon. Rub up a 6 oz shortcrust mixture using butter rather than margarine or lard, add about 2 oz demerara sugar and a good grate of nutmeg. Strew this mixture on top of the rhubarb (not too thickly or it will be stodgy, so use a big enough dish) and bake in a fairly hot oven about three-quarters to an hour or until the fruit is cooked and the crumble lightly brown on top and quite dry through the middle. Serve with plenty of thick cream.

SPICED RHUBARB TART

Another version of the crumble, from Glamorganshire, is from *Farmhouse Fare*:

Line a deep enamel plate with pastry. Cook rhubarb to a pulp, adding as little water as possible. Sweeten to taste, and add ¼ teaspoonful ground ginger and ¼ teaspoonful cinnamon. Allow to cool and spread on pastry. Over this sprinkle the following mixture: ½ oz margarine rubbed into 2 tablespoonfuls flour, with ½ oz sugar added.

Bake for 20 minutes, when the mixture on top will become crisp.

Rhubarb Shortcake

From Farmhouse Fare.

Another Glamorganshire recipe:

Take a few sticks of rhubarb and cook in a casserole in the oven with a tablespoonful of water and a little sugar till tender (but not broken).

Meanwhile you will need for the shortcake 12 oz flour, 3 to 4 oz fat, 2 oz sugar, 1 egg, 1 teaspoonful baking powder, and milk to mix. Rub fat into flour, add dry ingredients, and mix with egg and milk to a stiff mixture. Divide in two. Roll one half out to an oblong shape ¾ in. thick. Place on a greased baking tin. Spread with cooked rhubarb. Roll out other half and put on top. Bake in a hot over for 25 minutes. When cool, cut in slices.

Like rhubarb, gooseberries are a commonplace in Wales. So not surprisingly, there is a large clutch of recipes for them.

The use of breadcrumbs in the following recipe suggests 17th or 18th-century origin.

Gooseberry Pudding

From Glamorganshire *Farmhouse Fare*:

1 quart green gooseberries (topped and tailed)	1 oz butter
¼ lb sugar	¼ lb breadcrumbs
2 eggs	

Stew the fruit gently till it will pulp, then beat it up. Take 1 pint of this pulp, add the other ingredients, mix all together except the eggs which should not be added till the mixture is quite cool, and then stirred in thoroughly. Put the mixture into a buttered dish and bake for ½ hour. Strew a little sifted sugar over the pudding before serving.

Apple and Ginger Fool

To recreate Richard Llewellyn's recollection, follow any classic fruit fool recipe – cooled stewed fruit with thick fresh cream folded into it.

For this one, stew apples in as little water as possible, with sugar and ginger (powdered, or best of all, some of the syrup from stem ginger). When cold, beat up with enough cream to make it stiff. Chill well before serving.

QUINCE FOOL

Quarter and core the quinces but do not peel them; put them in a vegetable steamer – the kind known as an adaptable steamer, which looks a bit like a colander, and fits on top of the saucepan, *not* a *bain marie* or double boiler – over a pan of water, and cover them. Steam until they are quite soft. Sieve them. Into the hot pulp stir caster sugar (about 6-8 oz for 1½ lbs of quinces, but this is a matter of taste). When quite cold fold in about ¾-½ pint of fresh cream.

Elizabeth David's version of a quince cream recipe from the notebook of Mrs Owen of Penrhos in Wales, 1695, in 'Syllabubs and Fruit Fools'.

Trifle was of course adopted from English cookery, a dish which did come down from the *plas*. Its richness would depend upon funds, and some preferred the simpler versions:

TRIFLE WITH JELLY

From a Welsh wedding reception in Parrog, Newport, Pembrokeshire, c. 1950:

1 Swiss roll
a tin of fruit salad

1 pint red jelly
custard

Cut the Swiss roll into rounds and arrange in the base of a large glass dish. Make the jelly with a little less water than usual, and when nearly cold, pour it over the Swiss roll. Leave in a cold place until set firm. Arrange the fruit salad over the top of the jelly, then finish off with a deep layer of thick custard. Chill well before serving.

Trifle is still included as a dessert in Wedding Breakfasts of the more prosperous 1990's although the meal itself is now much more sophisticated as this example shows:

Roll with butter

Meats
Ham, Beef, Turkey with Sausage and Bacon stuffing

Fresh Salmon

Quiches

179

Help yourselves to
Lettuce, Tomatoes, Cucumber, Sliced Beetroot, Red Cabbage,
Vegetable Rice, Coleslaw, Potato Salad, Cheese, Pickles, Sliced Onions,
Peas, Chutney, Vol-au-vents, Sausage Rolls, Peppers, Crisps,
Fruit Bowl, Nuts, and all sauces

Sweets
Pavlova, Cheesecake, Lemon Surprise, Gateaux, Sherry Trifle,
Fruit Pie
All served with U.H.T. Cream

Tea or Coffee with mints
Squash for Children

VIOLET PUDDING

From the diary of an unknown farmer's wife for the year 1796/
97, probably living in Radnorshire. I am grateful to Mrs Geraldine
Barnes for this recipe.

6 handfuls (5oz) dried or preserved violets	1 tablespoonful honey
6 eggs	juice of a lemon

Boil the violets gently until tender, with just enough water to prevent
them sticking. Beat the eggs to a froth with the honey and lemon juice.
Put in a greased dish and bake in a slow oven until set – about an hour
but test after ¾ of an hour. The oven *must* be really slow (250-300
deg.F). Serve with chopped fresh violets sprinkled over the top and
with plenty of cream.
    The colour will be curious but the pudding tastes delicious and may
be rich enough without cream.

(See also pp 286-7)

VIOLET JELLY

Gather about 1½ oz fresh young violet blossoms, pluck off stalks and
calyx, wash and drain off all the moisture. Make a syrup of 1 pint
water and 1 lb sugar and add violets, stirring gently, bringing the
liquid to the boil. Simmer gently for about 20 minutes. Strain through
muslin and allow to cool. Add 1 oz powdered gelatine to each pint of
syrup and heat, but on no account allow the liquid to boil. Pour into a
mould which has been previously rinsed in cold water, and when
turned out, arrange violets around it. The addition of a few drops of
violet colouring may be needed to achieve the correct tint. Rose petals
may be used in the same way.

Contributed by Mrs Barker, Felin Cochwillan, Tal-y-bont, to the *Llandegai Recipe Book*, edited by the Lady Janet Douglas Pennant, 1959.

JUNKET (*SOPAS*)

I am surprised to find junket so far out of fashion nowadays. In hot weather its cool, simple slipperiness can be most refreshing. Teamed with the contrast of crunchy paper-thin oatcakes it provides an excellent summer breakfast – an idea suggested by Mati Thomas' note on junket with oatmeal bread being a summer breakfast on the farm.

On the Welsh farm, junket was simply a matter of scooping up some of the curds straining in the dairy for cheesemaking if a dish of junket were fancied for breakfast or supper.

These are Mati Thomas' instructions:

3 gallons of skimmed milk
1 tablespoon rennet

Put the milk into the cooker over a slow fire. Allow to reach blood heat. When this is reached remove from the heat and add a tablespoon of rennet. After it has set properly, cut up with a *sletten* (a wooden tool made specially for the purpose).

PRINCE OF WALES CREAM

A Victorian recipe, origin unknown. Eliza Acton gave a similar one, but recommended using water instead of milk:

Dissolve ½ oz gelatine in 1½ pints of milk. Add ½ lb loaf sugar and the very thin peel of one lemon. Boil for five minutes then very gently pour three well-beaten eggs into the mixture. When almost cold, add juice of two lemons and strain through a sieve into a mould.

WELSH CHEESECAKE

Kathleen Gooding, who has divulged so unstintingly to me her memories of the old food of Wales (see *Cawl*), says this is how her mother used to make a cheese or 'curd' cake on the Welsh farm where she was brought up: it is typical of the cheese cakes commonly made in Britain from medieval times onwards:

> "First we lined a shallow (2" high) cake tin with pastry. Then I was packed off to the dairy for a whacking basin of the Caerphilly cheese curds a-doing there. We used to squeeze them dry, put in enough egg yolk to make it yellow, plus one or two of the whites; sugar, dried fruit, spice, candied peel – it varied according to what we had because the nearest shop was 3 miles away. I used to get the job of rolling out the pastry scraps and making lattice work while mother got on with finishing off the cheese in the dairy. Our oven wasn't very reliable and never got very hot, so I suppose you could say bake it for about an hour in a moderate oven. Instead of the Caerphilly cheese curds you could make a junket and drain it, but I think it would be better made with commercial curd cheese."

TO MAKE A CHEESE CAKE PUDDING

Putt on a pint of new milk, let it boyl, thicken it with grated bread, stir in a good piece of butter, take it off the fire, and putt in as many curants, as you thinke fitt; putt it of your skellet, and cover it up; (turn it out the saucepan into a bowl to cool) when it almost cold, putt in a good deal of fruit shred small, with nuttmeg, and sugar, 8 eggs well beaten, leaving out half the whites, a little orange Flower water or Rose water, lay a thin puff past (short crust is easier and better) on the bottome, and sides of the dish, and bake it in a pretty quick Oven, a little time will bake it.

From a late 17th century MS recipe book found at Gogerddan, near Aberystwyth, once the home of the Pryse family, now the Welsh Plant Breeding Station. Despite interior alterations, the outside of the lovely low mansion is exactly as it was.

WELSH CURD CAKES

From Croeso Cymreig:

Junket made with Channel Island milk will produce richer curds.

1 pint firmly set junket	½ oz cake crumbs
2 oz margarine	rind of lemon
yolks of 2 eggs	1 teaspoonful brandy
½ oz sugar	pinch salt
½ oz currants	

Cut junket and drain through muslin to remove whey, cream butter and sugar, add eggs, crumbs, flavouring and curds. Fill into patty tins lined with short pastry. Bake in moderate oven for 15-20 minutes.

POTATO CHEESE CAKES

Spiced, sweet, potato cakes were popular in north Wales during the 19th century. Potato was also used for these little 'cheese' cakes:

½ lb mashed potatoes	¼ lb sugar
¼ lb currants	¼ lb butter

Mix all well together. Line patty tins with pastry and fill with the mixture. Bake in a fairly hot oven until golden brown.

2. Rice and other puddings

Simple, old-fashioned rice pudding is still much loved in Wales today. No workers' canteen dare omit it from their daily selection of puddings, and the men in particular are fussy about the way it is made. If it is not just to their liking, rich and creamy, there will be trouble. When food costs began spiralling a few years ago, one industrial canteen in west Wales tried substituting dried milk for fresh in the rice pudding – but it was no good, the men spotted the subterfuge immediately, and after a short but sharp struggle involving the threat of strike the outside catering management gave in.

When I went to live in Cardiff in 1971 I found an additional pint of milk on the doorstep on the first Sunday. Mystified, I asked the milkman, when I came to pay him, why he'd left it. He looked at me surprised – "for your Sunday rice pudding," he said.

Some rice puddings in Wales were made on top of the fire or stove, some in the oven (often after baking bread in the large brick oven). At harvest time, huge, solid rice puddings rich with eggs and dried fruit and brown sugar, were made and left to go cold, when they were cut into squares and taken out to the workers in the fields. This pudding recalls the very early rice puddings, boiled in a cloth.

MARY MORRIS' PUDDING (*PWDIN MARI MORRIS*)
From Welsh Fare *by S Minwel Tibbott.*

Rice	water
salt	currants (optional)

Wash the rice and put it in a linen bag. Sprinkle with salt and currants. Secure the bag tightly and keep it immersed in boiling water for two hours. Serve with sugar and cold milk.

RICE PUDDING FOR THE HARVEST
also from Welsh Fare:

1 lb rice	1 lb raisins
1 gallon milk	½ lb brown sugar
1 lb currants	1 dozen eggs

Bake the pudding slowly until it has the consistency of a cake. When cool, cut into squares and serve cold.

SUNDAY RICE PUDDING (*PWDIN REIS DYDD SUL*)

This recipe from *Croeso Cymreig* is interesting because it recalls the days when rice puddings were baked in a puff pastry shell. They come straight from country house cooking. A Haverfordwest man recalls his mother, before her marriage a cook at one of the south Pembrokeshire mansions, making rice puddings in the same way.

Boil 1½ oz of rice in about ½ pint of milk till soft, and add 1 oz of sugar.

Mix another ½ pint of milk and 1 oz of sugar with two beaten eggs and add to the boiled rice.

Pour the mixture into a pie dish lined with puff pastry. Bake for about ½ hour in a moderate oven till the custard is set and the pastry is browned.

GROUND RICE PUDDING

Another pastry-case bake, this one is adapted from Alice Tipping's MS cookery book in the NLW:

1 pint cream	6 oz sugar
2 oz ground rice	1 tablespoon each
½ lb butter	brandy and sherry
3 small eggs	½ lb puff pastry
2 oz ground almonds	

Thicken the cream with the rice over a gentle heat, then add the butter, ground almonds, sugar and beaten eggs. Before stirring in the brandy and sherry a dash of cold milk helps the mixture to cohere.

Lay puff pastry over a greased baking dish and pour in the rice mixture. Bake 20 minutes at 400 deg.F., Gas 6.

A more usual way with the Sunday rice pudding in Wales is to cover a cupful of rice with cold water in the pie dish, and leave it in a moderately hot oven until the water has evaporated. This helps to soften the rice and makes the final pudding creamier. Then pour the milk over and add the sugar and salt. Stir well and add a bay leaf, and a knob of butter, sprinkle a little nutmeg on top. Beaten eggs may also be added, but if so, the oven must not be so hot or they will curdle.

All rice puddings were once as delicate and appealing as this. But Victorian times brought the economical rice pudding for the servants and nursery – and it is this which survived to give modern rice puddings a bad name. The Welsh, however, were happy to borrow from the English tradition for this, which is almost identical to Eliza Acton's 'Rice Pudding Meringué' p.363

in *Modern Cookery for Private Families*, 1846, reprinted 1991 by Southover Press. Recipes from English cookery books of this period are a commonplace in Welsh collections, their origin obscured by having been given another title, as with this one.

2 oz rice	4 tbs caster sugar
2 oz demerara sugar	½ pint water
1 pint rich Jersey milk	pinch salt
1 oz butter	½ teas. nutmeg
2 eggs + 2 whites	

Simmer the rice in the water until the grains are swollen. Heat the milk, add it with the butter, sugar, salt and nutmeg and the beaten yolks of 2 eggs. Whisk the egg whites until stiff, folding in 1 tbs sugar for each white. Pile the meringue on top of the pudding and bake in a moderate oven for about ¾ of an hour (350 F, gas 4) until the meringue is pale and biscuity.

MONMOUTH PUDDING (*PWDIN MYNWY*)

A white and red confection, from Dorothy Hartley's *Food in England*:

Take the white crumb of a small loaf, break it into a hot basin, and pour on boiling milk till *just* soaked; cover, and let it stand for 10 minutes; flake up with a silver fork, adding 2 tablespoonfuls of rough white sugar, 2 tablespoonfuls of fine lard (or butter), and, lastly, the stiffly whipped whites of 2 eggs. Flavour delicately, pour into a buttered dish with a layer of red jam at the bottom; put other layers alternately on top and bake till set, in a *very* gentle oven.

SIR WATKIN WILLIAMS WYNNE'S PUDDING (*PWDIN WATCYN WYNNE*)

A famous, old bread pudding from the Welsh border family noted for their passion for hunting along the border counties. The original specified beef marrow, once popular for puddings. Beef suet can be substituted. Versions of the pudding sometimes appear in collections of Welsh recipes but the instructions are vague. The original is reproduced in *English Recipes* by Sheila Hutchins.

Mix 4 oz of beef marrow (or suet) with 4 oz of sugar, 4 oz of bread-crumbs, the grated rind and strained juice of a lemon. Beat the yolks of 9 eggs and the 2 whites separately. Beat in the yolks and then fold in the stiffly whipped egg whites. Steam the pudding in a mould or buttered basin for 2 hours.

This pudding should be turned out and served with a good sauce such as the following:

THE SAUCE:

Take 2 tablespoons warm water, the yolks of 2 eggs, 1 tablespoon of sugar, 1 tablespoon of brandy, rum or whisky. Put them into a pan and whip over a low heat until the sauce is very stiff. Put it over any kind of steamed pudding in spoonfuls, but serve it immediately, or the sauce will be spoiled.

SNOWDON PUDDING (PWDIN ERYRI)

One tends to feel this famous pudding is slightly suspect. Certainly it is not in the Welsh pastoral tradition – how could it be with lemon marmalade and wine sauce? But it belongs to Wales all right, to the Pen-y-groes Hotel at the foot of Snowdon – Eliza Acton, writing in 1845, publishes it with reference to the hotel. Probably it was taken there by a cook experienced in cooking for the gentry. It is typical of the bread puddings popular at the beginning of the 19th century. Miss Acton claims this as the 'genuine receipt' and states: *This pudding is constantly served to travellers at the hotel at the foot of the mountain from which it derives its name:*

INGREDIENTS:

Some fine raisins split open, stoned but not divided; butter, beef-kidney suet ½ lb; bread-crumbs ½ lb; rice-flour 1½ oz; salt a pinch; lemon marmalade 6 oz; (or orange if lemon cannot be obtained); pale brown sugar 6 oz; eggs 6 thoroughly whisked; lemons grated rinds of 2.

TIME:

To boil 1½ hours. This quantity will fill a mould that will hold a quart. If half the quantity be made up and put into a pint mould it will only want boiling one hour, or even a little less.

METHOD:

1. Butter a mould or basin rather thickly, and ornament it with the p repared raisins, pressing the cut sides well into the butter.

2. Mix all the dry ingredients well together.
3. And blend well with the well-whisked eggs till thoroughly mixed.
4. Then pour carefully into the decorated basin and boil as directed.
5. Serve with wine sauce.

WINE SAUCE FOR SWEET PUDDINGS

Beat gently together for ten or fifteen minutes the very thin rind of half a small lemon, about an ounce and a half of sugar, and a wineglassful of water. Take out the lemon-peel and stir into the sauce until it has boiled for one minute, an ounce of butter smoothly mixed with a large half-teaspoonful of flour; add a wineglassful and a half of sherry or Madeira or other good white wine, and when quite hot serve the sauce without delay. Port wine sauce is made in the same way with the addition of a dessertspoonful of lemon-juice, some grated nutmeg and a little more sugar. Orange-rind and juice may be used for it instead of lemon.

WELSH PUDDING

Half a pound of butter; yolks of eight, whites of four eggs; six ounces of sugar; peel of one lemon; puff paste.
Melt half a pound of butter gently, beat it with the yolks of eight, and the whites of four eggs, six ounces of loaf sugar, and the peel of a grated lemon. Put a puff paste into a dish for turning out, pour in the above, and nicely bake it.

An old recipe, origin of the title unknown, quoted in Warne's *Model Cookery and Housekeeping* edited by Mary Jewry, one of a spate of popular-priced Victorian books of cookery and household management extracted from Mrs Beeton's famous work – this one sold at about 2*s*.6*d*. (30p).

APPLE, OR EVE'S PUDDING (*PWDIN AFAL, PWDIN EFA*)

This pleasant little pudding is too complicated I feel to have come from the rural tradition in Wales. I suspect its origin is English, too.

2 oz plain flour	2 eggs
1 oz sugar	½ to ¾ pint milk
1½ oz butter	Stewed apples

Melt butter in a saucepan, stir in the flour and add the milk a little at a time. Bring to the boil to make a smooth sauce. Pour into a bowl and add the sugar, and the egg yolks. Then fold in the stiffly beaten egg whites.

Grease a pie dish, and cover the bottom with a layer of stewed apples. Pour the mixture over them and bake for three-quarters of an hour in a fairly hot oven.

BLACKBERRY BREAD PUDDING (*PWDIN MWYAR*)

This is simple enough for the kitchen of a holiday cottage or caravan and useful for smaller quantities of blackberries perhaps gathered on the walk back from the beach. It is undoubtedly a Welsh cottage-version of the better-known English Summer Pudding, to which the second recipe is even closer. In this informal handling of the bread and fruit partnership one can imagine the children coming home to the farm or cottage with a collection of blackberries, and mother too busy with kitchen or dairy to do more than put the berries on to stew, and to bulk them up with scraps of stale bread:

Put some blackberries to stew with enough sugar to sweeten and just a little water. When the juice is running freely throw in torn-up scraps of bread (I prefer brown) until nearly all the liquid is absorbed (not quite all, or the pudding will be too stodgy). Chill well and serve with plenty of whipped fresh cream. I have made this dish very successfully with tinned blackberries.

BLACKBERRY PUDDING (PWDIN MWYAR DUON)
From Welsh Fare.

a large, thick slice of white bread
blackberries
sugar

a little water
fresh cream

Put the slice of bread at the bottom of a pie dish. Simmer the blackberries in a little water, with sugar added to taste. When soft pour the stewed fruit over the bread and leave to cool. Finally, top with fresh cream.

189

QUARRYMAN'S FAVOURITE
From The Llandegai Recipe Book.

Wherever workpeople have to take portable food to their work-place, many of the traditional dishes evolve from this necessity. The Cornish pasty, the cotton-workers' 'butty' are two examples. In the Welsh Valleys, *teisen lap* was a miner's and tin worker's favourite for their dinner tins because of its moist quality. In north Wales this was a favourite of the slate quarrymen.

1 lb flour	pinch salt
½ lb lard	water to mix
½ lb currants	few dabs butter
¼ lb sugar	

Mix enough water with the flour, lard and salt to make a firm pastry. Roll out fairly thinly and place half over a large plate. Lay the currants evenly over the pastry and place a few dabs of butter here and there. Add sugar evenly all over and cover with the rest of the pastry. Join the edges, cut a hole in the top to let the air out. Brush all over with milk and egg to improve the appearance and cook until golden brown.

An entry in *Croeso Cymreig* haunted me for years because of its intriguing name. To the English eye, *trollins* conjures up visions of engaging little Scandinavian dwarfs with the music of 'Peer Gynt' somewhere in the background. But alas, in Welsh the name is probably a mis-spelling of Trollies *(trolis)* with the same derivation from 'troll' (roll) in both languages. These little boiled curranty puddings are very old: made with oatmeal and boiled in broth they are a substitute for potatoes (and rather unpalatable) but made with flour, suet, and a spicing of nutmeg, served with a sprinkle of brown sugar and a knob of butter after simmering in plain water they are nice:

TROLLIES *(TROLIOD)*

oatmeal or plain flour	a little broth
currants (if liked)	

When boiling broth, skim a little of the surface fat off and put it into a bowl together with some oatmeal or flour. Mix with a little broth to make a soft dough. Add a few currants if you wish. Divide the dough into small balls. Cook with the vegetables in boiling broth for a few minutes. Serve with the meat and vegetables instead of potatoes. These were often scarce in early spring.

'TROLLINS' (TROLIS)

From Croeso Cymreig.

6 oz self-raising flour   pinch of salt
2 oz suet   a sprinkle of nutmeg
2 oz currants

Mix ingredients with milk to a stiff dough. Cut into four or six pieces. Mould into balls or rounds and flatten these to about three-quarters of an inch thick. Dip each piece in flour, then drop one by one into a saucepan of boiling water. Cook about 20 minutes.

Serve hot, with a spoonful of demerara sugar and a nut of butter on each. Trollins make a nice change from milk puddings after dinner.

DOWSET

A Gower dish – one version a simple, pastry-baked egg custard stiffened with a little flour; the other resembling the Derbyshire Bakewell Tart. Dowsets were often baked in the wall oven on baking day and kept for Saturday dinner. Saturday morning on Gower was taken up with house-cleaning and there was no time to cook! S.Minwel Tibbott records both versions in *Welsh Fare:*

ONE:

Shortcrust pastry, 2 large well-beaten eggs, ½ pint milk; 1 dessertspoon plain flour, 2 tablespoons sugar; salt, nutmeg. Blend the flour with a little of the milk and then pour it into the remainder of the milk and beaten eggs. Add the sugar and salt and beat well. Line a deep pie dish with pastry, pour the prepared mixture into it and sprinkle the ground nutmeg on top. Bake in a moderately hot oven for about half an hour or until the mixture is set.

TWO:

Shortcrust pastry; 6 tablespoons plain flour, 2 teaspoons sugar, 1 egg, well beaten, ½ teaspoon baking powder; jam, ¼ to ½ pt milk. Line a pie dish with a thin layer of pastry and spread jam on it. Put the dry

ingredients in a bowl and gradually add the beaten egg and milk to
make a smooth batter. Pour this mixture over the jam and bake the
pudding in a fairly hot oven until golden brown.

This can be likened to a 'hasty pudding', often appearing in
18th century cookery books, an English standby for centuries
without the pastry case. Dorothy Hartley in *Food in England*
quotes an elegant Victorian development:

HASTY-BATTER, CALLED DOWSET

Take a pint of new milk, 3 laurel [bay] leaves, and a little of the yellow
rind of lemon; cook till the milk is well flavoured, and, with fine flour,
make it into a pretty thick hasty pudding. Stir in ¾ lb butter, 2 oz sugar
crushed, the yolks of 4 eggs, and their whites beaten separately. Whip
all lightly together and bake in a deep pastry-lined dish. It would have
a light sack or madeira wine sauce with it.

WHITEPOT (WHIPOD)

Another Gower speciality, but recipes are recorded elsewhere in
Wales. There was a lot of Somerset in the Gower dialect, as this
rhyme about the old white pudding reveals:

O then vile wretch, the oarms (worms) shalt thou devour
To spule a great panvul of white pot
For the sake of a doust o' vlour (dust of flour)

Whitepot was sometimes made with rice, sometimes with
flour. It was a harvest field dish, or, with bread and butter, a
worker's supper. Again there are two versions, both of which
Minwel Tibbott has recorded: one is essentially a rice pudding
enriched with egg and flavoured with lemon rind like the stiff
'portable' rice puddings of other parts of Wales; the other is an
old-fashioned flour-and-milk pudding with currants and candied
peel, very common to early 18th century English cookery. It seems
reasonable to assume that the ricepot was in the Welsh tradition
and the other pudding in the English tradition on the other side
of the Bristol channel.

WHITEPOT (with rice)

Half a cupful of rice
half a pint of boiling milk
1 tablespoon sugar
1 egg, well beaten

1 teaspoon butter
good pinch salt
shredded rind of a lemon

Soak the rice in warm water for 3 hours. Drain, put the rice in a saucepan and pour the boiling milk over it. Boil for half an hour, then add the sugar, butter and salt. Simmer another 10 minutes, then allow to cool before adding the beaten egg slowly to the mixture. Finally add the lemon rind. Stir, bring to the boil once more and continue to boil until the mixture thickens.

Note: I feel it advisable not to bring the pudding right to the boil after adding the egg, otherwise it will curdle.

WHITEPOT (with flour)

1 pint milk
2 tablespoonsful plain flour
2 tablespoonsful sugar
2 oz currants

1 oz candied peel
large knob of butter
salt
nutmeg

Blend the flour with a little of the milk. Heat the remainder of the milk and pour, boiling, over the flour mixture, stirring well. Add the other dry ingredients, pour the mixture back into the saucepan and boil for 15-20 minutes. Serve warm.

In the mid-19th century a group of Welsh pioneers founded a colony in the Chubut Valley in South America, where they could have freedom to worship in their own way, and speak the Welsh language. They called the colony Patagonia. Total disaster almost overtook the embryo state more than once, until the emigrants learned to control the Camwy river and to irrigate the land consistently.

By the turn of the century the situation was completely reversed: famine and starvation had turned to overplus, and there was more of everything in foods – especially dairy produce – than could be profitably sold or practicably transported as the railway was never completed. Richard Llewellyn describes the situation well in *Up, Into The Singing Mountain,* the sequel to *How Green Was My Valley.* So housewives contrived dishes to use up the surplus cream, eggs and butter, thus developing a cooking style the very opposite of the frugal fare they had left behind in their homeland.

Patagonian Cream Tart (*Teisen Hufen Patagonia*)
Ann & Mair Griffiths, Cwm Hyfryd, Patagonia.

8 oz flour	pinch nutmeg
4 oz butter	1 tablespoonful sugar
3 eggs, separated	vanilla
½ pint double cream	

Rub the butter into the flour and bind together with the egg yolks and a little milk if necessary – this will give you what the French call *pâte sucrée.* Put it to rest for several hours, then roll it out and use it to line a fairly deep pie dish. Beat the egg whites and fold into the pastry case, sprinkle nutmeg over the top and bake in a slow oven (Gas Mark 3, 325°F.) for 35 - 40 minutes. If liked, a layer of sultanas can be laid on the pastry base before adding the filling, and the top can be covered by a layer of pastry.

I am inclined to think that when this dish was originally made, a vanilla pod would have been used for flavouring. Leave one in the cream or sugar overnight if you don't keep a jar of vanilla sugar in your larder – the flavour is less harsh than that of essence.

Patagonian Carrot Pudding (*Pwdin moron Patagonia*)

Marion Rees, of Cardiff, who brought this and the Patagonian cake recipe back with her to present-day Wales from a visit to Patagonia, also had this one for a pudding which must have been carried over in the *Mimosa,* for when carrots are used in puddings and cakes the recipe is usually an old one from the time when they were employed for their sweetness when sugar was scarce and dear. In this recipe, for 'cup' read 'American cup'.

1 cup grated potato	1 cup raisins
½ teaspoon bicarbonate of soda	½ cup melted butter
1 cup grated carrot	2 teaspoons cinnamon
1 cup flour	pinch salt
1 cup sugar	

Mix the bicarb, with the potato. Add the raisins to the flour and then add all the other ingredients and mix together thoroughly. Turn into a basin or other receptacle and boil in a *bain marie*.

3. Pancakes and other quick girdle cakes *(Crempogau)*

If anything can be said to have endured from the 'old days' of Welsh cookery in addition to *cawl*, it is the love of pancakes, in all their many forms. Pancakes were (and still are) a birthday treat in Wales. Being quickly made, they could be whipped off the bakestone at a moment's notice, and were a traditional offering to unexpected visitors. Upon arrival, the bakestone quickly went over the fire to produce other good things for a Welsh teatime as well as pancakes.

When pancakes were on the menu in an industrial canteen in west Wales, I was amazed to see an old bakestone come out of its cupboard to be placed over a couple of bricks set on either side of a gas burner. On this, amidst the gleaming steel and steam of contemporary catering equipment, the cook stood patiently making pancake after pancake, hour after hour, until the men's demands for them were appeased.

What characterises most Welsh pancake recipes is that they reflect very old cookery traditions which were once common to Britain as a whole. They use a lot of butter – in them or on them. Some are made with yeast or oatmeal. And almost always they are stacked in a pile, butter oozing generously between them, and cut down in wedges, like a cake. They are all horribly fattening and difficult to make well, especially those which contain sugar.

Pancakes have many names in Wales:

'*Cramwythen;* (plural, *cramoth*), parts of Carmarthenshire and

Glamorgan; *crempog (crempogau)*, counties of North Wales generally; *ffroesen (ffroes)*, parts of Glamorgan; *poncagen (poncagau)*, parts of Cardiganshire; *pancogen (pancocs)*, parts of Pembrokeshire; *pancosen (pancos)*, parts of Carmarthenshire and Cardiganshire';[1] and they have brothers and sisters called lightcakes and batter cakes.

There are so many variations on the basic pancake theme in Wales that you will almost never see exactly the same recipe twice under the same name. . . the principle is the same while quantities vary slightly.

The *ffroes* of parts of Glamorganshire are virtually identical with Scots pancakes or drop scones. Did the Scots introduce them when they came to the Glamorgan coalfields? But the way of piling them up on top of each other, buttered, with a sprinkle of sugar on each, is, I think, Welsh.

The *slapan* (batter-cake) is another extension of the pancake, this time baked thick on the bakestone, then split and buttered.

The lightcakes *(leicecs)* of Wales again are similar to the Scottish drop scones, but with the added incentive of buttermilk and bicarbonate of soda towards a greater lightness. At one 500-year-old hill farm high above Aberdyfi, where the fire was still 'on the floor' and the 50-year-old daughter of the household (currently the farmer) was famous for her lightcakes, I learned that the farm had been for generations noted for these delicious little pancakes. Long ago, the young men of the district would walk out from Aberdyfi to the farm of an evening and vie with each other as to how many *leicecs* each could consume; remembering the precipitous climb up to the old farm which my little car had almost refused, I realised the *leicecs* must have been very good indeed to have lured those young men upwards on foot. Pausing, with a sudden recollection of oneself as a child running from teatime on Shrove Tuesday in Lancashire to boast to playmates of the number of pancakes one had eaten, the universality of pancake-eating contests is apparent: remember Little Black Sambo who ate 169?

---

1. *Welsh Fare*, S Minwel Tibbott.

Lightcakes should really be small – 3 or 4 inches across, no more. Some recipes indicate a larger pancake, but it is impossible to make them large on the bakestone, as it can't be tilted. If you do make them large, in a heavy iron frying pan, they will go much more holey than the smaller ones do and are very difficult to handle. The holes may account for their name, but the degree of holeyness depends on how much raising agent you use. Buttermilk gives them their true lightness; one recipe I've seen contains so much cream of tartar (1 tablespoon to 6 of flour!) that I daren't think what it would do to stomach insides. One thing's for sure with lightcakes – don't leave the batter hanging about for after a while it becomes runny and won't hold its shape on the bakestone. These pancakes contain no butter, so the bakestone must be kept well greased. I find cooking oil easier than butter for this purpose.

PANCAKES (FFROES)

1 lb plain flour	4 eggs
1 oz butter	a little milk
1 oz lard	(currants, if desired)

Sift the flour into a bowl. Melt the butter and lard and pour into a well in the centre of the flour. Beat the eggs, add a little milk and gradually pour into the flour, beating well to make a thick, creamy batter. Then add a little water and beat again for a few seconds to make it light in consistency.

Melt an ounce of fat on a frying-pan or on a bakestone and pour on it half a cupful of batter. (A few currants may be added at this stage, if desired.) Allow the pancake to bake until small bubbles appear on its surface, then turn and bake on the other side. Place on a plate and spread with butter and a little sugar.

Continue to bake the remainder of the batter, and pile the pancakes on the plate to keep warm.

PANCAKES (CREMPOGAU)
A recipe from Anglesey:

10 oz plain flour	2 eggs, well beaten
½ teaspoonful salt	3 oz sugar
2 oz butter	1 teaspoonful bicarbonate of soda
¾ of a pint of warm buttermilk	1 tablespoonful vinegar

Melt the butter in the warm buttermilk, pour gradually into the flour and beat well. Allow this mixture to stand for a few hours, if possible.

When ready to bake the pancakes, stir the sugar, the bicarbonate of soda and the vinegar into the beaten eggs. Pour this second mixture into the first one and beat well to make a smooth batter.

Drop the batter from a tablespoon on to a well greased and hot bakestone or griddle. Bake over a moderate heat until the pancakes are golden brown on both sides. Then spread butter on each pancake whilst hot and serve warm. (A cupful of sour cream stirred into the batter acts as a further raising agent.)

YEAST PANCAKES (CREMPOGAU BURUM)

12 oz plain flour	¼ oz yeast
2 eggs	a little salt
3 tablespoonsful sugar	milk or buttermilk
a large knob of butter	

Mix the yeast with a little sugar and warm water and leave to prove in a warm place.

Heat the milk or buttermilk and dissolve the butter in it. Sift the flour and salt into a bowl, add the sugar, make a well in the centre and pour the well-beaten eggs into it. Now gradually add the milk and beat the mixture well to make a soft, creamy batter. Lastly, add the yeast mixture and leave the batter to rise in a warm place.

Bake the pancakes on a heated bakestone or frying-pan in the usual way. Then split each pancake in half and spread with butter. Serve warm.

A similar pancake was made with oatmeal or barley meal and served with treacle or butter. This was often a pancake made for the farm servants. Yeast pancakes are worth trying if you have hungry men to feed. . .

LIGHTCAKES (*LEICECS*)

4 oz flour	milk or buttermilk
3 oz sugar	¼ teaspoon bicarbonate of soda
1 egg	pinch salt

Put the dry ingredients into a small bowl. Beat the egg well and then add a little milk, or dissolve the bicarbonate of soda in the buttermilk.

Make a well in the centre of the dry ingredients, pour in the egg and milk/buttermilk, and beat the mixture with a fork into a thick, creamy batter.

Drop the batter from a dessertspoon, or from a jug, on to a hot, well-greased bakestone or griddle to form small cakes 3-4 in. in diameter. Allow to bake until small bubbles appear on the surface and the lower surface is golden brown. Then turn with a knife and bake on the other side. Serve warm with butter.

Note: Take care not to have the bakestone too hot for these.

ANGLESEY BATTER CAKE (*SLAPAN SIR FÔN*)

This is a batter-cake mixture used to make small pancakes on the bakestone which are afterwards split and buttered while still warm:

½ lb plain flour	2 oz currants
¼ lb butter	a pinch of salt
2 eggs	a pinch of bicarbonate of soda
2 oz sugar	a little sour buttermilk

Dissolve the bicarbonate of soda in the sour buttermilk. Melt the butter over a pan of hot water. Beat the eggs and pour slowly on to the melted butter and then add the sour buttermilk mixture.

Gradually pour this liquid mixture into the dry ingredients in a bowl and beat thoroughly to make a fairly stiff batter. Drop the batter from a tablespoon on to a greased bakestone or iron pan, and bake as for pancakes. Then split in half and spread with butter. Serve warm.

DAVID'S BATTER CAKE (SLAPAN DAFYDD)

The batter-cake made large – another Anglesey recipe:

10 oz plain flour	3 oz sultanas
2 oz butter	1 tablespoonful vinegar
½ pint warm buttermilk	1 teaspoonful bicarbonate of soda
2 eggs	½ teaspoonful salt
3 oz sugar	

Melt the butter in the warm buttermilk. Put the flour, salt and sultanas in a bowl, gradually pour in the buttermilk mixture and beat well. Leave this mixture to stand for a few hours, if possible.

When ready to bake the cake, beat the eggs, add the sugar, soda and vinegar and then pour this second mixture into the first one, beating well.

Pour all the mixture on to a greased, moderately hot bakestone to make one large cake. Bake and turn as for pancakes. Then split in half while warm and spread with butter.

These last six recipes are from *Welsh Fare* by S.Minwel Tibbott. (See also Cream Pancakes p.297).

GRIDDLE CAKES (CACENNAU CRI)
Dame Margaret's Way

These 'pancakes' are really a rich paste made with butter and eggs, sugar and dried fruits, rolled out thinly. Their name is derived from the 'speckling' of air bubbles. Sometimes they are cut into rounds, but more often they are rolled out almost as big as dinner plates, buttered when they come off the bakestone and served hot. As with the other Welsh pancakes, it is usual to make them into a pile, with plenty of butter oozing between them, the pile cut down in wedges to serve, as in this recipe, a very special favourite of Lloyd George which he was fond of having by the fire when he came in cold and wet from a long afternoon walk. But only Dame Margaret could make *cacen gri* the way he liked it. 'She would plaster them with the lovely salty Welsh butter until they were absolutely soaking with it, and pile them on a plate – oh how he used to enjoy that!' So said Mrs Blodwen Evans, who worked for the family in Llanystumdwy for many years, in *Lloyd George's Favourite Dishes:*

1 lb flour	sugar to taste
6 oz butter	1 teaspoonful baking powder and
1 egg	as much bicarbonate of soda as a
a few currants	sixpenny piece will hold*
a little milk	

Mix the baking powder and bicarb. on your hand, then add to flour. Rub in the butter. Add the currants and sugar to taste. Beat the egg into the milk then beat well into the flour mixture. Roll out thinly and bake on a greased griddle.

BAKESTONE TURNOVERS (*TEISENNAU AR Y MAEN*)

These can be made from a circle of pastry folded over like a Cornish pasty, or from two small circles of pastry, 4-5 inches across. Either way the principle is the same – the fruit enclosed by the pastry is cooked without sugar. I find the little round ones easier to handle, particularly when it comes to lifting the top pastry to work the butter and brown sugar into the hot fruit. It is this butter and sugar treatment which gives the turnovers their special appeal. The are also very easy to freeze uncooked, and can be fairly quickly thawed and baked on the bakestone or griddle.

1 lb plain flour	cooked apple, rhubarb or other fruit
6 oz butter, or margarine	soft brown sugar and butter

Drain the cooked fruit really well and cool. Make pastry (do not make it any shorter than this or it will be difficult to handle), roll out and cut into rounds (a saucer is useful for this), damp the edges, cover with another round and pinch the edges tightly together. Cook gently on both sides on a moderate bakestone or griddle until mottled with gold. The trick now is to trim the edge of each turnover with a sharp knife before carefully lifting off the lid. Work sugar and butter into the hot fruit, close up again and serve at once – with whipped cream if real wickedness is your aim.

---

* the pre-decimalisation tiny silver sixpence. This is the old way of stipulating quantity – ½ teaspoonful.

Large turnovers were made like this on the bakestone, often called *teisen blat* ('plate cake'), with fruit, or jam. 'Harvest Cake' is an example – see p.272.

A GREEN PANCAKE (*CREMPOG LAS*)

½ lb flour
2 eggs
milk to mix

chopped parsley
chopped shallot or spring onion
pepper and salt

Make the flour, milk and eggs into a batter, which should be stiff enough to support the onions. Cook over a moderate heat on both sides, taking care not to burn and to cook right through. Spread with butter and eat hot with grilled bacon or sausages.

---

8. Cakes

1. Buns and small cakes

. . . And a couple of minutes later come out with big teapots, and home brew in jugs, and others again would come out with bread and cheese and cake.

HOW GREEN WAS MY VALLEY, Richard Llewellyn

Bread and cheese and cake. For how long has that simple combination sustained the Welsh? Here, they were singing, late at night, in a coal-mining valley. At harvest time, in the country, bread and cheese and cake were taken out to the fields. A woman whose father had farmed at Pontypridd before the land went to mines and building told me how unemployed men would be taken on by her father for a few hours' work to get the harvest in quickly. "Glad of the tea, they were, never mind the money," she said. "We never knew my father had taken the men on until the call came from the fields for food for about twenty people. . . I had to run to the shop then, I can tell you."

"For what?" I asked, stupidly.

"Bread and cheese and cake, of course," she replied, surprised by my ignorance.

Cakes which come from the oven on the whole are from the more recent tradition of Welsh cookery. Like so much of Welsh food, the cakes are full of surprises: gingerbread without ginger? Boiled cake? Cakes in scallop shells? And who was Ann Davies, whose fruit cake recipe turns up in almost every Welsh collection and housewife's notebook? What surprises me, considering the long involvement of the Welsh with tourism, at least in the coastal areas, and the proliferation of cakes of all kinds and varieties – never mind the pancakes and bakestone specialities – that Welsh Teas were never developed along the same money-spinning lines as Devon and Cornish Teas. And the Welsh are such *good* bakers, and enjoy this activity so much. Maxwell Fraser says there are over sixty different cakes, buns and breads in the Welsh repertoire, and I have no reason to doubt her.

Perhaps when first confronted by the English tourist they felt it would please more to provide strictly English fare rather than their own delicious specialities. Though 'Welsh Teas' are everywhere advertised now, the attitude remains much the same – except that the teas are more likely to be offered by an English tearoom proprietor. But whether English or Welsh, they are simply responding to the market, and the chance of finding a dedicated traditionalist along the tourist routes are slim. There may be some *bara brith* or Welsh cakes included in some 'Welsh Teas', but more often than not they follow the jam and scone 'Cream Teas' of Devon and Cornwall. There was a Welsh country house hotel set in the green hills of Carmarthenshire which became famous for its scrumptuous and real Welsh teas in the 1970's (they included the little bakestone turnovers *teisennau ar y maen* – see p.201) but to the best of my knowledge nowhere else is doing anything similar. Perhaps one day someone will be encouraged to do so.

The Welsh used spices extensively in their traditional cakes. Honey and ginger cake, cinnamon cake, caraway cake. They were resourceful, too, when time or essential ingredients were short. Bacon fat, for example, was always saved, and used for cake-making when there was no other fat available – as well as an economy, it added to the rich flavour of the finished cake. When there was not enough sour cream for a churning of butter it went into a cake instead – and the result was a quickly-made, shallow, scrunchy, batter-based fruit cake, the forerunner of the famous *teisen lap*, designed to cope with the inadequacies of a Dutch oven. (Later, when there were 'proper' ovens, this cake was made in the 'modern' way, with fat rubbed into the flour, but it remained essentially a shallow, moist cake, for *lap* means 'moist, wet', as the original batter would have been.)

It is possible that *teisen lap* was the very first of the Welsh cakes after the very early fruit cakes made with bread dough, of which *bara brith* is a surviving example. Many feel that it eventually evolved into shop 'slab' cake, still widely on sale in Wales today – it was one of these of course which the Pontypridd farmer's daughter was sent to the shop to buy.

The cakes made on bread-baking day, from a piece of bread dough specially kept back for this purpose, had many names according to the part of Wales in which they were made – in England they'd be known generally as 'lardy' cakes. They had to be made much as is puff pastry – dried fruit, fat and sugar being worked into the rolled-out dough on the same roll-and-fold principle.

PEMBROKESHIRE BUNS (*MIOGOD SIR BENFRO*)

These buns were a traditional part of the Pembrokeshire New Year celebrations for children, who went from house to house singing and chanting verses to announce their *calennig* (New Year) greetings. Each child would be given a couple of buns at each house, and the haul was carried home on their backs in clean pillow-cases.

That industrial canteen where they still make pancakes on a bakestone is only half a mile or so over the border from Pembrokeshire into Carmarthenshire, and another Welsh tradition still carried on there is a twice-weekly bake of these buns, sometimes listed in Welsh recipe collections more prosaically as 'Yeast Buns'. Freshly made and eaten warm they are delicious:

2 lb plain flour	4 oz currants or sultanas
2 oz yeast	2 oz candied peel
6 oz sugar	2 eggs
4 oz butter	milk to mix

Mix the yeast with a little tepid water and a teaspoon of sugar in a small bowl or cup. Put the flour into a warm bowl. Rub in the butter. Add the dried fruit and sugar. Beat the eggs, add them to the yeast and add sufficient warm milk to make up to 1 pint. Make a well in the centre of the flour and pour this mixture in. Mix and knead well. Put in a warm place to prove for about 45 minutes, covered with a cloth. When the dough has doubled, roll it out on a floured board and cut into about 36 buns. Put in greased baking tins to prove for about 30 minutes. Bake in a hot oven (400 deg.F., Gas 6) for about 15-20 minutes. Glaze by brushing the surface while still warm with a mixture of sugar and water.

SOULY CAKES

These were a Gower speciality, yeast buns formed into the shape of a person in the manner of a gingerbread man. I have been unable to trace a recipe for it, but am grateful to David Morgan of Dunvant, Gower, for the following description:

"Souly (or Soulee) Cake was a yeast bun, brown, spiced and shining, with a round head, currant eyes, semi-circular smile, two arms represented by cuts in the body, and two legs, made on All Soul's Day, the Christian version of the pagan feast of that day."

He likens it to the 'pop' dolly of traditional west-country fare and it is almost certainly a custom imported from Devon and Somerset via the limestone importers who came to Gower for centuries (many of them settled, too) and influenced the customs, speech and food of the peninsula, until the trade died in the late 1800's with the coming of the railways.

All Souls' Day in the Christian year is November 2nd, but on Gower they keep it in the 'old style', i.e., according to the Welsh year (which denotes January 13th as New Year's Day) on November 12th. On 'Souling Day' the children of Gower would call round the houses asking for cakes with this old souling song, according to H M Tucker's *Gower Gleanings:*

Souly, Souly, Christendom,
Every good woman give some
Give me some or give me none,
Give me an answer that I may be gone.

But 'souling' was carried out in other parts of Wales, too, though perhaps not with these 'dolly'-shaped cakes. Trefor M Owen gives a good account of the reasons for, and the practice of 'souling' in his *Customs and Traditions of Wales*. 'Souling', he says, was a form of socially acceptable begging which came about because the service for the dead became too costly for the common people. This service which, probably began after the Reformation, was to secure the release of the souls of the dead from purgatory: the cakes were given to the priests in payment for their prayers.

WELSH CAKES (PICE AR Y MAEN)

There are two ways of making these traditional little spicy cakes. The most usual is on the bakestone or griddle, which produces them in a rather dry, biscuity form – I cannot share the Welsh liking for them in this way. Nor do I like stodgy 'shop' Welsh Cakes, which are often not spiced at all and made with lard instead of butter:

8 oz plain flour	½ teaspoon baking powder
2 oz butter	¼ teaspoon mixed spice
2 oz lard	1 egg
3 oz sugar	pinch salt
2 oz currants	milk to mix

Sift flour, baking powder, salt and spice together, rub in butter, add sugar, currants, bind with a beaten egg to a paste, similar to shortcrust, but slightly more moist. Roll out to about ¼ in. thick, cut into 2½ in. rounds, preferably with a plain cutter and bake on a greased griddle (not too hot) about 3 mins. each side until golden brown. Sprinkle with sugar when cooled and eat hot or cold, but they are best warm. Spread with butter if liked. This moister mixture avoids the dry, biscuity result, but needs careful handling.

Should you find slightly varying recipes for Welsh cakes, do not be puzzled. Welsh cookery is essentially imprecise, as it depended upon what happened to be available. And as with all national dishes, regional variations occur.

Yield: about 20.

The other method is to make them, from the same mixture, in a Dutch oven, and this produces cakes which are firm on the outside, soft and melting within.[1]

To substitute for a Dutch oven, try making them under a medium hot grill.

Made this way Welsh Cakes are often known as 'round cakes'. Instead of mixed spice they are spiced with nutmeg only, and are a speciality of the Vale of Glamorgan. In *Good Cookery*, Lady Llanover gives a recipe recommending "sheep's-milk cream to bind the cakes, calling them 'Short Cakes of Gwent and Glamorgan' ".

---

1. Welsh Cakes to this recipe are available in Tesco's 'Traditional' range.

James' Cakes (*Cacennau Iago*)

Made from a shortbread mixture in the shape of a scallop shell, these little cakes are a speciality of Aberffraw on the west coast of Anglesey, and are nearly always called *Berffro Cakes* after the little village. But they were earlier and more appropriately named *Cacennau Iago* after St James, because of their scallopshell shape – pilgrims *en route* for the church of Santiago de Compostela in Spain's north-western province of Galicia wore a scallop shell as a hat badge to distinguish them, and it has been the pilgrim's motif ever since.[1] An interesting note is the sharing of a common name for James by the two Celtic countries.

In St Mary's Church, Haverfordwest, Dyfed, the 15th-century effigy of a pilgrim has three scallop shells on his scrip, signifying his pilgrimage to the Spanish shrine.

The scallop shells which were, and still are, found on the wide beach near Aberffraw are not true scallops, but the smaller 'queens' about 2½ in. across. Queens move about the sea-bed considerably – an acquaintance remembers finding them as a child on the south Pembrokeshire coast, where he knew them as 'hens'. They are now being commercially fished in Cardigan Bay.

These little cakes are not made on the scallop shells, as some recipes suggest, for they would be difficult to remove. The flat half of the shell is just used to imprint the cake with its shell motif. The recipe was included in *Cassell's Dictionary of Cookery*, 1885.

(The influence of the simple shell motif upon 18th-century design in Britain was extensive. Its effect upon architecture is particularly noticeable in Wales where so much of the great wave of late 18th-century house building still remains; over and over again the shell motif is there in a front-door fanlight or a canopy – remember Mr Gruffydd's house with the sea-shell porch in *How Green Was My Valley?*)

---

1. 'How should I your true love know
   From another one?
   By his cockle hat and staff
   And his sandal shoon.'
   W.Shakespeare, *Hamlet*.

| 3 oz flour | 1 oz sugar |
| 2 oz butter | |

Make the mixture entirely by hand as the hand's warmth is needed to make the dough soft and pliable.

Soften the butter and beat in the sugar. Add the flour a little at a time, work the dough on a floured board and then roll out thinly and cut into small rounds. If you have a scallop shell, sprinkle the underside with sugar and press on to each round to make an imprint. Place the cakes on a greased, shallow tin, leaving space between each one. Bake quickly in a hot oven (425 deg Gas mark 7). They should not turn brown. Sprinkle with sugar while still warm.

SPICED POTATO CAKES (*TEISENNAU* TATWS SBEIS*)
From Croeso Cymreig.

1 lb cold cooked potatoes	¼ teaspoonful cinnamon
3 tablespoonfuls flour	milk to mix a fairly stiff
2 tablespoonfuls brown sugar	consistency
1 teaspoonful baking-powder	

Put mixture into a greased tin, and put in a fairly hot oven to start with, then lower the temperature, and leave the cake to bake for two hours.

The cake can be eaten hot or cold, sliced and buttered.

---

2. Large Cakes

MOIST CAKE (*TEISEN LAP*)
From Welsh Fare *by S Minwel Tibbott.*

1 pint sour cream	3 oz butter
4 tablespoons self-raising flour	4 oz sultanas
4 oz sugar	1 egg

Rub the butter into the flour and work into the sour cream, together with the other dry ingredients. Lastly, add the beaten egg to the mixture before pouring it into a shallow tin. Bake in a low oven or in a low position under a hot grill.

---

* the south Wales word for 'cake'. *Cacen* is the north-Walian word.

This is an early version of *teisen lap* which would traditionally have been baked in a Dutch oven before the fire.

A modern recipe, adapted from *Croeso Cymreig:*

8 oz flour
2 oz butter
2 oz sugar
2 oz sultanas and currants
1 large or 2 small eggs

¼ pint milk (sour milk is delicious)
½ teaspoon baking powder
pinch salt
grated nutmeg

Sieve flour, baking powder, salt and nutmeg. Rub the butter in lightly, add sugar and fruit, then well-beaten eggs. Add the milk gradually, beating with a wooden spoon. The mixture should be soft enough to drop from the spoon. Bake in a fairly hot oven (375 deg.F., Gas 5) for about 30 minutes.

SEED CAKE (TEISEN GARAWE)

Caraway seed flavouring was one of the longest enduring spices after the availability of cheap sugar in Britain had reduced the need for spicing. Caraway seed cake is still liked by older people in Wales today, for whom it must be inextricably linked with memories of chapel and Sunday tea in the front parlour with everyone on their best behaviour.

1 lb flour
2 teaspoons baking powder
5 oz brown or caster sugar

8 oz dripping or butter
1 or 2 eggs
½ oz caraway seeds

Rub the fat into the sieved flour and baking powder. Add sugar. Beat a little water up with the eggs, mix very dry. Bake 1½ hours in a moderate oven.

Adapted from a recipe in *Lloyd George's Favourite Dishes.*

WELSH CINNAMON CAKE (TEISEN SINAMON)

An unusual cake with every indication of being in the Welsh tradition because of the shallowness of the baked base – a consideration for coping with the inadequacies of a Dutch oven. The saving of the egg white from the cake mixture to make into a sparse little meringue topping suggests ekeing out a few ingredients to make something a little more special than usual – perhaps for a birthday or an important visitor.

The possibilities afforded by enriching this cake a little led me to add an extra egg yolk to the base mixture, and two or even three egg whites to the meringue to make a really deep, white topping – which contrasts splendidly with the darkish, cinnamon-coloured base. In this form it makes a delicious dessert. I quote the original version here, which I found in *Croeso Cymreig*. For my 'development', just increase the egg yolk to 2 and the whites to 3.

½ lb flour	½ teaspoonful baking powder
4 oz sugar	1 teaspoonful cinnamon
4 oz butter	jam
yolk of one egg and whites of two	

Mix the baking powder with the flour and rub in the butter. Add the sugar and cinnamon and the yolk of the egg to make a stiff paste. Roll out and place on a shallow tin or plate – as for making a plate tart. Cook 'blind' in a hot oven. Allow to cool and spread with jam. Beat the whites of egg until stiff, fold in a little sugar, spread on jam and return to a cool oven to set.

Oven: 400 deg.F., Gas 6, for the base.
325 deg.F., Gas 3, for the meringue.

The base in my version is not meant to be rolled out like a dough. It is best if made like a fairly stiff sponge, with a little milk to moisten; the result is softer and lighter than the original. The base can be left to cool in its baking dish.

HONEY CAKE (*TEISEN FÊL*)

Perhaps because of its cinnamon content, this cake is sometimes confused with the previous cake. The Welsh love of spices, the absence of sugar in early days and honey's additional usefulness as a moisteriser gives us two Welsh recipes for Honey Cake, one with cinnamon and the other with ginger to spice it.

4 oz honey	½ lb flour
1 teaspoon cinnamon	½ teaspoon bicarbonate of soda
4 oz brown sugar	4 oz butter
1 egg, separated	caster sugar

Sieve together flour, cinnamon and bicarb. Cream fat and sugar and beat in egg yolk. Add honey gradually. Stir in the flour with a little milk if required and mix lightly. Whisk egg white until stiff and fold into mixture. Half fill small patty tins, dredge the tops with caster sugar and bake in a hot oven (400 deg.F., Gas 6) for 20 minutes. When ready spinkle with more caster sugar.

Though it was traditional to make small cakes from this mixture, it can be used to make one large cake, which will obviously need a longer baking.

ANN DAVIES' CAKE (CACEN ANN DAFIS)
From Welsh Fare *by S Minwel Tibbott.*

Because of the confusion of names in Wales (so many Joneses, Jameses, Edwardses, Davieses, Llewellyns and so on) the ubiquitousness of Ann Davies' Cake doesn't strike one at first. But after the name has cropped up in enough Welsh recipe collections the idea slowly filters through that this lady may be of some significance. She was in fact a baker in the early 1900's with a shop in front of her bakery in Kidwelly (Cydweli), the small town in south west Wales, important in medieval times for its impressive castle, situated on the Gwendraeth estuary and thus able to be supplied by sea. She was famous for her fruit cake, which sold at 6*d.* a pound, and was apparently prepared to part with the recipe, though whether for free or for money I am not able to say (bakers did sometimes sell their recipes). This recipe was much prized by housewives throughout the south of Wales.

1½ lb plain flour	½ a teaspoonful mixed spice
1½ lb currants	½ a teaspoonful baking powder
1 lb sugar	¼ teaspoonful salt
¼ lb butter	½ pt milk
½ lb lard	two eggs, well beaten
½ a teaspoonful nutmeg	

Rub the butter and lard into the flour and sugar and add all the other dry ingredients. Make a well in the centre of this mixture, pour the eggs into it and gradually add the milk, mixing all together to give a fairly soft consistency.

Grease two cake tins, divide the mixture equally between them and bake in a moderately hot oven (350 deg.F., Gas 4) for about one and a half hours.

CREE CAKE (*TEISEN GRIWSION*)

Cree, or scruggins, are the small crisp pieces left over when pig's fat had been melted down for lard. This type of cake often called 'Scruggins Cake' is by no means exclusive to Wales, but known wherever pigs played a major part in household economy.

This recipe is from Gwent, from *Farmhouse Fare.*

1 lb self-raising flour	½ lb granulated sugar
¾ lb chopped scruggins	milk and water for mixing

Chop the scruggins into small pieces, then put in a basin the flour, chopped scruggins and sugar; mix all the dry ingredients together, then make into a soft dough with the milk and water. Roll out the dough about 1 in. thick and press into a square tin, well greased with lard. Cut the top of the cake into squares, and sprinkle with a little castor sugar, bake in a moderate oven for about ½ hour.

Currants can be added to the basic mixture, and in some parts of Wales the rolled-out dough was baked on a bakestone.

BOILED CAKE (*TEISEN FERW*)

Medieval bakers used to part-boil, part-bake their light, biscuity confections called Simnels and cracknels (the name Simnel was later transferred to a spicy fruit cake).* Though not to achieve the same effect, the method is still in use in Wales today; I feel it may have been employed as a device to assist baking in a Dutch oven. I misunderstood the first recipe I was given for this cake. . . I thought the instructions were to simmer the dried fruit, butter and sugar for two *hours*! Nothing like studying a foreign subject which presents some odd aspects to an outsider to encourage you to accept any apparent oddity, and it has to be said that the result was a lovely, dark, rich cake. Like *teisen lap* this cake was a useful portable for meals eaten at the workplace. Some of my friends make it instead of the usual Christmas cake. This recipe comes from Mrs K L Edwards of Capel Seion, near Aberystwyth, a scattered parish in the lovely Vale of Rheidol

---

* *Food and Drink in Britain*, C Anne Wilson.

near the 18th-century mansion of Nanteos, where a relic of what was said to be the Holy Grail was once kept:

12 oz dried fruit	½ lb soft brown sugar
½ lb butter	½ pint milk

Simmer these ingredients together for 2-3 minutes; leave to cool for 15 minutes, then add:

1 lb plain flour	1 teaspoon salt
1 teaspoon mixed spice	2 eggs
1 teaspoon bicarbonate of soda	

Mix well together, turn into a greased cake tin and bake in a moderate oven (350 deg.F., Gas 4) for 1-1½ hours..

There are many little homely recipes for cakes devised around easy-to-remember measurements occurring in Welsh collections – 'three-quarter cake', 'weight of an egg cake' – to obviate the need for scales or more formal measurements. They were useful to pass on to young brides, perhaps nervous in the kitchen and having nothing but the simplest of measuring devices. An example:

The Weight of an Egg

From Farmhouse Fare.

A simple sponge mixture which makes about nine little cakes for tea, from Anglesey; useful to know because most bun-making trays have nine compartments:

1 egg and its own weight in sugar, self-raising flour and butter or margarine.

Cream butter and sugar; whisk in beaten egg and flour alternately. Divide into about 9 greased patty-tins. Bake in a fairly hot oven till well risen and nicely browned.

A delicious alternative is made by mixing double the quantity and substituting one pint packet of strawberry blancmange powder for the equivalent amount of flour.

ANGLESEY CAKE (TEISEN SIR FÔN)

3 teacups (8 oz) flour	3 teaspoons baking powder
1 teacup sugar	2 eggs
1 teacup butter	milk to mix
a little dried fruit	

Add the baking powder to the flour. Rub in the butter, add the sugar and well-beaten eggs, with a little milk if necessary, but keep the mixture fairly stiff. Fill two greased sandwich tins, bake in a fairly hot oven (375 deg.F., Gas 5) 30-40 mins. Cut each in half, spread with butter and eat hot.

OVERNIGHT CAKE (TEISEN DROS NOS)

½ lb plain flour	1 teaspoon ginger
¼ lb butter or lard	½ teaspoon bicarbonate of soda
¼ lb mixed dried fruit	1 tablespoon vinegar
1 teaspoon cinnamon	milk to mix

Rub the fat into the flour and work in the spices and dried fruit. Mix gradually with milk to give a fairly soft consistency. Dissolve the soda in the vinegar, pour it over the soft batter mixture and stir briskly. Allow this mixture to stand overnight. Line a cake tin with greaseproof paper, pour the mixture into it and bake in a moderately hot oven for about 1¼ hours.

The Women's Institutes in Wales are no less active than those in other parts, perhaps more so, having regard to the large proportion of rural areas. One of their frequent activities is to compile little books of their favourite recipes, which with the passage of time become interesting. Cricieth W.I. did this in 1920, when, with a clutch of the great man's 'favourites', they published with great aplomb and a fine disregard for the *double entendre* under the intriguing title *Lloyd George's Favourite Dishes*.

Or groups of women in town and country pool their culinary collections to make a little, often photocopied book to sell to raise money for the restoration of a church or to buy an invalid a much-needed aid, and the little pamphlets are tucked away and forgotten, to come out years later with a bundle of old papers to delight and to puzzle – for explanations as to source, etc. are seldom given. Many of these Welsh collections contain an American or Canadian Cake – a poignant reminder of the families left behind in Wales by enterprising sons and daughters who struck out for adventure in the New World?

But the emigration to South America and the setting up there of the Welsh colony produced its own cookery tradition:

BLACK CAKE OF PATAGONIA (CACEN DDU PATAGONIA)

At first glance this is just another rich, dark fruitcake – until one comes to the final stage of embalming it within a crisp casing of thin icing. With the rum thus entrapped and going about its good work amongst the cake's innermost recesses, this was a cake which could be made well ahead of times of celebration and could be kept, in cool conditions, maturing for months:

10 oz butter	4 oz chopped nuts
10 oz dark brown sugar	(walnuts or almonds)
4 eggs	2 teaspoonfuls baking powder
1 lb plain flour	1 teaspoonful bicarbonate of soda
1 teaspoon cinammon	mixed in 1 tablespoon of
1 teaspoon mixed spice	vinegar and 1 tablespoon
4 oz raisins	water
4 oz currants	1 teaspoon almond essence
4 oz sultanas	small glass of rum
8 oz mixed peel	

Grease and line an 8" deep cake tin. Cream the butter and sugar. Whisk eggs lightly and add a little at a time to the butter mixture, beating well. Fold in the sieved flour and spices, and the fruit and nuts. Pour the baking powder and bicarbonate of soda liquid, also the almond essence on to the mixture. Mix together. Lastly add the rum.

Bake cake at gas mark 3, electricity 325 deg.F. middle shelf for 3-3½ hours.

FOR THE CASING:

6 oz icing sugar	3 tablespoonfuls hot water

Mix to form a thin, glacé-type icing and brush over all the cake – top, sides and bottom to completely encase it in a brittle, sugar shell. You can do it while the cake is still warm from the oven or after it has cooled – the results seem to be pretty much the same.

From Ann and Mair Griffiths, Cwm Hyfryd, Patagonia and published in *Egg Recipes From Wales* collected and presented by Evan Rees, Egg producers and packers, Swansea, in conjunction with the Welsh Folk Museum, St. Fagan's, near Cardiff.

3. Gingerbread and cakes

GINGER CAKE WITHOUT GINGER (*TEISEN SINSIR HEB SINSIR*)

Why or how was ginger left out of this traditional recipe? Was it simply forgotten because so obvious an ingredient, or is it really meant to represent ginger cake without actually containing the spice? Because it does in fact have a gingery taste. I found the recipe first under the title, 'Old Welsh Gingerbread', with the explanation that it used to be sold at the old Welsh fairs:

½ lb flour   ¼ lb butter
½ teaspoon bicarbonate of soda   2 oz chopped mixed peel
1 teaspoon cream of tartar   6 oz black treacle
6 oz demerara sugar   1 gill milk

Warm treacle slightly and mix the milk. Sift together flour, bicarbonate, and cream of tartar and rub in butter. Add sugar and peel and stir in treacle and milk. Bake in a greased tin for 1½ hours at 350 deg.F.

TO MAKE GINGER CAKES THAT WILL KEEP ALL YEAR

Take a quarter of a p^d of Almonds Blanched, and put them in a morter & put to them a quarter of a p^d of sugar being beaten & ten Dates cut small, then beat all these togather untill they may be wrought like a paist, then put to it 1 ounce of cinemon, 1 ounce of Ginger scearced, a littel sanders & beat them togather one hour, then make littel thin cakes of it and lay them upon ye mold to print them & cast a littel powder of cinemon & ginger betwixt ye mold that it does not stick. Dry them before ye fire till they be hard & so lay then up in a box.

Old gingerbread moulds can be seen in many museums. The Welsh Folk Museum at St Fagan's has some Welsh ones.

'Sanders' – a preparation of sandalwood from India.

(See also p.294 and p.302)

4. Picnics

For those who worked on the land life was extremely hard in Wales (as in many other parts of rural Britain) until well after the turn of the last century. But from contemporary accounts and memoirs there is an over-riding impression of good companionship and spontaneous friendly fun which made the unrelenting round of toil tolerable. Local fairs and markets provided occasional cheerful relaxation, and once a year there was the Picnic, a tremendous Day Out to the sea, or nearby beauty spot if the sea was too far away, organised by the Sunday School or chapel. Dr James Williams described the annual outing for the children, *c.*1907, at Pen-y-bryn, near Cardigan, to Poppit, in *Give me Yesterday:*

> What a day for the carters! They had freshly painted the carts, spent hours grooming the horses and had gaily decorated their tails and manes with coloured ribbon with corn-dollies on their foreheads. They themselves were clad in breeches with impeccable black shining leggings and boots. There was considerable rivalry between the various équipes, much of it expressed in broad badinage mingled with loud guffaws. If there was a drizzle early in the morning the wise men would pronounce gnomically that it was only a 'shower before the tide' it would be lovely later, more often than not it was. Nothing was said or done that could possibly reduce the buoyancy of the occasion. I do not remember ever seeing a four-wheeled waggon – for the simple reason nobody used them in our part of Wales, apart from the carriers. Brakes or waggonettes could have been hired – but no, this was a proud do-it-yourself occasion, so carts it was – clean, with the axle tree greased, and to accommodate the load a *treble* was fixed on each cart – and on the treble sheaves of corn on which the passengers sat. The more crowded a cart was, the better. . . The minister, his wife and family would be transported in a gig or governess trap – out of respect for the cloth – but as their children grew up, they would gravitate to the carts where they could sit squeezed tight against their boy or girl friend. By about 8 am the superintendent of the Sunday School gave

the order to move off – except the cart remaining to pick up the stragglers, and the triumphant 4 miles progress to the sea began. Various hymns were sung: flippant greetings exchanged with all the people *en route* who came out of their houses and waved to each cart-load as it passed. The real singing was to be heard on the return journey in the gloaming. On arrival the carts were unloaded, the likely lads making much of their opportunity in helping the pretty girls down. There were coy blushes indicating some advance in their affairs – the silent language of pressure, pats and hugs being well understood and applied by all involved. The horses were taken out of the shafts, and there was much competition among the boys to be allowed to ride them to the stabling provided at the neighbouring farms. The ladies by this time had donned whiter than white aprons, and were calling us all to light refreshments – pop in those lovely bottles sealed by a glass marble, or tea with buns and cake. After this the mad rush over the strip of shingle to the long sandy beach if the tide was out, and a collection would be made of ribbon sea-weed, shells, pebbles and other treasure trove. There were rock-fish in the pools, and caves to be explored. Our elders forbade any one to bathe when the tide was going out, quoting in support of their prohibition the dire fates of those who had disobeyed in the past. Neither were we to go into the sea until at least one hour had elapsed since the last meal. A horn and a big hand bell summoned us all to lunch, a sumptuous repast of cold ham, beef, new potatoes, cabbage, broad beans, pickles, followed by massive portions of rice pudding. . . The food was eaten in a long, low shanty owned by Dinah and her husband the Captain. Inside were four long tables, the two farther from the door being set on a terrace a foot above the others. Light was shed on them by skylights fixed in the roof. Dinah charged a fee for the use of the shanty, all cutlery, plates, boilers, tumblers, tea cups. She also provided the long white tablecloths. The use of the nine-pin skittle-alley was included in the hire charge for the day. . .

Food has never tasted so good; everyone remarking on the way sea air had revived their jaded appetites. The great event of the day was the communal dip in the sea. The ladies formed themselves into a laager to undress – great care being taken to ask someone who understood the speed of the incoming tide, where their clothes would be safe. Men were perched on neighbouring rocks in various stage of undress, pale bodies in startling contrast with their very red faces, necks and arms. None had bathing drawers, but two bandana handkerchiefs were tied together to form an *avant garde* bikini. The ladies wore no costumes, but had summer weight petticoats which ballooned as they entered the water, much to the delight of the men who made teasing comments. The ladies would reply with equal spirit, and if they found a man had strayed near them away from the ready succour of his mates, several would grab him and dip him unmercifully. What a cacophony of Rabelaisian laughter and jokes!

What a good time was had by all, with the minister remarking that his hearing had much deteriorated since the previous year! And, bless their memory! did they not deserve this one day after the unrelenting swink of their occupations?

Sports were held when the tide was out, the prizes being packets of sweets – pear drops, humbugs, or three XXX* peppermints. The last meal of the day was tea – gallons of it – with bananas, cake, and meat sandwiches. Again nothing was rationed. Before the start for home some of the boys and girls would sneak off in couples into the wide expanse of sand dunes. Mothers who felt their offspring were ignorant of the facts of life, and feared lest they should learn them in Dame Nature's way of trial and error in the sand-dunes, would chase after them, calling out Davi John, Ann Jane, Marged or Wynford, much to the amusement of those parents whose children as yet were too young to involve them in such agony.

When the sun was right, some time after tea, an official photograph was taken of the whole gathering.

Further up the Cardiganshire coast, the fishing village of Llangrannog was another popular venue for the annual outing for people living inland. Anne Jane and her late sister Beryl Jones, who looked after summer visitors there for over fifty years and until recently were still active in their waterfront guest house, full of Welsh atmosphere and the good smell of carefully cooked food, told me how the carts and gambos would come from as far away as Newcastle Emlyn and Lampeter: "The poor horses were glad of a rest when they got to the beach at the bottom of the long *cwm*". The day trippers brought "enough food to supply a village – huge flat loaves, brown and white, *bara brith* and a *cosyn* of cheese" (a whole cheese). A fire would be lit in a cave or other sheltered spot to boil the water for tea; and here in Llangrannog the annual paddle was taken fully clothed, "not further up than the knees, with long skirts and hats on". Finally, a sing-song for a grand ending, everyone on the beach joining in and by the time they got to *Calon Lân* ('Pure Heart') some of them were halfway to Heaven!

Anne Jane was a local Llangrannog celebrity on two counts: she was an *eisteddfod* prize-winner and regular broadcaster in the Welsh language on BBC Cymru, and as a young girl she played a part in the film 'Torn Sails', from the novel by Allen

---

* very big, very strong white mints.

Raine, made in and around Llangrannog in 1920-21. In one scene she had to stand on the shore with her half-sister Beryl, then still a baby, in her arms. In another scene, she was out in the bay on a boat for hours and hours in an August so unseasonably cold that they all had to be rubbed down with rum when the day's filming was over!

9. Poverty

*Food got less. Tea we had without sugar and milk, and then no
sugar, and after, no tea. Meat came less and less. Bread was
sparse, thick in the slice, and presently, butter only on Sunday.*
HOW GREEN WAS MY VALLEY, Richard Llewellyn

1. Broths and Gruel

Right up to the Second World War, poverty was a factor in Welsh
life. For some, recurring; for others, a constant. Many left rural
poverty to work in industry, only to exchange what they had left
for urban poverty.

Emigration was one escape – to north America, Canada,
Patagonia, or to London (where the emigrant Welsh dominated
the dairy market for several centuries).

Rural poverty in Wales parallelled the condition in the rest of
Britain and Ireland, and had the same causes: the plague, crop
failure and famine, ruinous wars (especially the Napoleonic
wars), the Enclosure Acts, absentee landlordism, disastrous
agricultural policies. Terrible and widespread as it was in Wales,
on the whole the Welsh peasantry fared better, along with the
Scottish, on their particular diet than their counterparts in
England. But it lasted longer.

Poor and insubstantial as it may appear today, the frugal fare
of the Welsh peasant 150-200 years ago, as recorded by Mati
Thomas, bore a close resemblance to what today we call a 'health-
food' diet. It bred a notably strong race of men and women
characterised by their stamina and capacity for long hours of
work in the fields, with energy still for poetry and song. From
the earliest times the Welsh have taken pride in their strength
and energy – on the farms, in the mines, on the rugby field and
on the field of battle. . . Shakespeare leaves us in little doubt as
to the valour and value of Welsh soldiers.

As Eifion Wyn has it recorded as Yr *hen drugareddau* ('The Old Ways') in *Cerddi Eryri*, Carneddog.

> *Ymrown i gyd i ganu*
> *Hen fwydydd annwyl Cymru –*
> *Y bara ceirch a'r bara haidd,*
> *Yr uwd, y maidd, a'r llymru;*
> *Beth sydd yn fwy amheuthun,*
> *Neu'n well i fagu giewyn,*
> *Na sucan gwyn a brywas da,*
> *A bicws mali melyn?*
> *O, credwn fel ein teidiau*
> *Mai'r ffisigwriaeth orau*
> *Yw camomeil a wermod lwyd*
> *O flaen ein bwyd pob boreu;*
> *A da yw te rhosmari*
> *A thrwyth o ryw y gerddi;*
> *Er estyn oes mewn tref a gwlad,*
> *Mae rhinwedd rhad yn rheini.*

> Let us all join in singing the praises of the old foods of Wales.
> Oat and barley bread, porridge, whey and flummery.
> What is more tasty and better for strengthening muscles
> Than white sowans and brewis and yellow shot?
> Let us believe, like our grandfathers, that the best medicine
> Is camomile and wormwood, first thing every morning.
> That rosemary and other herb teas will prolong one's life in town and country
> All such inexpensive remedies.

Those who lived in this manner did not necessarily recognise it as poverty. On the contrary, words like 'plenty', 'wholesome', 'nourishing' occur frequently in reminiscences of the old Welsh pastoral life in even the meanest surroundings. The food is remembered with relish: 'Good food it was, and healthy, too' one old man said to me, and he was right, for in many respects the present-day diet in Wales in general has lost much of the former health-giving aspect.

Sir Henry Jones (1852-1922) writes in *Old Memories:* "But neither on Sunday nor on a week-day was the meal scanty, or the fun and chatter lean, or was there any faintest hint of scarcity or poverty. . . And the bread was of my mother's own making – the best in all the land!" His only criticism, "our food was somewhat monotonous, and possibly we might have done better with less buttermilk and more sweet-milk. But, while the latter was plentiful and cheap and good, the former was to be had in big canfulls for the mere fetching." He was describing his childhood as one of a family of seven reared in a tiny two-roomed cottage, where the kitchen, though ill-lit, was "rich with flitches of bacon". In the light of our present dietary knowledge about saturated fats, Sir Henry was perhaps fortunate in his 'deprivation' of full-cream milk. Increased affluence and the consequent change in diet and lifestyle, has, alas, resulted in a marked increase in heart disease in Wales.

But there were bitter memories, by L Wyn Griffith, in *The Wooden Spoon*:

> I want to forget those days, if I can, but I do not know how to set about forgetting. I can pretend to myself that they never existed, but that is not forgetting. I want to separate my memory of my father and mother from the remembrance of the hardship and poverty that clouded their lives, to remember their self-sacrifice without seeing their suffering. Perhaps it is impossible.

The recipes in this section are taken from this self-sufficient style of living which characterised rural Wales for so many centuries. We would not feel inclined to make many of them today even if we could obtain all the ingredients. Nor would modern gas or electric cookers reproduce their style.

THE SHEPHERD'S FIRST BREAKFAST (*SIENCYN TE*)

A slice of bread   sugar
butter   cold milk
hot tea

Break the bread into a basin and cover with hot tea. Add sugar and milk. Old people in Wales still enjoy a bowl of *siencyn te*. Its preparation has moved with the times though. The broken bread and butter, sugar and milk are often left ready in a bowl, with a tea bag on top. . .

Siencyn was a similar dish made with boiling water and sometimes dripping instead of butter with the bread, seasoned with salt and pepper.

In the Valleys they ate *siencyn* with a lump of cheese for supper or breakfast.

WHEY SKIM (GWYNEB MAIDD)

From the Mati Thomas' MS

three gallons of whey   a bowlful of buttermilk
half a bowlful of milk

Place the whey in a cooker on the fire, and when about to boil pour the milk into it. A little later add the buttermilk. This would appear as large lumps on the surface of the whey. Remove from the fire before it actually boils. To serve, break barley bread into bowls, sprinkle with a little salt. Then fill the bowls with the skim from the surface of the whey. To complete the meal it was usual to have a bowlful of whey and eat bread and cheese.

MILK BROTH (CAWL LLAETH)

From the Mati Thomas' MS

This was a meal for poverty-stricken people:

1 pint skim milk   salt
oatmeal

Put a cooker with the skim milk on the fire and bring to the boil. Mix two tablespoons of oatmeal with cold water to make a paste. Pour into the boiling milk. Add salt to taste. It was then boiled and served into bowls that had barley bread in them.

BREWIS (BRŴES)

From Farmhouse Fare.

2 tablespoonfuls breadcrumbs   salt and pepper to taste
1 tablespoonful crushed oatmeal   ½ pint boiling water
1 teaspoonful butter or dripping

Put the breadcrumbs and oatmeal into a basin, add salt and pepper to flavour, break in the dripping or butter. Pour the boiling water over it, and stand for 5 minutes before serving.

SHOT (SIOT)

From Welsh Fare.

a thick oatcake, made without fat
cold buttermilk

Crush the oatcake finely and put in a basin. Add cold buttermilk, stir
well and serve. Or leave the mixture to stand for about an hour and
add more buttermilk when serving if desired.

BREAD IN WATER (SGOTYN)

From Welsh Fare.

This is still a favourite with older country folk:

bread   boiling water
salt and pepper

Break a slice of bread into a bowl, pour boiling water over it and add
salt and pepper to taste. Serve immediately.

SOWANS (SUCAN)

From the Mati Thomas' MS

My son-in-law's late father, Biddyr, a north-Pembrokian of Breton
descent, said he knew this as *uwd* as a young man, and hated it
because it didn't contain enough nourishment to satisfy his
hunger for more than an hour or so. Nevertheless, every young
girl had to learn to make it successfully, encouraged by the dire
warning that if the surface should crack, she would marry a boy
with an ugly face.

What is it? Oats were roasted at the mill, then hulled to remove the
husk. It was then ground in the millstones. The meal was then riddled
and the material held in the riddle was Sucan, and was called Sucan
Meal.

sucan meal   skimmed milk or butter milk
lukewarm water   a little salt

Place the sucan meal in a cooker, pour lukewarm water over it. Allow
to steep for two days, then add a further quantity of lukewarm water.
It should be of a thick consistency. Pour into another cooker and boil. It

should be thicker than 'bwdran' and should cover the wooden spoon and form a mass that could be stretched to about two feet high from the cooker. Once to this consistency pour into an earthenware crock which had been chilled with cold well water. If correctly made it would set to a solid mass with a glossy surface.

It was served in portions into bowls and skimmed or buttermilk poured over it. Salt was not added to the *Sucan* but was added to the taste of the eater.

This was commonly served as a harvest dinner.

OATMEAL WATER (DŴR BLAWD CEIRCH)

This was a very popular drink consumed during harvest time, and considered to be very healthy.

oatmeal
cold water

Put three handfuls of oatmeal into a jug of cold water. Mix well and drink at once. It was unnecessary to allow it to settle and clear.

BREAD AND WATER SOAK (BARA DŴR)

wheatmeal bread   a little ginger and a little sugar
boiling water

Break the wheatmeal bread up into small portions into a bowl. Sprinkle with a little ginger and sugar. Pour boiling water over it.

This was an invalid food, and contained little nourishment, and was light on the constitution. It was eaten as soon as made.

BREAD AND BUTTERMILK (BARA LLAETH ENWYN)

This meal was eaten occasionally during the summer, especially when the buttermilk was at its best. Great faith was attached to the medicinal qualities of this meal and it was claimed to be a cure for tuberculosis.

barley bread
buttermilk

Cut slices of barley bread and toast well on both sides on the bake-stone. Then crush to crumbs and place in bowls. Pour buttermilk over the crumbs. Allow to steep for some time. It was ready for eating, and a meal in itself.

OATMEAL AND BUTTERMILK GRUEL (LLITH)*

This was a gruel of oatmeal and buttermilk.

three tablespoonsful of oatmeal
a bowlful of buttermilk

This was a very popular meal in days of old and eaten as a rule between dinner and supper during harvest time. It was called *Bwyd Ambor* or pasture meal. Taken to the men harvesting were a stone** of oatmeal, and a large earthenware jar full of buttermilk. Each harvest worker took three tablespoonfuls of oatmeal and placed it into their bowls. The buttermilk was then poured over the oatmeal. The contents of the bowl were thoroughly mixed and eaten with great gusto.

All these buttermilk dishes are remembered with great fondness and relish. Real buttermilk is much yearned after, and I found a bottle of it obtained from a churning of farm butter the best possible passport to talking to the older country people and eliciting their memories. The following recipes are from Mattie

---

* lit. 'mash'.
** the old British measure for 14 lbs

Thomas' MS.

Although not confined to lean times, when it was a godsend to families in abject poverty – sometimes trapped at great risk on the squire's land – rabbit was always a welcome addition of fresh meat to the country larder, in stew or pie, or stuffed and roasted. Farmers and tenants trapped them without fear, they could be bought cheaply from the local trapper, and in urban areas bought from market stalls. (See p.172 and p.273 for recipes.)

SHEEP'S HEAD BROTH (*CAWL PEN DAFAD*)

The sheep's head was often given to the farm worker by the farmer. The worker then took it home and prepared it for his usually large family.

sheep's head	salt
oatmeal dumplings	parsley and leeks
water	

Place a cooker full of water on the fire to boil. Wash the sheep's head well, keeping it in one piece. Place the head into the boiling water. Boil for an hour. Make the oatmeal dumplings and place in the cawl, then add the parsley and leeks. Add salt to taste.

When cooked there was a tasty meal for the family which was also free.

BARLEY MEAL DUMPLINGS (*TROLIOD BARLYS*)

a bowlful of boiling *cawl*
a bowlful of barley meal

Place the barley meal into a large bowl. Pour the boiling hot *cawl* into the meal a little at a time. Mix with a wooden spoon until it is a hard mass. Mould into ball shapes with the hands. Put into the *cawl* and bring to the boil. When the *cawl* is ready to serve, remove the dumplings and place in a dish.

They were eaten with *cawl* and bacon as a dinner in the spring.

2. Porridges *(uwd)*

OAT GROATS PORRIDGE *(UWD RHYNION CEIRCH)*

a bowlful of Groats   buttermilk or cows milk
boiling water   a little salt

Put 3 quarts of water into the cooker and bring to the boil. Mix the groats to an even paste with cold water. Pour into the boiling water stirring continuously with a wooden porridge stirrer. Put in a little salt. When it thickened it was ready to remove from the fire.
    It was eaten at dinner time with buttermilk or skimmed milk.

RICE PORRIDGE *(UWD REIS)*

a bowlful of rice   a tablespoonful of flour, and a little salt
a gallon of cold water

Wash and clean the rice. Place a gallon of water into the cooker over a slow peat fire, and bring to the boil. When boiling add the rice. Stir frequently, and when it thickens add a tablespoonful of flour to assist in the setting. The salt was added just before it was ready to remove from the fire. The salt being added to prevent burning during completion of the cooking.
    This was a harvest dinner.

BARLEY GROATS PORRIDGE *(UWD RHYNION BARLYS)*
All from Mati Thomas' MS

a bowlful of barley groats   buttermilk
cold water   a little salt

Put three quarts of water in the cooker and put on the fire. Bring to the boil. Mix the groats with cold water and put into the boiling water. Continue until thickening occurs. It must be stirred continuously with a wooden stirring stick. When cooked and before removing from the fire add salt. It was then ready to eat with buttermilk for dinner.

3. Puddings

RICE AND MILK (*REIS A LLAETH*)

a bowlful of rice   a little salt
a gallon of water   barley bread
a gallon of skimmed milk

Wash and clean the rice. Put the water in the cooker and place on the fire and bring to the boil. When the water is boiling add the rice. Allow to boil until it thickens. At this stage add the gallon of skimmed milk. Boil for a short time. Remove from the fire and add salt to taste. Serve in wooden bowls adding chunks of barley bread.
This was a supper suited to summer or winter requirements.

Compare it to the rich rice puddings of 18th century 'great house' cookery.

WHITE PUDDING (*POTEN GAN*)

half a bowlful of wheatmeal   brown sugar
two quarts of skimmed milk

Boil the skimmed milk. Mix half a bowlful of wheatmeal with cold milk to an even consistency. Pour this into the boiling milk stirring continuously with a wooden porridge stirrer. When it has thickened lift into a metal dish. Place in the cooker and bake until it colours slightly. It usually took about an hour to cook.
This formed part of the 'Harvest Home' supper. The harvesters expected a super supper after a successful harvest.

A whole meal was commonly cooked together in the one pot – sweet dumplings for pudding along with the meat:

Apple Dumplings (*Twmplins afalau*)

wheat meal

apples

cawl

brown soft sugar

Mix the wheatmeal to a dough with hot *cawl,* using a wooden spoon. Do not core or peel the apples. Wet the hands in cold water, and lift enough dough to evenly cover an apple. Spread the dough on the hand, place the apple in the middle and proceed to mould the dough around it, baking as many as would be required for the meal. Place the completed dumplings in the boiling *cawl* and cook until a fork test tells you that they are ready. Care should be taken that they do not break during cooking. When cooked remove from the boiling *cawl* and place in a large wooden dish.

Serve broken open and spread with the soft brown sugar.

Thin Flummery (*Bwdran*)

Put the boiled oatmeal gruel in a pan and pour the lukewarm water over it. Leave overnight. For supper the following night it was passed through a gruel sieve. It should be of a consistency that would only leave a trace on the back of a wooden spoon. Should it be too thick, a little water should be added. Place on the fire and bring to the boil, stirring continuously. When it had boiled for five minutes it is ready to serve with salted herring and barley bread as a winter supper dish.

All from Mati Thomas' MS.

Flummery (*Llymru*)

From Lloyd George's Favourite Dishes.

3 basinfuls of oatmeal

3 quarts water

2 teacups buttermilk

Cover the oatmeal with water and buttermilk, let it remain for two nights, until sour, then pour off the water and add a little fresh water to it and put it through a sieve. Then put it in a pan and when it begins to boil add two tablespoons white flour to it, mixed with cold water and free from lumps. Boil all together for ten minutes, stir all the time.

Note: *Llymru* was stirred with a special stick. When the liquid ran from it in a prescribed 'tail' this signified that it had reached the required consistency. For further details of *llymru* see introduction.

Routine on a north Pembrokeshire farm 50 years ago, described by the late Mrs Nellie James of Parrog, Newport, Pembrokeshire.

9.00 am	Bacon and egg, bread and butter, tea.
12.00 noon	Dinner – *cawl cig moch* (bacon broth). The broth first, then the bacon, potatoes and vegetables. Bread. Rice pudding.
3.30 pm	Tea. Bread and butter and cheese, cake and sometimes pancakes.
7.00 pm	Supper, after milking. Cold meat or broad beans with bread and butter – and anything available from the garden.
SUNDAY:	roast chicken or beef after a bowl of *cawl*.

When eggs were dear (1*d.* each) they were sold. When they were cheap (½*d.* each) there were plenty for the kitchen – and pancakes.

Fishmonger at Cardiff Market. Photo by Keith Morris.

10. Markets and Fairs

Long, wide and high, under an arch of glass, with the sun strong
about us and the stalls very tidy and full of good things and
voices coming happily from hundreds in a deep sighing sound
that echoed in warmth, and a lovely smell made of many smells,
of mint and cabbage and celery, and cured bacon and hams, and
toffee and flannels and leather and cheeses, and paraffin oil, and
flowers. . . Out we went with arms full of flowers, and parcels
of cheeses and a black ham, with a couple of bolts of flannel, two
pairs of solid boots for the boys and a hand-worked apron for my
mother, and both my pockets crammed with toffee, and our faces
paining with big lumps that tasted lovely.
HOW GREEN WAS MY VALLEY, Richard Llewellyn

1. Markets in Wales

In a society which was, and still is, predominantly agricultural, markets and fairs play a prominent part in the life of the people. There are lively markets still in both rural and urban Wales – the big town daily markets of Swansea, Cardiff, Llanelli, Pontypridd and Merthyr, and the weekly country markets are all colourful and rich in local produce and the unexpected – like piles of pigs' tails.

A more recent addition to the market scene are the W.I. (Women's Institute) markets, held weekly (not always in winter) in most country towns, often within or adjoining the permanent covered market halls. Otherwise, look for them in church halls. Even more recent are the hygiene regulations which ensure the foodstalls conform to EU standards, which have brought about the absence of one or two of the older, smaller stallholders unable to afford to achieve the new standards.

Cardiff covered market has an exceptionally fine fish stall, with a circular display offering every variety of home and imported fish and shellfish.

Swansea market dates from the middle of the 17th century; it was first erected in 1652 for the sale of corn, fish and vegetables, and if fresh-baked bread is substituted for corn the same produce could be said to dominate the market stalls today – with the addition of cockles and laverbread which almost seem to be on every second stall. Pontypridd market is noted for dress materials and old-fashioned Welsh sweets and toffee.

In Llanelli there's a stall where they have been baking Welsh cakes and sponges and custards and fruit tarts for eating with a cup of tea or coffee at the stall for thirty years, and a similar stall in Swansea market. Perhaps the most remarkable impression one gets from watching the mixing and baking going on is the homeliness of it all. . . it's as if one had stumbled accidentally upon some ladies who are preparing for a Sunday school treat or a crowd of hungry farm-workers about to come in from the fields for their tea-time break. I'm sure the customers find it reassuring in this age of packaged foods to see the boxes of eggs, packets of butter and lard and bottles of fresh milk ranged in readiness at the back of the stall, to leave no doubt that what goes into these Welsh tea-time favourites is the real thing. Wirt Sikes, the kindly American consul to Cardiff in the 1880's, commented extensively on the south Wales' markets of his day. This is what he had to say about Welsh market-women:

. . . they are generally the producers or gatherers of the things they sell. On the morning of a market-day you may meet on the high road – if you chance to be up early enough – a constant procession of market-women setting toward the market-town. There are men in this procession, but women are in the majority. They are of every age, and of varying conditions, and they bear to market all sorts of farm produce, as well as shell-fish, which they have gathered by the sea. One day, as I was returning from a visit to a friend who lives in one of the ancient castles on the southern coast of Glamorganshire, I passed a group of seven women striding along with a good swinging gait, each leaning far forward under the weight of a huge basket laden with water-cresses.

These women were in jolly mood, and chaffingly asked us to give them a lift with their baskets: 'Let us put 'em on your trap, master, won't you, now? *Wfft!* they're so heavy!' My driver, who was of the neighbourhood, told me these women had been to a point some distance beyond St Donat's Castle after their water-cresses – that is to say, twenty miles from Cardiff. Every week they made this journey, walking all night Thursday, gathering their cresses from certain lakes and pools by the roadsides on Friday, then walking back to Cardiff and making their appearance in the market early on Saturday morning. Such sleep as they had was got in the open air under the hedge-rows. This was in the last week of October, and it was pretty cold for such lodgings. For their forty miles' tramp, their discomfort, and their labour in gathering and selling, they would realize perhaps seven or eight shillings the basket.

Country markets in Wales still create a strong sense of market-day for their inhabitants, for here the weekly markets remain a focus for shopping, and social and business exchange. . . the personal encounter is infinitely preferable to that still suspect arm of communication, the telephone! This profoundly effects the pace of life in these areas – a blessing or bane according to the type of business or activity you are engaged in.

Fishguard's market-day is Thursday, and winter Thursdays probably saved our communal sanity in the 1960's; for the town, which spent the rest of the week in gloomy wintry desertion, sprang into comparatively feverish life as people from miles around hurried into and out of the market, or formed groups for animated conversation in the streets and town square. The Easter market, which fell on the day before Good Friday, surpassed even the height of summer markets for activity. You would have to be there very early indeed to be sure of getting everything you needed and avoid the frustration of a long wait in a cheerfully chattering queue of customers, for whom the occasion was a social one, with no herculean programme of final preparation of a small hotel for the first Bank Holiday weekend of the season to be completed by nightfall.

By mid-morning the noise of social exchange had reached a crescendo, audible several hundred yards from the market square; eventually the town almost took off in the excitement created by the imminence of the first open-air holiday of the year, with its traditional promise of children, grandchildren and other relatives heading for home on the longed-for visit. The housewives stocked up as for a month-long seige; far more food and drink was bought at the Easter market than for Christmas. Woe betide any disorganised hotelier who had forgotten anything vital for the Easter trade, for by early afternoon the town had been stripped of its food and drink supplies, and with trade virtually over for the day both market stalls and shops were tidying up and totting up the takings.

2. Fairing-Pies

Few, if any, of the pies and cakes once traditionally associated with the old Welsh fairs are made today. The travelling hot-dog stand and fish and chip vans satisfy popular demand at Welsh fairs and markets as in the rest of Britain. At the traditional Llanybydder horse sale, where horses and ponies have been sold on the third Thursday of the month for generations, the odour of fried onions and hot fat dominates even the horsey smell. . . while a group of burly farmers, eyes and ears fixed knowledgeably on the sale ring, tongues busily at work on the Mr Whippies clutched incongruously in their massive fists, provide an unconsciously comic picture.

The disclamatory *Teisen sinsir heb sinsir* (Ginger cake without ginger) mentioned earlier, with its old-fashioned candied peel content, was a popular seller at the old Welsh fairs.

KATT PIES

At Templeton Fair (November 12) in south Pembrokeshire, Katt Pies were the speciality. Thanks to Dillwyn Miles, the Herald Bard of Wales, I think I have at last found an explanation of the name – an immediate puzzle as Katt is in no way Welsh – and explanations on the lines of pussy patties are not allowed. It seems that Katt pies may have originated in Christopher Cat's Shire Lane pie-house where in James II's time leading Whigs of the day – Steele, Addison, Congreve, Vanbrugh – met and formed the Kit-cat Club, dining of course on Cat's mutton pies which became known as 'kit-cats', abbreviating finally to 'katt'. All we need to know now is how the pies reached Templeton, Pembrokeshire, in that name, for in themselves mutton and currant and sugar pies were not uncommon mid-18th century offerings in England and Wales. In fact they are said to have been sold on Gower, and at another November Pembrokeshire fair – on Old St Martin's Day (22 November), in Trefin on the north coast of the county. I speculate whether the name might have been carried west by Whig politicians amongst the Halls of Pembrokeshire, whose home was at Gumfreston near Tenby, not far from Templeton (the family of which Benjamin Hall, Baron Llanover [q.v.] was a member and who was himself a prominent Whig politician and reformer) who could conceivably have been members of the famous Kit-cat Club.

Katt pies are also in the medieval British tradition of meat plus dried fruits and spices and sugar. In the cooking the meat has a curious way of all but disappearing; eventually it was left out altogether leaving *mincemeat* to come down to us with only the suet to remind us of its one-time beef content. Mutton was the meat used in Katt pies. Katt pies are still being made today, by housewives in Templeton:

KATT PIES

From Croeso Cymreig

1 lb flour	½ lb currants
½ lb suet	½ lb sugar (brown)
good pinch salt	salt and pepper
½ lb minced mutton	

Make hot-water pastry by boiling suet in water, add to flour and salt, stirring well with wooden spoon. When cool make into pies about 4 ins. in diameter. Arrange filling in layers – mutton, currants and sugar, salt and pepper; cover with a round of thin pastry. Bake in hot oven 20 to 30 minutes. Eat hot.

At Llanmadoc Mapsant (fair) on Gower a report of 1885 tells of 'a particular sort of pie, made of chopped mutton and currants', which was a feature of the fair. The same report mentions a kind of plum pudding called 'Bonny Clobby'.

LLANDDAROG FAIR CAKES (*CACENNAU LLANDDAROG*)

Llanddarog is a village in Dyfed positioned, in contemporary terms, on what was until the by-pass the main Swansea-Carmarthen road, but more significantly, it lay on the old drover's route. Maxwell Fraser writes about the traditional fair cakes in *Wales*: 'Llanddarog. . . used to be well-known for its fair cakes, which the cattle dealers and drovers bought for 2*d* each. They were about 6in. long, 3in. wide, and a ¼ of an inch thick, and were made of flour, kneaded with beer, butter and eggs. They kept in good condition for a long while, which made them particularly acceptable to drovers on their long journeys.'

12 oz plain flour	3 tablespoons beer
8 oz butter	currants
6 oz sugar	

Mix flour and sugar and rub in butter. Mix to a stiff dough with beer (or water). Roll out ½" thick and cut into rectangles 2" x 3". Dot with currants to look like dominoes. Bake in a moderate oven for 20-30 minutes.

Finally, an older recipe than any of the foregoing:

TO MAKE SWEET LAMB PYE

(late 17th century, from the MS recipe book from Gogerddan, near Aberystwyth)

Cut your Lamb in pieces and season it with cinnamon, mace, nuttmeg, and salt, sugar a little, then putt it into your pye with butter and reisins of the sun (big raisins), bake it: then melt some butter and beat 2 yolks of eggs with a little sack (sherry), and sugar, then putt your melted butter to it, and when your pye comes out of the oven, putt in your cawdle (the egg, sherry, butter and sugar mixture), you may putt in hard eggs, sweet meats and citron if you please.

Dolgellau mart. Photo by Keith Morris.

3. Welsh Toffee and Rock *(Cyflaith)*

Originally made in domestic kitchens and sold from trays at the fairs and markets, traditional Welsh toffee is manufactured today by a few small firms proudly adhering to family recipes and as much hand-production as possible to maintain the traditional appearance and true Welsh flavour of the peppermints, hard treacle and butter toffee and the streaky brown minty rock. Some of these firms make for and sell only at the fairs and markets while others supply both shops and fairs. At the open market and fair stalls there will usually be a plate of opened toffee and pieces of rock for customers to taste before buying: this is not a gimmick or a trap for unwary parents but a genuine service – the Welsh know the true taste of their traditional sweets and there are now so many imitations on sale that they want reassurance before they buy.

It was the hard, boiled sweets and particularly the peppermints which formed the basis of the Welsh sweet and toffee industry (more peppermints are reputed to be sold west of Offa's Dyke than in any other region of Britain). They are still made, and as popular as ever, but in recent years there has been an increasing liking amongst the Welsh for fudge. It was doubtless due to the proximity of the mining areas as well as being centres of population that the south Wales' peppermint and hard sweet manufacturers were established in Cardiff, Barry, Newport, Merthyr Tydfil, Pontypridd and the Swansea areas. The Welsh miner had a liking for a peppermint in his snap-tin – as essential an item as his slice of *teisen lap* and an apple. Perhaps for men working in the old, terrible, cramped coalface conditions a peppermint soothed after-dinner attacks of indigestion as well as ensuring a moist mouth against the all-pervading coal dust. In north Wales the industry grew less around the indigenous population than to supply the tourist resorts. Much of the pink peppermint rock was made in Lancashire, and still is, but until a few years ago the former Caernarfon Rock Co. was run by a Yorkshireman attracted to north Wales and motivated by a belief that the genuine Welsh rock and toffee industry was worth preserving. Fortunately he had the necessary skills to fulfil his aim – until his retirement, which effectively ended the independent north Wales rock and toffee-making industry. There is, however, still a wholesaler in Caernarfon, R J Jones Ltd., who carries the traditional Welsh rock and toffee lines.

The old 'figure-of-eight' brown and cream rock isn't often seen now. I used to love to watch this being made. The figure of 8 in its centre was engineered by hand by means of a skilled pulling and rolling until a shiny brown roll the size of a tree trunk was reduced to a thin stick capable of being cut into short lengths. The rolling was a process for which girls' hands seemed the best suited as they worked side by side in cheerful rows, their delicate touch exerting just the right pressure to obtain an even circumference along the gradually lengthening and thinning rock. This brown rock became popular at the old hiring fairs when the lads had six months wages burning holes in their pockets.

Soft brown, rather than demerara or white sugar, was used for the traditional toffees because it was then marginally cheaper than the former and much cheaper than the latter. In those days coppers counted. What they probably didn't realise then was that brown was a slightly more wholesome form of sugar.

The last remaining south Wales firm, Brays of Barry, is now the guardian of all the old Welsh confectionery manufacturing traditions. They might have lost out in the struggle against the giants in the mass sweet and toffee market, as so many of the original firms did, but for a continuing family involvement. The founder's grandson, Stephen Bray, is now firmly and happily in charge of the family business, which gradually incorporated, as, one by one, they faltered for want of a succeeding generation, the old established family firms, retaining their recipes and familiar packaging. Thus Franks' 'Special Mints', a firm favourite with the Welsh, are still sold in their distinctive tins with the two little girls in Welsh costume* decoration. Far from being at risk themselves, Brays have expanded, twice, to new and bigger

---

* The two little girls were sisters, daughters of the then manager of Franks. One of them grew up to be the beauty queen who took part in the Esther Rantzen 'Big Time' programme.

factories in Barry, where the firm originally began. They make the familiar lettered pink rock for Welsh resorts, and still have the order for barley sugar for lifeboat provisions. The popular *Lossin Dant* Welsh Mints, especially mild, striped, suck-or-chew peppermints, and Franks' beautiful shiny brown-and-cream striped extra strong 'Special Mints', are the hardcore of their business, recently augmented by the acquisition of the formerly Swansea-based 'Conway Confections', yet another victim of the threat of extinction through lack of a new generation to carry it on. This firm was noted for its 'olde fashioned' boiled sweets.

Brays still make sweets, as they always have done, for the local south Wales markets – Cardiff, Aberdare, Bridgend, Neath, Swansea, and they still make their *'Lossin Cymru'* – Welsh butter toffee, another old favourite, along with 'Clove Sweets', the unusual round, red and white striped clove-flavoured sweets popular in the Valleys, and their popular pear drops. But they also move with the times, making an increasing amount of fudge every year. Their liqueur fudge, made with 'the real stuff' is especially popular. Conscious of the contemporary issue of tooth decay, Stephen experimented a few years ago with sugar-free sweets designed for children. They were not a success – perhaps a bit too far ahead of their time, he thinks, but nothing daunted, is prepared to try again in the future.

Brays were a widespread family, making toffee and mints in various parts of south Wales. One firm, F W Bray, in Merthyr, made among other items the enduring Valleys' favourites, 'Winter Warmers', a round cough sweet for Aberdare market. Brays of Barry now produce the sweets formerly made by Fred Bray to his recipes. Fred Bray told me a nice tale about Stephen's great-great-grandfather who sold a recipe for toffee from an old family recipe book to a man called Mackintosh. . . for £5.00 – a princely sum in those days.

Stephen says he has retained as much of their oldtime cottage-industry image as possible, but the 1991 Food Act has inevitably meant some changes to their former largely hand-crafted methods. Machinery has had to be introduced, and production methods modernised, but confined as much as possible to the end part of the production line – the wrapping and packing stages. The sugar is still boiled in open copper pans and poured on to steel cooling slabs and thence to marble slabs. The machines I find the most fascinating are those that 'pull' the brown toffee to make it a lighter colour for the humbug stripes. 'Pulling' aerates the toffee (the tiny air holes are just visible in the finished toffee) lightening it to a rich cream colour. As it is being 'pulled' it resembles nothing so much as a hank of silky platinum hair.

The simple pleasure of making toffee at home was expanded into a social activity in north Wales, especially at Christmas-time and New Year, when a *noson gyflaith* (toffee evening) was part of the traditional festivities. (This custom travelled south to become part of the servants' Christmas Eve celebrations at Llanover Court in Gwent in the 19th century.) Friends came to join the family for a supper of Christmas fare, afterwards there would be games, story-telling and toffee-pulling. At the appropriate moment the boiling toffee in its copper saucepan was taken off the fire, poured on to a well-greased marble slab, and while still warm grasped by willing, buttery hands to begin the 'pulling'. In medieval times a honey and ginger *confit* is reputed to have been made in Wales (ginger having arrived with the Romans, but sugar still unknown) but it did not survive the centuries, and when toffee was made it was just with the simple ingredients ready to hand for all home toffee-makers – brown sugar, treacle, butter – and peppermint.

TOFFEE (*CYFLAITH*)

one pound black treacle	one pound brown sugar
quarter pound butter	one teaspoonful vinegar

Put all the ingredients in a large saucepan (enamel or copper) and melt slowly over a moderate heat. Then boil mixture briskly for about twenty minutes, stirring it continuously. Test its consistency at the end of the twenty minutes by dropping a teaspoonful of the boiling mixture into cold water. If it hardens at once leaving the water perfectly clear it has boiled to the required degree. Remove from the heat and pour the boiling toffee on to a stone slab or shallow dish, previously greased with butter.

Butter both hands and 'pull' the toffee into long golden strands while hot. Cut into smaller pieces before the toffee hardens.

TOFFEE AND FANNY (*TAFFI A FFANI*)

Both recipes from Welsh Fare by S.Minwel Tibbott.

one pound soft, brown sugar
one large cupful cold water
two teaspoonfuls vinegar

a knob of butter
oil of peppermint

Put all the ingredients (except for the oil of peppermint) in a cast iron saucepan over a moderate heat, and boil, stirring continuously, for fifteen minutes. Test a teaspoonful of the boiling mixture in cold water (see previous recipe) and if it hardens immediately remove the mixture from the heat.

Pour out the bulk of the mixture on to a greased slab or dish but retain a small amount in the saucepan. (Keep this in a warm place to prevent it from hardening.) Grease both hands with butter and 'pull' the toffee while it is hot, as quickly as possible, adding a few drops of the oil of peppermint while pulling. Continue pulling until a creamy colour is attained.

Place in long, flat strips, about an inch wide, on the table and pour the toffee that was retained to form a thin brown line along the centre of each strip. Cut into smaller pieces before it hardens.

TREACLE TOFFEE (*LOSHIN DU*)

From Croeso Cymreig.

½ lb treacle (syrup)
½ lb demerara sugar

1 tablespoonful butter

Melt butter in a saucepan, then add treacle and sugar. Stir gently. Boil until a few drops poured into cold water set crisp (about 10 minutes). Pour into rectangular greased tin. When nearly cold cut into sizeable squares.

CONFITS (*CWNFFETS*)
(Medieval)

From Bwyd y Beirdd (Food of the Bards) by Enid Roberts.

Warm some honey, and add eggs, nuts and fruit, then pour into a dish or slate slab, and before it is cool break into small pieces.

4. Fruit Preserves

All the usual country jams are made in Wales – rhubarb, blackberry, gooseberry, blackcurrant, raspberry and strawberry – and their method is much the same as elsewhere. But there are just a few special preserves for which recipes turn up in Wales and which are worth noting. The first, 'Apple Ginger', is an old-fashioned preserve, possibly coming from the kitchen of a Welsh *plas* and originating probably from the late-17th to early-18th century. The cayenne pepper is a clue to its age, for at that time it tended to go into everything. Somehow the recipe found its way into *Croeso Cymreig:*

APPLE GINGER

From Farmhouse Fare.

4 lb apples	3 lemons
2 lb granulated sugar	2 oz root ginger
4 lb lump sugar	½ teaspoonful cayenne pepper

Peel and core the apples and quarter. Make syrup from 2 lb granulated sugar in a pint of water. Let it boil, then pour over the apples. Let it stand for two days. Add 4 lbs of lump sugar, the rind and juice of the three lemons. Add the ginger (after bruising in a bag). Add the cayenne, let it all boil until the juice is clear. Simmer about one hour.

DAMSON AND APPLE JELLY

From Farmhouse Fare.

Using equal quantities of damsons and apples, add ½ pint of cold water to 1 lb of fruit. Boil until fruit is quite soft. Strain through muslin; weigh the juice, and allow 1 lb sugar to 1 lb of the liquid. Boil the juice quickly for 15 minutes, then add sugar and boil together for ½ hour. This jelly is perfectly clear, and will keep for 12 months at least.

MEDLAR JELLY

From Lloyd George's Favourite Dishes.

Take medlars when quite ripe, wash them, and put them into a preserving pan with as much water as will cover them. Let them stew slowly till they become a pulp. Then put them through a jelly bag, and to every pint of liquid put ¾ lb of loaf sugar. Boil it quickly for half an hour or until it jellies. It should be clear and bright in colour when done.

11. Drinks in Wales

. . . and a hot poker with honey, in home-brewed beer. . .
HOW GREEN WAS MY VALLEY, Richard Llewellyn

1. Mead *(medd)* and Beer *(cwrw)*

Mead made its appearance in Wales as elsewhere as the first-known intoxicating liquor. Designated a Royal beverage, its glories and pitfalls were sung by the Welsh poets and bards. In the mid-10th century the swarms and hives and the honey from which it was made were regulated by the Welsh Laws. *Hywel Dda* himself pronounced:

> Bees derive their noble descent from Paradise: when owing to man's transgression, they were hence expelled. God gave them his blessing; on this account mass cannot properly be sung without their wax.

Hywel Dda held his great law-making convention of lawyers and Welsh princes at Whitland near Carmarthen in Dyfed *(Hendygwyn ar Dâf* – the White House on the Tâf), where it has been suggested that the impressively-stocked mead cellar contributed to the codification of Welsh Law in a mere six weeks.

Several wines have evolved from the basic fermented honey formula. The recipe for one, Hippocras, a spiced variant of *pyment,* which incorporates grapes into the basic mead, is often quoted as a method for making mead. The Welsh drink, *Metheglin,* is often confused with mead.

Mead is currently enjoying a slight revival and is being drunk again in Wales, though not seriously – usually as part of the attempt to re-create the roistering atmosphere, and the food and drink of the Middle Ages, in the 'medieval' banquets staged as tourist attractions in various Welsh castles.

People who keep bees may like to make mead, but with honey as expensive as it is now the cost could be prohibitive for those who must buy the necessarily large quantity.

MEAD (*MEDD*)

This recipe from Mati Thomas' MS utilises the honeycomb rather than a quantity of honey, and would produce a mead of less cloying sweetness than most other recipes. Note particularly the addition of hops. It was brewed in June and kept in large earthenware jars buried in boggy land until the following spring when it was 'greatly appreciated drunk with *sucan*':

honeycomb after extraction of the honey	brewers' yeast
cold water	hops and cold water

Allow the honey to drip from the honeycomb. After this is completed place the honeycomb in a large bowl. Pour a gallon of water over it. The quantity of water is dependant on the amount of comb available. Allow to steep overnight. Next day filter through a wine sieve into a cooker. Boil over a slow fire and skim the surface regularly. When it breaks to the boil add a handful of hops and allow to boil for a quarter of an hour. Remove from the fire and allow to cool to lukewarm. Add a pint of yeast. Cover with a cloth and allow to ferment overnight. Next day skim the surface and pour into large earthenware jars. Cork the jars securely tying down the corks. Hide the jars in boggy land until spring.

BEER (*CWRW*)

Welsh ale was a distinct brew from the earliest times. Its special character came from the barley from which it was brewed being kilned so as to give the liquor a smokey taste and render it 'glutinous, healthy and soporiferous'. It was known in Saxon England by the 7th century, where it began to take its place in food rents in company with the traditional clear ale of England. Welsh ale was often spiced and sweetened with honey, when it was known as bragot – a much-esteemed drink at the courts of the Welsh princes, second only to mead.

Historically, the development of brewing is much the same in Wales as in England: small-scale brewing until in Norman times the abbeys and monasteries took the activity over and organised it, laying as they did so the foundations of the British brewing industry. Though it has to share the honours with tea, beer is very much the national drink of Wales: *allwedd calon cwrw da* – 'good ale is the key of the heart'.

Welsh ale *(cwrw)* retained its individuality right up to the end of the 18th century, as long as the traditional method of kilning barley continued. George Borrow appreciated its quality in *Wild Wales:*

> 'I suppose you get your ale from Llangollen? . . .' 'No, nor anywhere else. . . It was brewed in this house by your honour's humble servant. . . There, your honour, did you ever see such ale? Observe its colour? Does it not look for all the world as pale and delicate as cowslip wine? . . . Taste it, your honour! . . .' The ale was indeed admirable, equal to the best that I had ever before drunk, rich and mellow, with scarcely any smack of the hop in it, and though so pale and delicate to the eye, nearly as strong as brandy.

But in the mid-19th century, when brewing moved out of the comparatively small scale of the little breweries attached to the inns and taverns and into larger scale, Welsh beer, like others, derived its flavour from the water used by the different breweries.

The development of the coal mines, the ironworks, steelworks and the ports drew the bigger breweries to south Wales, where they eventually brewed vast quantities of low-gravity beer for the miners, steel and dock workers, whose arduous work created a demand for copious liquid refreshment of some kind to replace the body-fluids they lost in their work. Many drank ginger-beer or lemonade, but for those who wanted it, the low gravity beer had a fairly weak alcohol content and was reckoned to be reasonably harmless even if drunk in large quantities. All the same, drunkenness was a widespread problem in both town and country. The Temperance Movement fought with intensity for a total ban on drink, but in the end the battle was only won for Sundays with the Sunday Closing Act of 1880 – echoed for decades in Wales by the county by county seven-year referenda to decide for and against Sunday drinking.

When the Welsh prohibitionists were sweeping strongly through Wales many were persuaded to 'sign the pledge' – including the founder of George Bennett's wine and spirit merchants' business. There used to be a framed copy of the old fellow's 'pledge' in the firm's former Fishguard premises: considering the nature of his trade I always felt his was an exceptionally noble undertaking.

But in the end it was the big, commercial brewers, when they got themselves properly organised and eliminated the small corner brewers, who succeeded in bringing about a better control of drunkenness, where the Government's mass of regulations to control private brewing had failed.

The bigger breweries all brewed from the same basic raw ingredients and achieved their distinctive differences of taste by the varying qualities of local water (known in brewing as the 'liquor') available to them. Even today, despite a growing standardisation in beer-brewing, they say the water makes a discernable difference – and the customers endorse the brewers' assertions.

At Brain's, Cardiff's own brewery, hemmed in tight by shops and stores but surviving still in its late 19th-century premises at the top of St Mary Street, and with only a few 'tied' houses, they set great store by the water from their own artesian well. With the judicious addition of a measured proportion of 'Welsh Water', it provides the 'liquor' which marks Brain's beer from the rest.

This brewery is sited upon an earlier brewery (and an even earlier malt house) built in 1713 adjacent to what 'was then Cardiff's dockland, where the Glamorgan canal wharf and the Customs House were situated. When the 2nd Marquis of Bute built West Dock, the first to accommodate sea-going vessels, Cardiff's dockland shifted into the area once known as Tiger Bay, but now demurely re-named Butetown. Cardiff in the ferment of the Industrial Revolution was a wretched place for those who were crowded into its mean streets and courts, but temporary anaesthesia from the miseries of noise, filth, disease and poverty could be had for the price of a drink in one of the scores of little public houses and beer shops which clustered within easy reach of the brewery.

A national preference for mild ales of low gravity, both pale and dark, developed and persisted until bitter beers were introduced to the Welsh after the first world war. There was, however, one astonishing exception to the uniform beer situation in Wales in the late 19th century: in the north-Wales border town of Wrexham a quixotic German brewer persuaded Welshmen to accept a radically different lager beer. The brewery he established in the face of predictions of total failure succeeded, and still flourishes as part of the Allied Breweries brewing empire for whom it now produces 'Wrexham Lager'. In the light of the current drinking revolution in Britain which has brought lager to a point of hitherto undreamed-of popularity that little island of lager-brewing in Wrexham of nearly a hundred years ago is interesting to say the least.

After the Second World War the pure Welsh beer strain was even further weakened by the introduction of English beers from the Midlands and the North of England as the major Welsh brewers coalesced with each other and signed treaties with brewers on the other side of Offa's Dyke. Though these mostly pasteurised and pressurised (brewery-conditioned 'keg') beers proliferated throughout Wales, the independent Welsh breweries were largely unaffected, and continued to produce their cask beers, many of which were brewed to cater for specific local preferences, though these are perhaps not as strong as they once were. The Llanelli-based Felinfoel brewery, for example, brews a beer that pleases the west Wales taste. In recent years the independents have widened their distribution, so that Felinfoel beers are now sold throughout the UK, and exported also to Canada, USA, Europe and Japan. Still a family firm into its fifth generation with every intention of continuing as such, Felinfoel is remarkable for having pioneered canned beer as long ago as 1935. The original founder was both brewer and tinplate manufacturer and the canning quite logically began as a means of stimulating the local tinplate industry during the inter-war Depression. Their gold-medal winning beer is 'Double Dragon', its Welsh colours of red and green appropriately appearing on their signs.

Buckley's Brewery also caters for the west Wales area though they are no longer independent, but part of the Crown Brewers empire. Thus they also produce 'Harp' lager. The mergers which began in the 1950's have continued through the decades, so that with beer as everything else, it can sometimes be difficult to know who owns who.

Brain's have also extended their distribution the length and breadth of Britain since their Cardiff-preferred beers, such as the famous 'Brain's Dark', have found equal favour far beyond the Welsh capital. This brewery's production has always been based upon cask beers, so it's no surprise to learn that their cask 'Dark Mild' was winner of its class in the CAMRA Great British Beer Festival 1991, and that their 'Dark' came third overall. There is a smaller production of keg and canned beers from this brewery.

Between the efforts of CAMRA and evident popularity of cask beers, especially in Wales, the brewery giants were eventually persuaded to devote some of their production to cask beers, some of which were inconsequently called 'Home Brew' for a while. . . but with the real thing there can be no comparison.

HOME-BREW

The tradition of brewing beer at home persists to the present day in rural Wales, by no means a part of the current trend in home-brewing beers and wines. In 19th-century Wales, home-brew was a kind of public relations factor in farming life; the farmer in fact employed it to keep his workers happy. Farm-workers expected beer or cider with every meal, and every social occasion in the countryside was an excuse for copious brewing and consumption, thus weddings, christenings, Christmas and New Year – and even funerals – were occasions for celebrating with plenty of beer. Again, because of the Welsh farming tradition of sharing labour between neighbouring farms, times in the agricultural years like shearing and harvest, farm auction sales and ploughing matches, were notable social occasions: harvest particularly was a time when the home-brew flowed liberally. And because mechanisation came to farming so late in west Wales, and to Pembrokeshire in particular, the custom persisted there until comparatively recently. Men in their forties today can remember farm-workers rolling in from the harvest fields long after nightfall, tired out, drunk as owls and happy as kings.

Home-brew, or *cwrw bach*, is strong stuff and can taste

marvellous – much nicer than commercial beer. Once they get wind of a home-brewing, Welshmen will travel miles to track it down; and when they find it, wheedle and cajole until they are given a glass or two. Part of the enjoyment of real home-brew must be in the excitement of the chase! Mrs Nellie James, of Parrog, Newport in Pembrokeshire, was renowned locally for her home-brew and as a result she was more often looking ruefully at a row of empty bottles than with satisfaction at a store of full ones. Related to her I may have been through her son, who was carried off to England by my eldest daughter, but it was not at all easy to obtain her family recipe:

a handful of nettle-tops   half a pound of hops
half a bushel of malt   5 gallons of water
1 cup brewer's yeast (barm). This is a liquid yeast.

Mix the dry malt with a little boiling water to make a mash. Leave it in the cask overnight, uncovered. Next day, boil the 5 gallons of water and pour slowly over the malt mash in the cask, which must have the bung-hole stopped with gorse in flower. Allow the liquid to filter through the gorse, into a bowl. Now boil this liquid for about 1½ hours – the longer the boil the stronger the beer. *Note:* the discarded mash is usually given to cows or chickens as it is considered too good to waste.
    When cool, add the hops and sugar to the liquor and strain back into the cask, with the gorse removed and the outlet completely stopped. When quite cool, add the barm and leave to 'bubble' for 2 to 3 days. When the top is clear, after about a week, bottle and store. Mrs James said you should use the barm again and again because each use adds to the flavour of the next brew and said that the gorse in flower, for filtering, is important to the flavour of the beer. But many west-Walian home-brewers are less dogmatic, and use wheat-straw instead.

Many now resort to the commercial kits of course, but the old methods have their special appeal. If your local home-brew shop cannot supply the ingredients, try the agricultural feed merchants, who will have the appropriate measures. (A bushel in my part of west Wales is a *'winshin'*, but more usually a *bwysel* elsewhere.) Brewers' yeast in liquid form can be obtained from some home-brew shops, but if you buy your malt from the agricultural merchant he will doubtless offer you 'Maxi-malt', which contains the yeast.

BRAGGET (*BRAGOD*)

A mixture of mead and spiced beer especially associated with Easter Monday, for which it was specially brewed.

THIN BEER (*DIOD FAIN*)

A medicine rather than a satisfier or thirst-quencher. Its composition was based on the old herbal laws:

water	brewer's barm
hops	agrimony
brown sugar	blind nettle

Chop the herbs up finely and place in a large cauldron. Pour five gallons of boiling water over them. Allow to steep overnight. Next day transfer to a large cooker, place on a slow fire and bring to the boil. When breaking to the boil throw a handful of hops into the cooker. Allow to boil for ten minutes. Place in a little brown sugar and allow to cool to blood heat. Then add a half a pint of brewer's barm. Allow to stand overnight. Fill into large stoneware jars. It was ready for consuming the following morning.

From Mati Thomas's MS

James Williams recalls in *Give me Yesterday*:

On 19 July 1906, mother paid 5/6d. for a bushel of malt and 1/3d. for a pound of hops. There was usually several gallons left over after harvest, and although the beer would progressively become flatter, it was a fine drink, and when we were children we were allowed a spoonful of demerara to sweeten it. It was not only the family that enjoyed this home-brewed beverage, for after brewing, the pigs were given the malt and the hops mixed in their swill and a dusting of barley meal, and we would occasionally witness the edifying spectacle of a pig who too much had taken, and was so high, that dignified progress was impossible through frequently collapsing on to its hind quarters to the accompaniment of unmistakeable porcine laughter. . .

2. Country wines and ginger-beer

The alternatives to beer were the country wines made from wild flowers and hedgerow fruits, vegetables and weeds: herb beer and ginger-beer – homely brews equally suited to the harvest field or the blast furnace. Ginger-beer was especially popular with avowed teetotallers, who saw the road to ruin starting at the beer shops, temptingly sited in close proximity to the gargantuan thirst with which the dehydrated men emerged from the heat of the ironworks. Of the flower wines, James Williams, chronicler of childhood at the turn of the century near Cardigan, put gorse-flower wine as the best of them all: 'an Olympian effect, imparted by a fragrant, golden wine endowed with all the qualities of greatness, surely greater than the wines of antiquity – those of Chios, Lesbos, Peparethos, Thasos and Samon. . . could it have been made from the long-lost recipe for the milk of Paradise, re-discovered on the slopes of Preseli mountains in Pembrokeshire?'

The earlier popularity of home-made wines and beers declined sharply when tea, so much quicker and simpler to brew, became cheap enough to oust them as a household beverage. But they were still made as a regular country occupation, and long before the current revival of interest, good chemists in rural Wales were distinguishable by their stock of pickling herbs and spices and condiments for simple wine-making.

There are old-fashioned instructions for all the usual country wines in Welsh collections: Elderflower, Elderberry, Sloe, Damson 'Port', Blackberry, Apple and the lesser-known Daisy. Out of interest, I've given details of the gorse-flower wine James Williams so cherished even though it can be found elsewhere, as can the others. They are all more likely to be made now by more up-to-date methods with the yeasts and nutrients which have been developed for home wine-making in more recent years. One of the reasons for my return to west Wales to live in 1982 was to have the time and opportunity to be able to make country wines. But I confess I have not yet tackled gorse-flower. These wines are often unpredictable, so your local 'home-brew' shop will be your best friend until you become an expert in your own right.

GORSE FLOWER WINE

3 pints of gorse flowers
1 gallon water

Pour the boiling water over the gorse blooms, let it cool and leave to steep for a week. Strain the liquor off, heat to tepid, then add 2½ lbs sugar, and when dissolved, add ½ oz of yeast on a small piece of toast.*
Cover and leave for 10 days. Strain and bottle.

Recipe from Mrs Davies of Haverfordwest, Pembrokeshire.

NETTLE SYRUP (*GWIN DANADL POETHION*)
From Croeso Cymreig.

I am also always intending to make this – a medicinal potion which the Welsh felt had great health-giving powers as a blood-purifier. Diluted with soda water it makes a cooling drink.

Gather the tops of young nettles, wash well, and to every 1 lb of nettles add one quart of water. Boil for one hour, strain, and to every pint of juice add 1 lb sugar. Boil for 30 minutes, and when cold bottle.

SIR WATKIN WILLIAMS WYNNE'S ST. DAVID'S DAY WASSAIL BOWL

Served at Jesus College, Oxford, on St. David's Day, in an immense silver-gilt bowl presented to the college in 1732 by Sir Watkin of the famous and many-branched Border family:

Into the bowl is first placed ½ lb of sugar in which is placed one pint of warm beer; a little nutmeg and ginger are then grated over the mixture, and four glasses of sherry and five pints of beer added to it. It is then stirred, sweetened to taste and allowed to stand covered for two or three hours.
    Roasted apples are then floated on the creaming mixture and the wassail bowl is ready.

The Curiosities of Ale and Beer, by John Bickerdyke, published about 1860.

* Use yeast + nutrient in place of this.

WELSH GINGER-BEER (DIOD SINSIR)

There were two kinds of home-made ginger-beer in Wales, one was a gingered herb (or 'small') beer, the other a straightforward ginger-beer made conventionally from lemons, ginger and sugar. This recipe for the former was given to me by Mrs Lizzie Griffiths, whose spotless little roadside cottage with its colourful garden spilling over into the surrounding hedge banks makes it a local north Pembrokeshire landmark. Then in her 70's, but still bright and energetic, for forty-five years this remarkable lady looked after the village school, situated an appreciable distance away from her cottage and at the foot of a steep hill, enough to have daunted a lady of less fortitude. Before the arrival of a more up-to-date heating system, her duties included the provision of wood for the school fires. In May each year she would chop over two tons of firewood in readiness for the next winter. In winter she ploughed her way through the snow in the early hours of the morning to light the school fires before the pupils arrived, breaking the ice on the water she drew and subsequently heated to scrub the classroom floors.

Almost always in rural Wales the talk between older women turns to recollections of slogging hard work like this which they have somehow survived with an amazing brightness of spirit miraculously intact.

4 lbs sugar
1 or 2 lemons, sliced thinly
1 stick rhubarb, cut in chunks
1 cooking apple
pinch hops
bunch of dandelion leaves

½ carton powdered ginger
a few blackcurrant leaves
goosegrass (gwlydd y perthi)
a little wormwood (wermod)
1½ gallons water
½ oz yeast

Boil until tender all these ingredients except the yeast and sugar. Strain and add the sugar to the liquid, stirring until dissolved. Mix the yeast with a little lukewarm liquid in a cup, then stir into the remainder. Leave overnight. In the morning, skim off the yeast and bottle the liquid, but do not cork tightly ar first. Drink in a week.

GINGER-BEER

1 gallon water	1 oz root ginger
1½ lbs sugar	½ lemon
¼ oz cream of tartar	1 oz baker's yeast

Bruise the ginger, put in to the water, add the sugar and boil for an hour. Skim. Pour on to the sliced lemon and cream of tartar. When almost cold, add the yeast. After two days, strain and bottle. Drink in 3 days.

'BERRY CIDER'

A localised drink made in the Cadair Idris area of Merionethshire. Boiling water was poured over rowanberries, left for a month or so, when the result would be a 'pleasant acid drink'. Trefor Owen, who records this in *Customs and Traditions of Wales*, also mentions 'Birch Wine', made from the sap drained from the tree. These two drinks were of course a product of poverty.

3. Tea and coffee in Wales

It's hard to believe tea was once a rarity in Wales. Nowadays it shares with beer the honour of being the national beverage. Mati Thomas writes of tea still being very precious in the middle of the 19th century, kept under lock and key in a special casket: a lady of property would buy an ounce of tea at a time '. . . on rare occasions she would prepare a cup of tea each for her husband and herself, after a breakfast of third-heating *cawl*. Great care was taken to see that the children and the workers were well out of sight before indulging in this delicacy'.

In the rest of Britain, tea was certainly the drink of all classes by 1850, although it was still relatively expensive – tea never cost less than 2/6d. a pound until Lipton sold it at 1/7d. in 1889. By the times Miss Thomas was describing, this attitude to tea would not be universal in Wales. But in some parts it was still scarce and expensive enough to be regarded as the luxury she describes, and the ritual associated with its use for almost a century still observed. The major reason tea was slow to take on in Wales was not so much its unavailability, as an unwillingness to drink a beverage which has to be bought, when buttermilk and home-brewed cost nothing. Thus tea tended to be reserved for special occasions: for the farm workers a Sunday treat, for the farmer and his wife a daily indulgence quietly taken together in private.

When tea was finally absorbed into the daily pattern of life in Wales, it was still greatly valued and relished, and employed in what may seem strange ways to those who valued it less; for example – *siencyn te* – the shepherd's first breakfast, hot tea poured over bread and butter mentioned earlier.

Social historians may class this as a hardship dish, but it was greatly enjoyed in Wales, and many old folk relish it to this day, when they can well afford 'something better'.

It is not easy to get good coffee in Wales, except in the best hotels and restaurants. There is a strong preference for milky coffee at all levels of society. Perhaps these amazing instructions, in a Welsh language book of household management with a wide circulation in Victorian times, had something to do with it:

MILKY COFFEE

INGREDIENTS:
    Dessertspoonful of coffee   some eggshells or isinglass
    1 pint milk

METHOD:
    Boil the coffee in the milk for 15 minutes, then add the eggshells to clear it; and boil for a few more minutes.
TIME:
    20 minutes. Enough for one person.

From *Coginiaeth a Threfniadaeth Deuluaidd* (Cookery and Household Management) by Mrs S.A.Edwards, Ty'n-y-cefn, Corwen, 1881.

Ernest Jones with the last bottle of Fron-goch whisky. Photo by courtesy of the National Library of Wales.

4. Welsh Whisky

Like their fellow Celts in Ireland and Scotland the Welsh had a predilection for producing whisky on a small scale – not surprising considering the rigours of life in early times. The practice persists to the present day – not so much amongst the Celts of the British Isles (or at any rate, if there is any going on in Wales I haven't heard of it) but most markedly with the French *vignerons* who still produce their individual *eau de vie* ('water of life').

Little is known about it, but Wales has an early history of commercial whisky distilling, beginning with the Evan Williams family of Dale in Pembrokeshire in the early 18th century. By the middle of that century the Daniels family of Cardigan were also distilling whisky: the surprise is that both families, after emigrating to America were reponsible for founding the famous Kentucky Whisky industry.

Whisky was commercially distilled at the end of the 19th century, at Fron-goch near Lake Bala *(Llŷn Tegid)*. It was a perfectly genuine grain whisky produced at a purpose-built distillery by a company founded in 1887 by Mr Robert Willis and the local squire, Richard Lloyd Price of Rhiwlas, Llanfor. Bala was served by three railway lines, thus admirably situated for industrial development; in a public-spirited attempt to create local employment at a time of great depression and poverty, Price had already got a small industrial estate going.

There was a thriving brush-making business in a water-powered mill; a 20,000-acre Game Farm, Fuller's Earth and Blue Clay excavation; slate-mining, and the bottling of Rhiwlas Table Water. The idea of Welsh whisky came to Price and Willis simply because of the alliterative appeal. Upon further consideration they decided that there was no practical reason why 'gallant little Wales should not turn out quite as good a spirit as either Scotland or Ireland'. Samples of various Welsh waters were promptly sent off for analysis and the sample from Fron-goch came out amongst the best. The realisation of Welsh Whisky went ahead at full speed: capital of £100,000 was quickly found, most of it raised from within the whisky trade. Plans and specifications for the distillery were obtained and a solid construction of the local grey granite went up in record time between the rivers Mynach and Tryweryn 600 yards from Bala railway junction. Within two years, under the expert guidance of an experienced Scots distiller, Welsh whisky was a reality.

In 1889 a silver-embellished presentation cask bearing the company's Welsh lady trademark was given to Queen Victoria on a royal visit to Bala, earning the whisky the prefix 'Royal'. A few years later a similar cask went off to the then Prince of Wales. What became of the contents of these two casks I am unable to say, but if they had had any sense, the Queen and her son would have drunk the whisky – contrary to popular derisory misconception, Welsh whisky was very good whisky: light, pale, straw-coloured, with a degree of austerity and a peaty similarity to Irish whisky.

The reason behind the Fron-goch distillery's closure just before the Great War was not due to the whisky's inferiority; on the contrary, it was because it was too good. It became a threat to the Scotch whisky distillers who were at that time concerned with establishing their brands on the English market. So the Welsh distillery was bought up by the Scotch whisky distillers and the lusty little infant Welsh whisky snuffed out.

When the New Distillery was eventually demolished just after the Great War, after being used as a POW camp during the war, its stones were snapped up by the Methodists to mend Tal-y-bont chapel walls – which is how the notion that the Temperence Movement had been responsible for closing the distillery down took root.

A blurb from the company said that 'Welsh Whisky is the most wonderful whisky that ever drove a skeleton from the feast of painted Landscapes in the brain of man. It is the mingled souls of peat and barley, washed white within the waters of the Tryweryn. In it you will find the sunshine and shadow that chased each other over the billowy fields, the breath of June, the carol of the lark, the dew of night, the wealth of summer, the Autumn's rich content, all golden with imprisoned light'.

One regrets, sometimes, the passing of the Trades Description Act.

George Bennett's, the former Pembrokeshire wine merchants, managed to acquire what they believed were the last eight bottles of whisky from the Fron-goch distillery. One bottle was sent to Prince Charles on board *Britannia* while she was anchored in Fishguard Bay during the 1969 Investiture tour. The bottle was suitably if slightly funereally housed in a custom-made coffin-shaped box lined with rich green velvet. Prince Charles, nobly resisting temptation, ultimately sent it intact to the Welsh Folk Museum at St Fagan's, where a dedicated staff strong-mindedly allow it to remain untouched in its velvet shroud.

Bennett's opened one of the other bottles and gave their customers a taste: as far as I was concerned it went down very well if unexpectedly at ten in the morning on top of nothing more substantial than my *siencyn* of cornflakes and milk, and I felt I could confidently endorse most of the distillers' claims. . .

Whisky is once again being distilled in Wales, appropriately enough on another industrial estate, this time in Brecon. The company responsible, the 'Welsh Whisky Company Ltd', was formed in 1990, but the proprietors had been working on the project for some considerable time. They have been producing a blended 'Welsh whisky' since 1974, infused with herbs in the style of the Welsh whiskies of early times attributed to the monks of Bardsey Island off the tip of the Llŷn peninsula. Known first as *'Sŵn y Don'* ('Sound of the Wave') and later, after more experimenting with the blend, it was superseded by *'Sŵn y Môr'* ('Sound of the Sea'). This is the malt whisky which is being distilled at Brecon.

In addition to the whisky, the company produce a range of spirits and liqueurs including vodka, gin and 'Merlyn Liqueur', and their single malt whisky, 'Prince of Wales', first introduced in 1986. Thus many public houses, restaurants and hotels have been enabled to offer a range of spirits and liqueurs, distilled and blended in Wales with a distinct Welsh connection.

Perhaps one day they will revive the once-triumphant 'Royal Welsh Whisky'. . .

A cask of Fron-goch whisky with its distinctive trademark of a Welsh lady in national costume.
Photo by courtesy of the National Library of Wales.

12. Festivals

*That night we had supper all over the house. The tables were not
big enough for all to sit down at once. So we had to manage.*
HOW GREEN WAS MY VALLEY, Richard Llewellyn

Festivals in Wales were largely those associated with religion
and the farming seasons. Sheep-shearing, hay and corn harvest
and threshing-day were all occasions to celebrate completed
work and reward neighbourly or hired help. Customs varied: a
'harvest mare' *(caseg fedi)* – the last remaining tuft of uncut corn,
later developing into the 'corn dolly', was the feature of the corn
harvest, involving a certain amount of horseplay as attempts were
made to smuggle it into the house without being discovered by
the women busy preparing the harvest meal, which was usually
taken in the house. This was a substantial affair of roast lamb
and vegetables and *whipod* (see pp 192-3), washed down of course
by a liberal supply of home-brew. Afterwards there would be
dancing to a fiddle.

The hay harvest was also characterised by hijinks – a toss in
the hay for anyone entering the harvest field, where the feast of
more simple food – *sucan,* cold milk or beer, bread and butter,
and a simple tea later on – was taken in a shady corner. The
emphasis here was on thirst-quenching, cooling drinks, usually
siot – crushed oatcake steeped in buttermilk.

Sheep-shearing day meant an elaborate meal for the co-
operative work team – a dinner of cold beef, potatoes and peas,
with rice pudding to follow and a plain tea in the afternoon.

Only the shepherds provided their own food for their *ffest y
bugeiliaid* held on August 12th on a hilltop or bank. Racing and
jumping and similar activities came afterwards, for the shepherd
lads were often only 10-13 years old.

Wales' major festival, the 'National', i.e. the annual Royal
National Eisteddfod held alternately in north and south Wales,
has not produced anything at all in the way of an eisteddfodic

culinary ritual other than the celebration meals arranged off the field when the day's competitions are over. No question why not, for those attending traditionally took their own portable food and drink, and still largely do, for the present day has brought little but the most ordinary commercial refreshments to the field.

1. Shearing and Harvest-time

SHEARING CAKE (CACEN GNEIFIO)

Sheep-shearing time was, and still is, one of the major social occasions in Welsh rural life, for in the difficult hill districts especially, farmers help each other with the rounding-up and shearing of their enormous flocks of sheep on a rota basis, and the host farm kitchen is busy for days beforehand preparing pies and tarts and cakes ready to feed the shearers. A good account of this and the responsibility for its success felt by a farmer's wife new to the occasion is in Thomas Firbank's *I Bought a Mountain*:

> Esmé has a hot meal for us. At shearing-time the kitchen is full of food. In a slow oven a huge round of beef is roasting against the hungry morrow. There are bowls and bowls of fruit jellies and custards. There are more jam tarts than the Knave of Hearts could ever have tackled. A stack of home-baked loaves is on the window-sill. Carrots, ready scraped, and peeled potatoes stand waiting in crocks of water. A big pan of porridge is slowly simmering for the gatherers' breakfast. It is often eleven o'clock by the time we have eaten, and in another four hours we must be on top of the Glyder once more to clear the remaining half of the mountain. Some of the men will vote for playing cards all night. But Thomas and Davies usually invite a few to snatch what sleep they can in the cottages, and Esmé and I provide some sort of sleeping quarters for the rest. We double-lock the kitchen and its eatables against dogs and go to bed.

This cake, with its caraway seed flavour, is traditional to shearing time:

½ lb flour (plain)	¼ pint milk
6 oz moist sugar	1 teaspoonful baking powder
4 oz butter	2 teaspoonfuls caraway seeds
rind of ½ lemon	little grated nutmeg

Rub butter into flour, mix all dry ingredients together and then stir in the milk and beaten egg. Bake in a greased cake tin lined with buttered paper, in a moderate oven for one hour.

From Croeso Cymreig.

THRESHING CAKE (*CACEN DDYRNU*)

A Montgomeryshire recipe from Welsh Fare.

This cake is also associated with sheep-shearing:

3 large cupfuls plain flour	1 lb mixed currants and raisins
8 oz sugar	2 or 3 eggs, well beaten
8 oz bacon dripping	buttermilk
a little bicarbonate of soda dissolved in a little tepid water and buttermilk	

Rub the fat into the flour and work in the other dry ingredients. Mix gradually with the beaten eggs and add sufficient buttermilk to give a fairly soft consistency. Bake in a greased cake tin in a fairly hot oven for about an hour and a half.

The combine-harvester came late to the remoter areas of rural Wales. This meant that the tradition of harvest as a great social occasion, when everyone helped his neighbour in turn, to be paid, not with money, but with plentiful food, lingered on until comparatively recently. West Wales was notably late – it was not until the mid-1950's that machinery put an end to the old ways in Pembrokeshire. The old spirit of co-operation lingers on there, particularly over the hay harvest, but the old days of twenty or thirty men coming to the farm to work and be fed are over.

In what was in any case a memorable year for the British harvest, the sound of the combine holds a particular memory for anyone who was near the shores of Milford Haven in the summer of 1974. Never before in living memory had the success of the British grain harvest been of equal importance to town and city dwellers alike. Perhaps for the first time in a hundred years, in the weeks of August and September the whole population had an eye on the sky and a sharp awareness of the importance of fine weather for something more than mere holiday pleasure.

Our anxiety was because of the catastrophic failure of the Russian grain harvest the previous year; as a result they had been buying on a vast scale which became known as 'The Great Grain Robbery'. Prices on the world market were such that if we'd had to rely too much on imports we risked a balance of payments problem – not to mention difficulties with the EEC, which we'd only recently joined. We needed all the home-grown grain we could muster. Town and city folk, for so long removed from the risks and rigours of life on the land, were uncomfortably reminded of their dependence upon the labour and skill of those who hopefully sow, and thankfully reap.

I remember walking the cliff-tops of southern Pembrokeshire that August in an unfamiliar silence. A week before, a bumper harvest had been assured. Then had come a week of wet and storm, now thankfully over. The sun shone benignly in a polished blue sky. Red Admirals and blue periwinkle butterflies crowded colourfully but noiselessly above the heathery, thistle-clumped turf. A soft breeze ran about, efficiently gathering the starry white thistle seeds and stacking them inches deep against the side of the path. Beyond the cliff a field of ripened grain lay shining in the hot August sun.

The sound I was missing was the urgent, noisesome clatter of the combine-harvesters which ought to have been busy about the fields. The sun had returned, but its beneficence was double-edged: it was drying-out the crop, but an oil tanker was grounded fast on the rocks of the Haven. A stray spark from a combine could easily set off a deadly explosion.

In the perfect weather the whole area seemed to be holding its breath.

A bumper harvest? A terrible explosion?

Then, as I rounded the last curve of the cliff path, I heard at last the sound I'd been missing, and away across the blue bay saw a combine-harvester at work on the curve of a field, and the

Tea at shearing time in Tryweryn. Photo by courtesy of the National Library of Wales.

first heavy load pulling away. The danger of explosion was over.

Next day, the air was alive with noise as harvesting got under way in earnest.

The harvest workers were often in the fields from dawn to midnight. The food they had there, seated in a companionable circle, was plain but nourishing. Plenty of oatmeal or rice porridge, cut cold in great slabs, with buttermilk poured over it; *sucan, cawl ffa, bara ceirch,* the traditional oat cakes, thin and crisp as paper and as big as dinner-plates, were much preferred to bread by the harvest workers. Oatmeal and buttermilk drinks, ginger-beer, nettle beer, cider, mead and 'home-brewed' were the traditional drinks to wash it all down. Farms which were rigidly teetotal tended to excel in the food they provided to compensate for any alcoholic shortcomings – and were just as generously helped as their more lenient neighbours.

When the harvest was all safely in, all the farmers' wives would get together for a tremendous bake-up for the 'harvest home' supper. There was usually some form of *cawl,* with cold joints, pies, pasties and cakes, and *poten gan,* a white pudding made with wheat flour – a great treat. Rice pudding boiled on top of the stove was another favourite. It contained currants and was thin enough to drink.

HARVEST CAKE (*TEISEN BLAT*)

This was often made by cooking the fruit filling without sugar, which was added afterwards by raising the lid of the cooked pie and working the sugar into the fruit. The lid was then carefully replaced. The tarts, or cakes, were made with very thin shortcrust pastry, often spiced with cinnamon, sometimes without a supporting plate base, which must have required considerable skill, considering the size of the tarts. Buttermilk was frequently drunk with this.

See *teisen ar y maen*, p.201.

Rabbit Stew (Stiw cwningen)

As the uncut area of the harvest field grew smaller, many rabbits would be caught to provide a seasonal dish for the harvesters.

a rabbit, skinned and cleaned
half a pound bacon
swede
carrots
one ounce flour

two or three onions
a little chopped parsley
a little fat
salt and pepper

Joint the rabbit and coarsely cut the bacon and vegetables. Put into a large saucepan, season with salt, pepper and parsley, cover with water and simmer slowly for about an hour and a half. Lastly, thicken with flour mixed with a little cold water, and re-boil for a further few minutes.

A recipe from Llŷn in Welsh Fare.

Rook Pie (Pastai Brain Bach)

Rook shoots organised to clear an area of troublesome rooks in spring were common in England and Wales. This recipe occurs in many old English cookery books and tends to find its way into Welsh collections. I give this one which Sheila Hutchins quotes in *English Recipes* because it is a more explicit version than the one to be found in *Croeso Cymreig.*

Rooks are about as big as pigeons; only the breast meat and sometimes the legs are used because the back is black and tastes bitter:

Steep the rooks' breasts in milk for several hours. Then lay a piece of lean tender steak in the pie-dish and put the rooks' breasts on top, seasoning them well with salt, pepper and nutmeg, dredge them with a little flour and cover them with strips of bacon. Fill the pie-dish up to two-thirds with water, cover the top with greaseproof paper or foil. Bake the contents in a moderate oven (350 deg F./Gas 4) for about an hour or longer, until a fork will pierce the meat easily. Let it grow cold, then cover the top of the dish with pastry as usual, and bake the pie for about 35 minutes first in a very hot oven (450 deg.F., Gas 8) and then with the heat reduced to moderate when the pastry has risen.

HARE BROTH (*CAWL COCH YSGYFARNOG*)

The acquisition of a hare in the old days would be the cause for a celebration. For a variation on the more usual jugged or stewed hare, consider Mati Thomas' instructions:

1 hare	oatmeal
a little swede	potatoes
a small quantity of leeks	parsley, salt, water

Skin and clean the hare. Place in a bowl of salt water overnight. Next day, cut the hare into portions and place in a cooker. Pour over a gallon and a half of cold water, placing in at the same time the finely chopped swede. When the water has boiled for a short time, add the parsley and leeks which should be finely chopped, then add the salt. After a short time add the oatmeal and water mix. Remove the hare meat, and add potatoes. Continue boiling until the potatoes are cooked.

Serve the *cawl* in bowls, the meat shared onto wooden plates. This dinner was of the highest order, and not often available.

2. Goose, Christmas and New Year

MICHAELMAS GOOSE (*GŴYDD MIHANGEL*)

Geese are still popular eating today in Wales at Christmas, a reflection of their importance in early Welsh rural life. The *Laws of Hywel Dda* decreed that 'the turbulent goose could be summarily executed' if found damaging standing corn, or corn in barns.

Goose-feather beds traditionally insulated against the cold of unheated Welsh hill farm bedrooms, while certain of the bigger feathers were employed in the kitchen – the large wing pinion for sweeping the hearth, and the smaller wing feathers for brushing flour or oatmeal during baking.

Mati Thomas tells us about the Michaelmas Goose *cawl* which the farmer would offer his tenants at the time of their payment of rents. It was considered a meal 'of the highest order'.

274

After the harvest the geese would glean the harvest fields and fatten very quickly. Roasting methods were unknown in rural Wales, and the goose was made into *cawl*.

one goose	onions
water	oatmeal

Place the prepared goose into a cooker full of cold water. When the water has boiled turn the goose over. Allow to boil for about an hour and three quarters. Put into the *cawl* a bowlful of finely chopped onion and oatmeal paste. Turn the goose occasionally. When ready remove from the fire.

Serve with mashed potatoes with the thick *cawl* poured over the meal.

NEW YEAR GOOSE

Christmas in the 1820's, the period Mati Thomas wrote about for the *eisteddfod* entry, was primarily a religious occasion, and meals on Christmas Day were the same as any other. New Year's Day, or *Dydd Calan*, on the other hand, was a very important festive occasion. In some areas of Wales, principally in the Gwaun Valley in Pembrokeshire, the old Welsh New Year (13 January) is still celebrated. For New Year, boiled goose, potato pudding and rice pudding were traditional, and everyone joined in the feast – the farmer and his family, the farm-workers and their families.

In west Wales the relationship of the large tenant farmer to his neighbours was interdependant, creating a special community spirit. In August, on *Dydd Iau Mawr* (Big Thursday), the families who had helped him with harvest were taken by the farmer in his wagons for a day at the seaside, and on New Year's Day he entertained them to a special dinner:

NEW YEAR'S DINNER (*CINIO CALAN*)

THE GOOSE

The goose was boiled in a cooker on the fire. Large amounts of finely chopped parsley and onions were added. The contents were boiled for around three hours, until the *cawl* was thick with nourishment.

POTATO PUDDING

Potato pudding. Peel half a peck* of potatoes, and put into boiling water, add the salt. When cooked pour off the water and allow the potatoes to dry in the hot cooker. Remove from the cooker and mash with a wooden masher. Adding an egg-size lump of butter. Sprinkle the tablespoonsful of dry flour into it. Allow to cool and place into two metal bowls. Place into the heated wall oven, and allow to cook to a rich brown colour.

RICE PUDDING

Place a large basinful of cleaned and washed rice in a cooker of boiling water. Allow to boil for half an hour. Pour in a gallon of skimmed milk. Allow to thicken and add a little brown sugar and salt. It was then put into two metal bowls and placed in the heated wall oven, and cooked until attaining a rich brown colour.

The rice pudding and the potato pudding were made the day previous to Dydd Calan, but the goose was cooked that day.

Between the three dishes they had a superior dinner for the festive occasion.

Rumours exist of an elaborate Christmas goose pie being made in Llansanffraid ym Mechain, Montgomeryshire, near the Shropshire border, but I suspect their authenticity, as the pie probably originates in Yorkshire. It was, however, the custom to send these elaborate pies, made specially for the Christmas trade, from Yorkshire to London (and possibly to other places, too) as presents, which accounts for the necessarily thick pastry cases ('the walls must be well built') to enable the contents to survive the journey and arrive intact. The inclusion of a large amount of butter on the top, beneath the pastry crust, also enhanced the pie's keeping qualities. Hannah Glasse, in *The Art of Cookery* gives a detailed account of a Yorkshire pie containing a turkey, a goose, a fowl, a partridge and a pigeon, each fitted inside the other on the Russian doll principle, a daunting prospect for a present-day cook to tackle. This recipe, origin unknown, is simpler, and similar to the one attributed to Llansanffraid. Jane Grigson gives it in *English Food*, together with her adaptation:

* 1 gallon or 4½ litres

To Make a Goose Pye

Half a peck of flour (5 lb) will make the walls of a goose-pie. . . Raise your crust just big enough to hold a large goose; first have a pickled dried tongue boiled tender enough to peel, cut off the root, bone a goose and a large fowl; take half a quarter of an ounce of mace beat fine, a large teaspoonful of beaten pepper, three teaspoonfuls of salt; mix all together, season your fowl and goose with it, then lay the fowl in the goose, and the tongue in the fowl, and the goose in the same form as if whole. Put half a pound of butter on the top, and lay on the lid. This pie is delicious, either hot or cold, and will keep a great while. A slice of this pye cut down across makes a pretty little side-dish for supper.

A splendid centre-piece for a party. Unless your pie has to go by train to London. . . there is no need to make such a thick crust. However, it must be thick enough to keep in the juices as far as possible. I recommend a hot-water pastry made with 3 lb of flour and a roasting pan 11½" x 9" x 2" deep as a mould (unless you have something of a comparable size which is deeper). It seems that the varieties of poultry in Hannah Glasse's day were not so large as they are now, because you need to increase the seasonings. My ingredients worked out like this:-

For 20-25

hot-water crust made with 3 lb flour
1 10 lb goose, boned
1 5 lb farm chicken, boned
1 2½ lb pickled tongue, soaked, boiled, trimmed and skinned

¼ oz mace
2 heaped teaspoons freshly ground black pepper
5 rounded teaspoons sea salt
2 oz butter

To bake the pie, put it into a hot oven, 425 deg.F./Gas 7 for 20 minutes. Then lower the heat to 350 deg.F./Gas 4 and cover the top with brown paper to protect it from becoming too brown too soon. Leave for 3 hours.

It is only prudent to check the pie from time to time. Lower the heat, if it is bubbling away too fast, to 325 deg.F./Gas 3. Towards the end of this time, push a larding needle or skewer into the pie through the top central hole; if the juices come out very red, leave the pie a little longer. On the other hand, if they come out a pale pink, that is all right – the pie continues to cook as it cools down. (I took mine out of the oven at 1 am, and it was still not quite cold by lunchtime next day, with the juices still liquid: it should have been left until the evening, with an hour or two in the refrigerator to set it properly).

The Celtic New Year is the 1 November, *Calan Gaeaf*, the first day of winter. In north Wales, up to 100 years ago, the more well-to-do farmers would slaughter an animal round about this time, and invite friends, neighbours and relations along to share in a feast. The origins of this custom are probably pagan – the celebrations of the coming of winter. The round of festivities provided by the north Wales custom would come as a welcome break in routine for the farming folk, for the feast was always followed by singing to the harp, and there would be fiddle music and clog dancing. It was a time for the poor to be thankful for, too, for the farmer always made sure the cook had plenty of broth to fill the bowls of the needy when they made application at the kitchen door. In some north Wales areas it was the custom to light bonfires, though this had no connection with the later celebration of Guy Fawkes night. Traditional bonfire food was white cheese and oatcakes and nuts roasted in the fire.

Roast goose is rich and fatty – this stuffing of Lady Llanover's from *The First Principles of Good Cookery* traditionally combines sage and onion with some apple to counteract the richness of the goose. Use fresh sage if possible, and Lady Llanover's recommendation to scald the onions is worth taking:

GOOSE OR DUCK STUFFING

Two ounces of scalded onion, one ounce of green sage leaves, four ounces of breadcrumbs, yolk and white of an egg, pepper and salt, and some minced apple. The flavour is much milder if the onions are scalded previously.
Note: Mix the ingredients together with the yolk of an egg, then fold the stiffly-beaten white into the mixture.

STUFFING FOR ROASTED DUCK

Medieval – from *Bwyd y Beirdd* (Food of the Bards) by Enid Roberts.
Boil parsley and pig's fat in Water or fresh potes (broth, stock). Add the yolks of hard boiled eggs, pepper, ginger, cinnamon, grapes and plenty of cloves.

'Oranges were a great treat for New Year's Day. Two or three shops in our village would have them in especially and they would set aside perhaps a whole boxful for the children. The shopkeeper would come out and throw them one by one to a crowd of children, who jumped to catch them. The tallest had the advantage, and I was one of them. . . ! We ate the peel as well,' so a retired solicitor's chief clerk remembers his Kidwelly (Cydweli), Carmarthenshire, childhood.

When times were very hard in Wales a simple fruit cake had to suffice for Christmas. Icing it would be out of the question, so the peel from the children's precious Christmas oranges would be carefully saved, shredded fine and put on top of the cake for decoration.

CHRISTMAS CAKE (*TEISEN NADOLIG*)

This recipe from Cardiganshire has home-brew instead of brandy or stout to give the cake keeping quality. In the absence of home-brew, use pale ale:

1½ lbs flour	4 oz sweet almonds
½ lb butter (or margarine)	half a nutmeg grated
1 lb caster sugar	½ oz yeast
¼ lb mixed peel	mixed spice (if wished)
½ lb currants	home-brew or pale ale
½ lb raisins	juice of half an orange and
½ lb sultanas	half a lemon

Rub yeast into flour, when well mixed rub in the fat, sugar, fruit and spices, and fruit juices, mix with pale ale. Do not allow mixture to become too soft. Bake in a moderate oven for three hours.

From Croeso Cymreig.

WORKMAN'S CHRISTMAS PUDDING (*PWDIN NADOLIG Y GWEITHIWR*)

Those who don't like an over-rich Christmas pudding might like to size up the possibilites of this economy recipe from Mrs S.A.Edwards of Corwen's book of cookery and household management, *Coginiaeth a Threfniadiaeth Deuluaidd*:

3 oz beef suet	2 oz currants
3 oz flour	2 tablespoons sugar
1 teaspoon raising agent	2 eggs
3 oz breadcrumbs	½ grated nutmeg
2 oz raisins	

Grate the suet finely, wash the currants, stone the raisins and beat the eggs well. Mix everything well together, then put in a floured cloth and boil for 3 hours.

GIBLET PIE

A recipe from the Swansea valley quoted in the magazine *South Wales:*

This recipe will make a supper dish for four. A little well-chopped fresh or dried thyme may be added.
Boil goose or turkey giblets with an onion. Boil long and slowly, approximately two hours. Include the neck and wing ends. When well cooked, remove all the meat from neck and wing bones and cut up finely. Chop onion and giblets, too. Thicken the liquid with a paste made with one dessertspoon of flour and a little water. Mix all together and add a little chopped parsley and a tablespoon of peas (optional). Season well with salt and pepper. Place in a deep pie dish or casserole and cover with pie pastry. Bake in hot oven for half an hour or until pastry is golden and ready.

The *Mari Lwyd* (grey mare) of Wales was a mock horse, or hobby-horse, carried by a wassailing party from house to house during the twelve days of Christmas. The horse party instigated a poetic exchange with the occupants of the house in an attempt to be let in and given appropriate refreshment.

'There were jumping sausages, roasting pies,
And long loaves in the bin,
And a stump of Caerphilly to rest our eyes,
And a barrel rolling in.
O a ham-bone high on a ceiling hook
And a goose with a golden skin,
And the roaring flames of the food you cook:
For God's sake let us in.'
'Ballad of the Mari Lwyd*': Vernon Watkins.*

13. The Cookery of the *Plas*

At one point in my studies of traditional Welsh food, being – not for the first time – temporarily stumped, I asked Jane Grigson: Where would she begin? "With the medieval Welsh poets," she replied in the off-hand way of a Cambridge scholar with a poet husband. Too humbled to protest that they weren't at that time in English translation and that the pressures of my life as a hotelier and restauranteur didn't allow for investigations into the subject (never mind the brush-offs I'd already encountered from Welsh academics and librarians!) I set aside that avenue of enquiry.

Then, a good few years afterwards, when I was free of the catering business, came the discovery one day in Oriel bookshop in Cardiff of *'Bwyd y Beirdd'* (Food of the Bards) by Dr Enid Roberts. From one of the recipes I got the title of this book, as referred to earlier.

Here was a record of the cookery of the later medieval period in Wales as practised by the *bonedd* (nobility) – praise and criticism of the food and drink they gave the poets on their tours around Wales – amounting to what you might say was a 'good food guide' to the halls of the castles and mansions of the day. It was of course much more than this, for the *bonedd* of that time ranked among the most learned noblemen in Europe and the poetry composed for them reflected this. As for judgement of the hospitality, some of the poets themselves were familiar with the English court – Iolo Goch and Guto'r Glyn knew men who were in the company of kings; Siôn Tudur served Edward VI, and later as Yeoman of the Crown at the court of Elizabeth I.

Then came Henry Tudor in his quest for the crown of England, wading ashore at Dale, in Pembrokeshire, and marching with his swelling army up through Haverfordwest, over the Preseli hills, down to Cilgwyn in the Gwaun valley and on to *Trefdraeth* (Newport). A turn off the present-day main coast road here marks where they turned down towards the sea along *Feidr Brenin*

(King's Lane) to cross the sands of Newport bay and up the other side – where the golf course is now – to Cardigan and on up the coast through Llwyn Dafydd, Llanilar, Aberystwyth. Then inland to Machynlleth, Mallwyd, Gartheibio, Llangadfan, Dolfor, Welshpool, where he was joined by Rhys ap Thomas and his army which had come up from Carmarthen. Two days later the combined armies entered Shrewsbury, then marched eastward to Bosworth field. Where, as everyone knows, Henry won the great battle there – and the English crown.

After that the inevitable happened. Anyone who was anyone in Wales flocked to London and the English court if they could, (see how St Peter threw the Welshmen out of Heaven [*caws pobi*]) and by and by the great Welsh patronage tradition of the arts by the *bonedd* and the *uchelwyr* (gentry) was lost for all time. The cookery of the Welsh upper classes from then on became the fashionable style of the English. But I want to record it here because it was a part of the cookery of Wales – that cannot be denied – and its influence did marginally affect the traditional cookery in places where mansions were plentiful, such as the Teifi valley in west Wales, and along the eastern border with England. And that is the great pity, for those who could have written the traditional cookery down, didn't do so – until 1928, when Mati Thomas wrote it down from the memories of the then old people, as she said in the introduction to her manuscript, a prize winning *Eisteddfod* entry. The desperate enquiries I made of Welsh libraries at the time had not revealed it – mainly, I have to say, by a profound lack of interest on the part of those who might have put me on to it. What I was trying to find was something I could trust to be authentic, to tell me what I needed to know about the traditional food – and lacked for want of a Welsh upbringing.

Fortunately there was in the National Library of Wales one man who had heard of my search and understood my motive: Ben Owens, a native of Pembrokeshire, the then Keeper of Manuscripts and Records at the National Library of Wales. "I think I have what you're looking for", he said on the telephone. "Come up and I'll show it to you. It's all in Welsh, mind you." It was to be a year before I had it translated into English; the

National Library weren't able to do it for me. . . eventually I found someone with sufficient knowledge of Welsh *and* of cookery to be able to translate successfully and type it out efficiently – Ieuan Griffiths, at that time farming in Tre-fin, between Fishguard and St Davids. This may seem an odd way of going about things, but at the time I was not only tied to Fishguard by the demands of business and children, but woefully lacking in the kind of friends and contacts I later made when I left west Wales to work in Cardiff. It was, after all, over 30 years ago.

At this time I was already studying the National Library's splendid collection of MS cookery books whenever I could get a day up in Aberystwyth. Later, I delved into the history of the houses with which they had been associated. What now follows is a selection of the recipes I found, and have often used.

In the 1970's I wrote a series exploring the history of the great houses and the MS recipe books which had been found in them for that much-missed quarterly *South Wales.* In the 1980's, Mid Wales Development asked me to write a similar series for a novel 'kitchen hanger' which they used as a gift for the wives of industrialists they hoped to attract to invest in Wales. This, I am told, has gone out to Disneyworld!

I could have turned many of the histories into novels – they ranged from romance to lost fortunes and eccentric owners – like the much-loved Sir Pryse Pryse of Gogerddan, who kept stuffed peacocks on the stairs, and the redoubtable Lady Llanover, better-known for having closed all the pubs in Llan-ofer than her sterling work in the Welsh language cause. Over the years I began to feel the writers of these MS books were friends, and to have my favourites. Some of the recipes have already been included in the text, as appropriate, here now are some more, together with a little about the women who wrote them down and the mansions with which the books are associated.

I have to begin somewhere, but it's difficult to decide. Perhaps the most beautiful and oldest of the handwritten cookery books to be found in the archives of the National Library of Wales, Aberystwyth, is that of 'Madame Sydney Wynne, – her Boke

1715'. It is in the Peniarth collection, notable for the large number of handwritten cookery books, as well as an extensive collection of priceless MSS. It's a large book, part leather-bound, its carefully laid out pages of heavy-quality paper reflecting a lifetime's scribing; the recipes indexed, the headings elaborately scrolled. Madame Wynne was the younger sister of the first Sir Watkin Williams Wynne, of the notable border family, who gave his name to the famous old bread pudding, and a Wassail Bowl traditionally served on St David's Day at Jesus College, Oxford. (See p.258.) Is his pudding good!

SIR WATKIN WILLIAMS WYNNE'S PUDDING

Mix 4 oz/125g beef marrow (or suet) with 4 oz/125g sugar, 4oz/125g breadcrumbs, the grated rind and strained juice of a lemon. Beat the yolks of 2 eggs and the whites separately. Beat in the yolks and then fold in the stiffly-whipped egg whites. Steam the pudding in a mould or buttered basin for 2 hours.

Turn the pudding out and serve with this sauce:

Take 2 tabls. warm water, yolks of 2 eggs, 1 tbls. sugar, 1 tbls. brandy, rum or whisky. Put them in a pan and whip over a low heat until the sauce is very stiff. Serve at once.

Another early handwritten book was found at Gogerddan, near Aberystwyth, home of the Pryse family. The present Georgian mansion was built by the kindly Sir Pryse Pryse on the site of the first house built in the early part of the 14th century. The first Sir Richard Pryse was created Baron by Charles 1st in 1641. By their marriage his parents had united two princely families (John Pryse, descended from the 11th century Welsh Lord of Cardigan, *Gwaethfod Fawr,* and Elizabeth Perrot of Haroldstone, Pembrokeshire, descendent of Edward 1st through Lord Berkley and the Duke of Norfolk).

This princely background seems to have had little effect upon the outlook of succeeding generations of Pryses, who farmed the great low-lying estate in the Vale of Clarach with exemplary husbandry, and fought the Liberal cause for generations, representing the constituency without a break for centuries. In the latter half of the 19th century an election song was sung with fervour to the tune of 'Plas Gogerddan' at Party meetings and rallies.

The mansion is a long, low building lying at the foot of gentle, shallow hills, its fascia quite unspoiled by the present owners, the Welsh Plant Breeding Station, whose laboratories now occupy the many graceful rooms. The former library is distinguished by a beautifully-painted dome.

Sir Pryse Pryse is reputed to have kept stuffed peacocks on the grand staircase; sadly there is no trace of them now.

A handwritten recipe book found in the mansion probably dates from the late 17th century.

The practice of cooking meat with dried fruit, sugar and spices dates from the time of the Crusades, when these additions became available, first brought back by the Crusaders, paving the way for importation. One explanation often given is that the combination was a way of disguising meat that had 'gone off'. This was not the general rule, however, except perhaps towards the beginning of Lent, when stores of salted and dried meat tended to deteriorate. Otherwise, spices were used purely for their taste. Medieval butchery was governed by strict rules and severe penalties were imposed for transgression. Our present regulations for hygiene in the preparation and sale of meats, fresh and cooked, are only just beginning to match those of the Middle Ages.

It is true, of course that the 'mincemeat' we use today to make our Christmas mince pies did once contain beef, which was eventually omitted, the suet remaining as a reminder of its former presence. Similar pies to this late 17th century example continued to be made virtually until Victorian times when the fashion for spiced food gave way to that of plainer food, thought to be an indication of high thinking as well as being morally healthier – an eating habit which has left its unfortunate legacy in Wales, where many older folk – particularly men – are stubborn in their refusal to accept anything other than the plainest of plain cooking.

TO MAKE A SWEET LAMB PIE.

Cut your Lamb in pieces and season it with cinnamon, mace, nuttmeg, and salt, sugar a little, then put it into your pie with butter and reisins of the sun,* bake it: then melt some butter and beat 2 yolks of eggs with a little sack** and sugar, then put your melted butter to it, and when your pie come out of the oven, put in your cawdle,*** you may put in hard eggs, sweet meats and citron if you please.

Merryell Williams
Ystumcolwyn Farm, Meifod, Montgomeryshire

'A prudent, virtuous and tender wife' runs the commemorative tablet in Meifod church to the woman who grew up on the family farm, where she compiled her charming book of early 18th century 'receipts' in the Peniarth collection, NLW. Her husband did not include her culinary skills in his tribute, but I'm sure they must have been exemplary as her instructions are so clear and detailed.

The transportation of oysters in water-tanks to inland areas was sufficiently well-established for them to have made regular appearances on the tables of the well-to-do, as the MS books of the period confirm, for ways of dealing with oysters feature in all of them. (See pp 81-3)

TO MAKE A VIOLET PUDDING

Before chemical flavourings and colourings were developed, flowers were used for this purpose; preserving violet and rose petals by crystallising survives to the present day.

---

*   big raisins
**   sherry
*** the egg, sherry, butter and sugar mixture

Take a pound of white grated bread & a pound/450g of suett and
Mince it into ye bread, & season it wth nutmegs and Rhose water and
collar (colour) it with syrrop of Violetts and soe boyle it.

(See also p.180)

Anne Phelps
Withybush House (Poyston East) Haverfordwest, Pembrokeshire

The area of Withybush is now indissolubly linked with Pembrokeshire's General Hospital, but long before anything of that kind was even thought of, there were two mansions there on the old Poyston estate, over on the other side of what is now the A40 trunk road. Poyston West is well enough known as the birthplace of Sir Thomas Picton, hero of Waterloo. Withy Bush House, on the other hand, was something of a mystery when I attempted to research what was already a wreck 20 years ago – and more so now as it is no longer standing. It existed alright (I have a photograph of it) and Fenton mentioned it in his *Guide to Pembrokeshire*, 1811, as 'the seat of John Phelps Esquire, called Withy Bush'.

The Air Ministry had much to do with the decay of the house and its environs – during World War 2 they built an airfield across the middle of the estate, effectively slicing it in two which may account for the substitution of 'Poyston East' for Withy Bush. The Ministry also left a litter of Nissen huts which eventually formed the nucleus of an unofficial industrial estate. Much of this activity is still there, expanded and official, while the airfield is used for peaceful purposes.

Who was Anne Phelps? John Phelps' mother? His sister? Probably the former, but there is no evidence to say. Her recipe book, stored in the Pembrokeshire Records Office is real enough. It was compiled about 1770, its content typical of the period – the presentation ordinary, almost untidy, but the recipes are very sound.

For the recipe below we now have to use lamb, but note how haricot beans are back in favour as an accompaniment:

HARICOT MUTTON

Cut a neck of mutton in pieces about two bones a stake [1], season it with pepper and salt, then fry it, just to turn it brown, then put it in your stewpan, with water enough to cover it, then add a bunch of sweet herbs, lemon peel, mace, Anchovy Onion and more pepper, stew it gently four hours, when ready take out the meat, cover it over by the fire, then strain the gravy, put to it some walnut liquor, two or three pickled walnuts bruised [2], mix some flour and butter to thicken it [3], it must be made pretty thick, then put in your meat give it a warm in the same, you must have a plate of Turnips and Carrots cut in squares, fry them then serve it.

The term 'haricot', though it originated to describe a stew of meat, vegetables and beans, came to be used loosely to indicate a stew of any kind, whether haricot or any other kind of bean were included or not. In the old books one sometimes sees 'haricot', sometimes 'haricood', sometimes 'harico', all with the same meaning; the term was often applied to root vegetables to determine the casseroling of turnips, carrots etc, in rich meat stock. Personally I am fond of haricot beans provided they are cooked to the right creaminess, and would feel quite happy to make this mutton stew with about a pound of white haricot beans, previously soaked in cold water overnight, half the quantity placed at the bottom of the oven dish with a few slightly browned onions, then the meat, browned, and the *bouquet garni*, finally the rest of the beans and about a pint of good meat stock poured over all. The dish is cooked when most of the liquor has been absorbed by the beans which should be tenderly soft. Eighteenth-century recipe books also suggest cooked haricot beans as an accompaniment, either hot or cold, dressed with oil and vinegar after sprinkling with chopped chives and parsley, or stewed for a few minutes in a little finely-chopped onion, parsley and butter, well seasoned, then placed under a roast of meat to absorb the gravy for additional flavour. Or they can be served in a hot tomato sauce.

---

1. steak
2. pickled walnuts can be bought at good delicatessens.
3. *beurre manié* i.e. slightly more flour than butter worked together and added, little by little, to the boiling liquor to thicken.

To make Green Pea Soup

Take a peck [4] of pease, boil them in three quarts of water with two or three roots of celery, two onions, two cloves, some split peppercorns and salt to your taste, when the pease are boiled tender, pulp them through a colendar, half a pound of butter to be melted over a fire till it boils, then put in three cucumbers pared and sliced, to be boiled in the butter till they are done enough for eating, then add a pint of very young peas boil these with the cucumbers ten minutes, the soup to be made scalding hot, and the butter, cucumbers and pease stirred into it until they are well mixed – when it begins to boil to be taken up, if it is suffered to boil many minutes it will lose colour.

Baked Beef

On a round of Beef rib ¾ lb of coarse brown sugar and 3 oz salt Petre – Let it lie 24 Hours, then salt it with common Salt, turn it and baste it very well every day for a fortnight.

Take of cloves, Mace, Allspice, Black Pepper and Nutmegs a quarter of an ounce each pounded, rub them well into the Beef, and make deep holes with a large skewer which fill up with spices. Fillet it and put it into a deep baking pan, with a good deal of suet at top and bottom to prevent it burning and a little water. Stop it down close with a coarse paste and bake about 4 hours.

N.B. a little common salt is sufficient – Too much Salt renders the beef too hard.

Yes. A wise comment on the seasoning of roasted or baked beef of which British housewives are all too often ignorant: season beef with black pepper and mustard but not with salt, which as Anne Phelps indicates, hardens beef; leave the salting until the gravy stage. I have not yet dealt with a round of beef in this way and am determined to do one for next Christmas.

---

4. 8 quarts

Trawscoed Hall
('Crosswood')

The original Montgomeryshire manor was built by Sir Rowland Heywood in the 16th century of grey stone from the quarry at Welshpool. He was lord of two manors in Kent and several in Shropshire. In 1777 Edward Heywood rebuilt part of the manor in the late Georgian style from local red brick. The house was originally known as Trawscoed Isaf ('Lower Trawscoed') anglicised in 1770 to 'Crosswood' – not unusually for that part of Wales, so close to the English border. The original Welsh name was re-adopted in 1926. The house has never been on the market: in 1898 the last of the Heywoods died, leaving the property to a god-daughter, and it has remained in the Trevor family ever since. When I wrote to enquire about the hand-written cookery book in their collection, the owners filled me with alarm by sending it to me in the post. . .

The small, hand-made, hand-written book is attributed to 'Rebekah Jones her Book 1741'. The handwriting is wonderfully clear for the period; moreover the recipes are of special interest as many of them are what I call 'bridging' recipes between an early version and the dishes we know today. Part of the fun of delving into old cookery is tracing the development of a dish from its earliest appearance. For safety's sake I took the little book to the National Library of Wales, where they made two copies – one for me and one for themselves – before returning it in person to Trawscoed.

Almost every dish here is finished by being 'scraped with sugar' – a reminder of the medieval practice when sugar went on everything, sweet and savoury, because it was so costly and the confirmation of wealth so necessary at that time. As a young woman I remember watching a catering cook sprinkling her fruit tart with sugar before putting it to the oven: she was unwittingly carrying on the old tradition when every dish carried the instruction to 'scrape with sugar and so *ice your tart*'. The italics are mine. The sugar melts in the heat of the oven and forms a crisp frosting – the beginning of the idea of icing I assume.

The recipes for 'a tart of green peas' seasoned with saffron, verjuice and sugar, and 'artechoak pie' – artichoke hearts, dates and raisins, seasoned with vinegar and sack, ginger and sugar, mace, and orange peel, together with the frequent references to 'coffins' for containing the meats while they baked are typical of an earlier period. If the idea of baking long, rectangular pies containing meat and hard-boiled eggs strikes you as odd, have a look at the pies of similar shape (perhaps now extra long) next time you're in the deli. . . the pies of the Middle Ages are indeed still with us.

HOW TO MAKE A TART OF CHERRIES

take out the stones and lay the cherries into your tart with sugar Ginger and cinnamon then close your tarte for bake it and ice it then make a sirrop of muskadine [sweet sherry wine] and damask [rose] water and pour this into your tart scrape on sugar and serve it.'

It should be noted that spelling did not settle down for quite some time yet, thus the many variations in spelling (even in the same sentence) are quite normal – and not the fault of the proof-reader!

Hengwrt
('The Old Court')

Hengwrt and its sister estate Nannau, both in the Dolgellau area, have yielded several hand-written cookery books, all in the Peniarth collection NLW. By far the most significant is the one in the neat hand of Elizabeth Baker – not so much for its cookery content as for the role its author played in rescuing the family fortunes. For here is a saga of debt and disgrace as thrilling and complex as any present-day Sunday newspaper revelation. . . but the fight to save Hengwrt from its creditors, and its owner from Carey St. took place over 200 years ago, in the second half of the 18th century.

Hengwrt, home of the Vaughan family, was mortgaged over and over again for forty years, plunging ever deeper into debt, as both father, Robert Vaughan, and after his death, his son Hugh, were equally financially incompetent. In 1775 Hugh inherited Nannau, at the time unencumbered by debt, assuming its rents would be sufficient to clear Hengwrt's mortgage. But records had been so badly kept that Hugh Vaughan was swiftly declared bankrupt and fled from Wales, the bailifs at his heels.

It is at this point that Elizabeth Baker enters the story. As Hengwrt's housekeeper, it was only a short step for her to take on the secretarial work for one of the two solicitors appointed to sort out Hugh Vaughan's affairs, and fortunately she recorded everything in her diary. She took on the mammoth task of sorting out Hugh Vaughan's tangled financial affairs. Working under the solicitor's instructions, she gathered evidence of all sales, rents and mortgages for the past 12 years, at the same time arranging for Hengwrt's most valuable possessions to be hidden at Nannau, safe from creditors. First to go were the priceless manuscripts (now in the Peniarth collection), then the other valuables – the stallion, the cattle and the hounds. From time to time her work on the accounts was interrupted by having to defend Hengwrt and Nannau from the bailiffs – by literally barricading herself in one house or the other, depending upon where the valuables were currently hidden.

Finally evidence of a massive double-cross emerged – Hengwrt was not bankrupt at all, in fact it was in funds to the tune of £12,000. The mortgagors were now in default, and after an exile of nine years, Squire Hugh Vaughan returned to Wales.

The solicitor was rewarded with an annuity of £150 a year, plus his fees of £3,000 for the six years' work. Elizabeth Baker, on the other hand, for all her devoted work, was poorly rewarded. She was allowed to continue living in the Dower House for a year or two, then in an apartment on the estate, but in 1784, the work on Hengwrt's affairs being virtually finished, she had left Merionethshire and was living near the English border in a rented cottage. Entirely dependent on subscriptions from her friends, she died in acute poverty and was buried in a pauper's grave.

There are several hand-written cookery books connected with Hengwrt and Nannau. One is clearly by Elizabeth Baker, distinguished by its careful neat script and concerns about the plight of the poor, compiled about 1796. Another, older book, is by Catherine Nannau. Unusually, a few local recipes are recorded. The shortages of the Napoleonic Wars, especially of wheat flour, are recorded, thus a recipe for 'a cheap soup for 120 persons' sits next to a copied extract from a London newspaper of the times on the raising of subscriptions by a Committee for Reducing the Price of Provisions – £2,994.7.6d resulted, distributed 'for the immediate relief of distressed inhabitants'.

OWEN GLANDWR'S LEMON PUDDINGS *

(so named by Sir Robert Howel Vaughan Bar[t] the *real composer Certain.*)

These were served at the launch of the first edition of *Peacock* at Lear's bookshop, Cardiff, in 1980. They were a tremendous success.

> Grate off the rind of the Lemons, scoop out the pulp and mix the juice and what has been grated with a few crumbs of bread as much beef suet chopped fine and the yolk of an egg, a little white wine and sugar; boil the rinds tender, let them cool, then fill them with the mixture and tye them in a cloth and so boil them. Sauce is melted butter, white wine, sugar and a little juice of Lemon; three lemons make the dish as they must be divided in halves, a few plumper currants must not be omitted in the mixture or a little Raspberry jiam (sic) by some palates has the preference, but the currants looks the prettiest.

This is a delicious pudding. I adapted it as follows:

3 lemons, juice and zest	6 tbls caster sugar
3 tbls white sweet white wine or cider	1 egg yolk
3 tbls suet	currants
14 tbls white breadcrumbs	

for the sauce: a good knob of butter, juice of ½ a lemon, 3 tbls caster sugar, 8 fl.oz white wine or cider. Heat gently until the sugar is melted. Boil the lemon halves for about 10 mins in enough water to just cover. The pulp will now scrape easily from the rinds.

for the puddings: mix all the ingredients together, including the pulp, and either fill the lemon rinds, packing them close into a baking dish –

---

* The spelling here has a waywardness typical of the period. But what moved the spendthrift Squire to descend to the kitchen to invent these delicious little puddings?

or little well-greased ramekins. Bake for about an hour in a *bain marie* in a very moderate oven. This is preferable to boiling in a cloth. Serve with the sauce or thin cream if preferred.

SPINNAGE OR SORRIL TARTE

Shred ye herbs small y^n wring out a little of ye juice y^n to a quart of shred herbs put sugar of Currants of each 4 ounces mix it y^n fill and lid yr tart and bake y^m y^n put in half a pint of Cream mix it dust onfine Sugar and serve it hot or cold y^r Cream must be boyled a little and w^n Cold put in.

'Herbs' here denotes vegetables, i.e. the spinach or sorrel. A dish which if it contained eggs would be a quiche, and which demonstrates the lack of our present-day concept of the division of sweet or savoury seasonings. Here again we have the 'icing' of sugar on the tart.

GINGERBREAD, MRS GRIFFITHS JONES' MANNER

An early, and very good mixture for ginger biscuits, with the other spices which have made this biscuit such a long-standing feature of the British tea-table. Cut the quantities down but don't omit the ground caraway seeds. A friend who is an expert biscuit-maker (which I am not) recommends putting the biscuits into a fierce oven for the first few minutes of cooking time (this will prevent the biscuits from spreading) afterwards lowering the heat to ensure the biscuits are really dry and crisp.

Take three pounds of flour, two pounds of Butter without salt, two pound and a half of Treacle: rub into the flour one pound of brown sugar, with one ounce of grated Ginger, a large Nutmeg, and half an ounce of Caraway seeds either ground, or beaten, melt the butter and work the above articles with it adding as much Pearl ashes (bicarbonate of soda) as will lie upon a shilling (see Griddle Cakes p.200) pour into the Treacle a glass of Brandy or Rum and mix the whole well together, drop it with a spoon upon tins buttered and floured, take care the Oven is not too hot to burn them.

Slebech Hall

The 18th century cookery book which was almost certainly compiled here was the very first MS cookery book I consulted. I was in one of those bleak periods which happen to all of us: nothing was going well with the restaurant, it was winter, and a wet, miserable one at that – I had got what was locally known as 'Fishguard Depression'. One grey day of rain the then Pembrokeshire Archivist brought me a little book which had just been attributed to Slebech Hall. Until then, very old cookery had been an unknown world to me. I was instantly captivated by it as I struggled to decipher the often difficult handwriting and to understand the old terms for cookery. Presently I began to try the recipes and to adapt them for the present day. I have been hooked on the subject ever since. In an age of precision cookers – gas, electric and microwave – its good to be reminded of times when fuels were not very reliable and part of the cook's skill lay in handling them successfully. At the time, I still had an Aga, which was sufficiently capricious to make cooking on it a challenge; now I have to be content with the occasional use of my younger daughter's in London. A childhood spent with an Aga certainly made an impression on her.

With its mock battlements, Slebech Hall is a comparatively recent architectural echo of nearby Picton Castle – less than 300 years old. But the site itself has a long history of occupancy, most notably by the Knights Hospitallers of St John of Jerusalem. The Commandary at Slebech was for centuries the resort of pilgrims, devotees and mendicants. The charity is still strongly active throughout Pembrokeshire, and the old parish church in the Park still belongs to the Knights, and though in ruins, a service is held there once a year. In the latter half of the 19th century and the beginning of this, Slebech was owned by the de Rutzen's. The old church had been built uncomfortably near to the Hall, in time the family objected to the parishioners passing so close to their windows and so built another church situated as far away from the Hall as possible, at the extreme edge of the parish boundary where it has stood in its Victorian glory for more than a hundred years, a familiar landmark beside the A40 at the

Slebech Hall. Photo by courtesy of the National Library of Wales.

approach to Haverfordwest. To the casual observer there is something vaguely puzzling about this church, but anyone familiar with church architecture soon realises it is sitting contrariwise as it were, with its nave and tower positioned in the opposite direction from the norm.

At one time it was believed that gold was to be found underground at a place in the grounds of Slebech called Mynwear – fanciful etymologists hopefully trying to link this name with *mwyn aur*, (gold mine). One wealthy owner was lured into sinking a mine. . . alas for the golden dream – all he obtained was an unprofitable amount of coal.

Two brothers named Barlow at one time lived in the two houses that then stood in the Park. Their brotherly affection was a local byword, extending to dining together each evening. Though they each maintained separate households, and dinner was prepared in each, they had developed an eccentric way of determining who entertained who, the menus being announced by trumpet voluntary, the best performance deciding the host.

But who enjoyed the other's dinner isn't recorded, not even in the 18th century cookery book found in the Hall, most of which was compiled there.

CREAM PANCAKES

These are deliciously extravagant for an occasional luxury treat. Don't forget to use small eggs, as eggs at the time this dish was composed were much smaller than those of today.

2 large spoonfuls of flour	4 whole eggs plus yolks of 4 more
1 pint thick cream	

Mix together 2 large spoonfuls of flour, a pint of thick cream, 8 eggs leaving out 4 of the whites and fry them in the usual manner.

BAKED HERRINGS

When you have scaled and washed your herrings, lay them in a dish with a Jamaican pepper* bruised, a few spoonfuls of port wine and bay leaves, add as much liquor (made of vinegar and water with a little salt) as will cover them and let them bake in a moderate oven till the bone is nearly all dissolved. When cold cover them close and they will remain good for several days.

MR ANSON'S PUDDING

A relation by marriage to the early owners of Slebech who later became the Earl of Lichfield. Perhaps he expressed a fondness for this pudding when he went a'courting there? In those days such a dish would not be thought extravagant, as the Home Farm always had a good supply of cream and eggs which often had to be used up, hence the preponderance of this apparently lavish type of dish (in fact a real old English custard) in the recipe books of the time:

Mix together a pint of cream and two spoonfuls of fine flour. Set it over the fire and stir it until it is thick. Let it go cool and add to it 4 eggs well beaten and a spoonful of fine sugar, with a very little nutmeg and a little salt. It will bake in half an hour. Pour over wine sauce.

I suggest a slow to moderate oven for this, and an ovenproof glass baking dish, well greased.

LEMON SPONGE

2½ oz of Isinglass, 1 pint water, the juices of 7 lemons and the rind of 2, and 16 oz sugar to be mixed together and when melted and cold, beaten up with the whites of 4 eggs for 1 hour till it becomes a thick sponge and then put into a shape. The shape must be filled with cold water before the above is put in.

---

* Another name for Allspice which is normally sold in the ground form, therefore a small pinch.

Make this the day after you've made the cream pancakes, to use up the egg-whites. Recipe books of this period always abound in lemon recipes (one is tempted to conclude that that generation were as preoccupied with the problem of scurvy as is ours with cholesterol) which are usually deliciously refreshing, and this one is no exception.

It isn't a sponge at all in the sense of a cake-sponge, the particular texture being obtained by the whipped egg-white. It is virtually a sorbet recipe, and if made in much the same manner as a sorbet, but without actually freezing the mixture, the hour-long beating can be avoided – as indeed it must be in this day and age! The finished dessert bears an uncomfortable resemblance to a sweet I claimed to have 'invented' and thereby called my 'Raspberry Fancy' – which proves all over again that there is very little new in the world of cookery. The Slebach Fancy however refused to adapt to the quick and easy way of making a Raspberry Fancy – in the end I experimented so much my family took to fearfully peering in the refrigerator each evening to see how many useless versions of the Slebach Fancy they were to be expected to eat up!

Boil the water and dissolve the gelatine in it. Add the lemon juice, sugar and grated rind and re-heat until the sugar is quite dissolved. Set aside to become really cold and just on the point of setting. Fold in the stiffly-beaten egg-whites and place the mixture in a shallow bowl either in the freezing compartment of the refrigerator or in the deep-freeze if you have one. As it sets, the mixture will be trying to separate itself, and to avoid this you must interfere and stir it up thoroughly every ten minutes or so during a half hour period. When the amalgamation is secure and the mixture soft enough to transfer to individual glasses or a large mould remove from the freezer and leave the sponge-filled glasses or mould to set in the main part of the refrigerator or other suitably cold place.

BOODLE CLUB CAKE
Contributed by Lady De Rutzen, October 1916.

This recipe, the last in the book, indeed refers to the fruit cake associated with Boodle's Club, London. The present secretary confirmed for me that this was the recipe for the cake regularly baked in the Club kitchens until a short time ago. Originally the cake was made to serve to Members who ordered a bottle of vintage port, in the days when port was ordered by the bottle and not by the glass and Members were known as 'one-bottle', 'two-bottle' or even 'three-bottle' Members: before the last war it was considered a very poor show not to be able to consume at least one bottle of port in an evening. In those days of course Members never drank spirits before a meal and the evening began with the serving of port; the cake was no doubt used as a mopping-up operation. In the end, with the decline of port-drinking, the cake had to be charged for separately until at length it was hardly ever eaten and therefore discontinued.

1 lb flour	½ pint milk
1 lb raisins	1½ teaspoons soda (bicarbonate)
½ lb butter	2 eggs
½ lb moist brown sugar	

Rub the butter into the flour, mix the eggs in the milk and put into a greased tin and bake for 2½ hours. If liked as a change add a pinch of ginger.

I baked this in 375 deg. oven and found it needed no more than 1½ hours with the heat lowered a little during the final ¾ of an hour.

To cheer up the end of winter, why not try a Port and Cake Party instead of the more usual Cheese and Wine?

AN AMBER PUDDING

Put a thin puff paste all over the dish, then slice very thin 1 oz of candied orange peel, 1 oz of lemon and 1 oz of citrons* and lay them in the bottom of the dish; then beat together the yolks of 8 eggs and the whites of 2, with ½ lb lump sugar and ½ lb melted butter quite cold and pour it over your sweetmeats. It will bake in about an hour, the oven must not be very hot.

---

* limes

Stackpole Court
Pembrokeshire

Stackpole is still a magical place – a great estate unfolding inland in vista upon vista of woods and water from a stretch of the southern Pembrokeshire coast and the famous Bosherton lily-ponds. But the beautiful expanses of waxy blooms upon the surface of the waters of the natural and artificially-created lakes are only one of the many glories of Stackpole.

The tragedy is that the glory of the great mansion on its magnificent site above a long, lovely creek is gone. In 1963, two weeks of gargantuan demolition wiped out eight centuries of history during which Stackpole had never been without its Court. All that is left are the remains of the terrace and the bleakly grassed-over foundations; with down below a few tumbled piles of masonry compassionately covered by the protective tangle of the woods.

The once-invincible Court was built upon the site of an 11th century Norman castle by Elidur de Stackpole. In the late 13th century it was a strong house strengthening the square of castles which held 'Little England Beyond Wales'. Roger Lort held it for the Royalists in the Civil Wars – changing sides when it became clear Cromwell was winning. In 1689 came the marriage with the noble Scottish Cawdor family we instantly associate with Macbeth. The Cawdor name occurs most markedly in the Llandeilo and Dinefwr area, as well as Pembrokeshire, a puzzle to those who don't know the story of how the connection came about. It's a romantic tale: Alexander Campbell, heir to Cawdor Castle, Nairnshire, and Gilbert Lort, Roger's son, heir to Stackpole, were undergraduate friends at Cambridge. By far the easiest way home to Scotland for Alexander was to travel with his friend to Stackpole, spend a night or two there, take ship up the west coast to Fort William, then ride across the Great Glen to Cawdor.

On one occasion young Campbell was delayed at Stackpole for several weeks by storms, long enough for him to fall in love with Elizabeth, Gilbert's sister. They were married in 1689, and when she inherited Stackpole from her brother the estate passed into the Campbell family. Their great-grandson was created Baron Cawdor, and his son the first Earl Cawdor, who increased the estate even more by his friendship with John Vaughan, heir to Golden Grove, (*Gelli Aur*) Carmarthen. The grounds are open to the public.

GINGERBREAD

From Mrs Vaughan's Book, c.1780, Golden Grove.

1½ lbs/675g treacle, ¼ lb/125g butter, melted together over the fire. Pour into a pound of Flower and Ginger to your Taste mix well together.

THE DUKE OF MARLBOROUGH'S WHITE FISH SAUCE

Three anchovies chopped small, a quarter of a pound of butter thickened with flower, 2 (table)spoonfuls of Veal Broth, 3 (table)spoonfuls of cream and 3 (table)spoonfuls of White Wine

---

This sauce resembles the Granville Sauce from Lady Llanover's 'Good Cookery'. I have my doubts about the quantity of butter specified – 'thickened with flower' means flour and butter worked together, a *buerre manié* in fact: slightly more flour than butter, and for this amount of liquid I wouldn't use more than an ounce of flour. When you have the sauce thickened, take it off the heat and add the anchovies.

DOCTOR OLIVER'S BISCUITS

Dr Oliver made what were to become his famous plain, baked biscuits in Bath (hence 'Bath Olivers') when it was the fashionable centre for 'taking the waters'. Recipes for them are usually found in 18th century collections, though it is doubtful if any of them are the original recipe, but I would think this one is closer than Mrs Raffald's* for Bath Cakes, which are set to rise, and are less

---

* 'The Experienced English House-Keeper'

Stackpole Court. Photo by courtesy of the National Library of Wales.

than spartan as they contain double the amount of butter, also cream, and caraway seeds.

> 1 pound/450g of flower, 2 ounces/50g of butter, a large spoonful of yeast, well water, and stir it with a little milk into a light dough. Pat it out excessively thin and bake in a slack oven.

A RECIPE FOR CURRIE

An interesting recipe indeed for it gives the lie to the popular notion that 'curry' is a universal word for a fearsomely hot, spiced dish of left-over cold meat the British acquired in the years of the Raj. And that a proprietory 'curry powder' is what it is made with. I think in this context the 'gravy' would be meat juices, not the thickened kind we might otherwise assume.

> Recipe given by Mirza Abu Taub to Warren Hastings, Esq. (first English Governor General of Bengal): Brown half a pound/225g of fresh butter, slice 2 large onions and fry them, put the above into a stewpan, add a hard, sour apple – the heart of a white cabbage, both shred very fine, 1 teaspoon cayenne pepper, 1 teaspoon black pepper, 1 teaspoon tumeric in fine powder, the juice of half a lemon and a gill/5 fl.oz of good strong gravy and a fowl or rabbit cut in pieces. Cover up the stewpan to keep in the steam – and let it simmer gently 3 hours.

What isn't said here is that the spices for this simple 'curry powder', including the essential tumeric, would have been freshly-ground.

A PATTY

> Pull a cold chicken. Chop finely 2 anchovies with parsley and shallot. Slice 1 cold boiled sweetbread and some ham or tongue. Put into a pan with some artichokes bottoms and season lightly. Add some good gravy and a little cream, bind with butter and flower. Stir in some sliced truffles and coarsley-chopped hard-boiled egg. Alternate layers of this mixture and the chicken until your dish is full.

Artichoke bottoms and truffles can be bought in tins nowadays.

To make British Champagne

Take gooseberries before they are quite ripe – crush them with a mallet in a wooden bowl, and to every gallon of fruit put a gallon of water, let it stand 2 days stirring it well. Then squeeze the mixture well through a hop seive with your hands, then measure the liquor and to every gallon put 3½ pounds of loaf sugar, mix it well in the tub and let it stand all day. Put a bottle of the best brandy in the cask – leave the cask open for five or six weeks taking off the scum as it rises – then make it up and let it stand one year in the cask before it is bottled.

(NB: one pint of brandy is put to 7 gallons of liquor.)

The Duke of Norfolk's Punch

Take 6 oranges and 6 lemons. Pare them very thin. Put these peels to steep in 2 gallons of the best brandy stopped close 24 hours. Take 6 quarts of water 3 pound loaf sugar clarified with the whites of 6 eggs, let it boil a quarter of an hour scum it and let it stand to cool. When cold strain out the peels and put as much juice of orange and lemon as you think fit to your taste so turn it all up in the vessel stop it close and when fine bottle. It will be ready in 5 or 6 weeks.

Of interest rather than for practical use today, I would think, although it might be fun to try a very much reduced quantity.

White Sauce (1)

These two recipes for white sauce are pleasantly flavoured with lemon and spices and quite specific as to their method of preparation, needing no comment from me:

Boil a quarter of a pint of milk with a bit of lemon peel, a sprig of lemon thyme and a blade of mace. Add to it half a pint of cream and about 2 oz of fresh butter rolled in flour.* Let simmer 5 minutes, stirring it carefully one way, then take it off the fire, and take out the lemon peel, thyme and mace – chop a little parsley into it but do not let it boil afterwards.

---

* Another way of saying *beurre manié*.

WHITE SAUCE (2)

Put equal parts of broth and milk into a stewpan with a blade of mace – have ready and rub together on a plate an ounce of flour and slightly less of butter,* put it into the stewpan, stir it well till it boils up – then let it stand near the fire or stove, stirring it every now and again till it becomes quite smooth, then strain it through a seive into a basin – put it back in the stewpan, season it with salt and the juice of a small lemon – beat up the yolks of 2 eggs with a scant three tablespoons of milk, strain it through a sieve into your sauce – stir it well and keep it near the fire but be sure do not let it boil for it will curdle.

Lady Llanover
The First Principles of Good Cookery 1867

Although in almost every other way Lady Llanover was a Victorian, in her cookery she reflected the 18th rather more than the 19th century. This was because of the influence, through her mother, of her great-great aunt Delany, a prominent and much loved figure of the 18th century. Yet the cookery expressed through the remarkable *Good Cookery* was essentially and idiosyncratically her own. Moreover, unlike most gentry cookery writers of her day, she knew her subject inside out. You know, from the detail, from the authority, that she was active in the kitchens of Llanover Hall, near Abergavenny, Gwent, training her kitchen staff to her own ways, for I do not feel she ever employed a professional cook. What does surprise me, considering the amount of hospitality offered at the Hall – including Royal visits – is that she appears not to have employed a *chef*! If she had, he would certainly have had to shape his ways to hers, and sparks would surely have flown, for her methods were her own.

Her 'first principles' are expounded through the complication of a tale of a Traveller who encounters a Hermit sitting by the Well of Gover on the Llanover estate. Having failed to obtain a decent meal anywhere on his travels the Hermit condescends to

---

* *beurre manié* – 1½ oz butter, 2 oz flour worked together and added in small pieces.

explain the way to culinary success. She was allegedly persuaded into print by her gentry friends eager to know the secret of the superb-tasting food they always enjoyed at Llanover.

Her book is also valued for the collection of traditional Welsh recipes obtained from friends in South Wales.

As Augusta Waddington, one of three daughters of a retired Nottinghamshire gentleman and businessman, she grew up at Llanover, which she was always to love more than any other place (and she travelled widely). In 1823, when they were both 21, she married Benjamin Hall, of the well-known Pembrokeshire family. It was a true love-match – he tall and handsome, she petite, golden-haired and blue-eyed – both active in the Welsh language cause, both dedicated teetotallers – no alcohol was ever served at Llanover, and it is a sad fact that she is remembered for having closed all the pubs in Llanover, rather than for their joint good works. His political work for the Liberal Party was rewarded with a Baronetcy, but a more heartwarming gesture was the affectionate naming of 'Big Ben' after him, when as Commissioner of Works he arranged for the casting of its great bell in Tredegar.

The Halls built Llanover Court in the Jacobean style, its massive entrance hall designed for entertaining, but it is no longer standing. *Tŷ Uchaf* ('Upper House'), where Lady Llanover grew up, is still there – and occupied by her great-great grandson. It was a memorable moment for me when I offered him her Welsh Salt Duck at the launch of the first edition of this book.

GRANVILLE FISH SAUCE

From Lady Llanover's Good Cookery, *(1987).*

One small anchovy well pounded in a mortar, one shallot chopped fine, two tablespoonfuls of sherry, half a tablespoonful of best vinegar six whole black peppercorns, a little nutmeg, and a very little mace. Simmer the above ingredients altogether in a double saucepan, stirring well all the time, until the shallot is soft: then take an ounce of butter in another double saucepan, with as much flour as will make it into a stiff paste: add the other ingredients which have been stewing, and stir it well till scalding hot for about two minutes, then add six tablespoonfuls of cream: stir well, and strain. This sauce was considered by the Hermit to be a difficult and complicated recipe to execute. The only written recipe he possessed was old, very vague, and unsatisfactory: but, nevertheless, the sauce was made in perfection under his directions, and the Traveller wrote down as well as he could what he saw executed, and was informed that when properly made it was even better the second day than the first, and only required to be warmed over a saucepan of hot water. It is suitable for salmon and every other sort of fish: but the Hermit drew his attention to the impossibility of any one making it either good or twice alike who was deficient in the organ of taste: as if the anchovy or shallot was larger or smaller, or the butter not the very freshest and best, or if there was too much or too little nutmeg and mace, or if the cream was of a different consistency, the flavour would be altered, and the greatest discretion is necessary in using mace, which, if overdone, the whole is spoiled.

Though this sauce is thought to be named after Lady Llanover's illustrious ancestor, Sir Richard Granville of the 'Revenge', there is no clue as to its origin. Maybe it was of her own invention, but it could have been one of great-great-aunt Mrs Delany's who had such an influence on her upbringing, and was a Granville before her marriage. Lady Llanover, however, though precise about the ingredients, tends to flounder when it comes to the actual instructions, which is not like her at all. I suspect she hadn't really succeeded with the old recipe, lost patience with it and surprisingly for her, made the rather feeble excuse that it was an old recipe, difficult to execute and seldom produced the same result. Whatever, it *doesn't* work too well. I have experimented with adjusting the ingredients and obtained better results, but I propose Franco Taruschio's version, prepared for the lunch held for the launch of *Good Cookery* 1991 facsimile edition in the 'Walnut Tree Inn', Llanddewi Skirrid, near Abergavenny, which he and his wife, Ann, have run so successfully for over 30 years.

Franco Taruscio's adaptation:

1 shallot, finely chopped	nutmeg
4 anchovy fillets, mashed	30g/1oz butter
2 tbls dry sherry	1 level tbls flour
½tbls white wine vinegar	6 generous tbls double cream
6 whole peppercorns, cracked	pinch ground mace and of freshly-grated nutmeg

Cook the shallot, anchovy, sherry, vinegar and spices in a *bain marie* until the shallot is soft. Meanwhile melt the butter in a small pan and add the flour. Stir in to make a roux. Cook the roux well, then add to the shallot mixture. Mix in well and cook for a few more minutes, stirring all the time, then add the double cream. Beat it in well and cook for 2 minutes, then strain through a fine sieve.

This quantity serves 2-3.

QUEEN CHARLOTTE'S ORANGE PUDDING

A favourite of the Queen, with whom Mrs Delany enjoyed a long friendship. In her later years she lived in one of the houses in Windsor Great Park: from time to time the Queen would call for her favourite pudding – but it had to be made in Mrs Delany's kitchen and sent across the Park, as the Royal kitchens could never get it quite right!

Take two oranges and one lemon, grate the peel off them and mix with the juice, into which put a quarter of a pound/125g sugar and the yolks of five eggs; then make a little paste for the bottom of the dish. It must be baked slowly in a moderate oven, but yet be browned at the top.

Bibliography

(all London, unless otherwise stated)

Aylett, Mary, & Ordish, Olive: *First Catch Your Hare,* MacDonald, 1965.

Bessinger, Bernard: *Recipes of Old England, Three Centuries of English Food,* David & Charles, 1973.

The Best of Eliza Acton; Ed. Elizabeth Ray, Longman's, 1968.

Borrow, George: *Wild Wales.*

Burnett, John: *A History of the Cost of Living,* Penguin Books, 1969.

Burnett, John: *Plenty and Want,* Thomas Nelson, 1966.

Conway, David: *The Magic of Herbs,* Mayflower Books, 1975.

The Cooking of Germany: Hazeltone, Nika Standen and the editors of Time/Life books, Foods of the World Series, Time/Life Publications,1969.

Croeso Cymreig (A Welsh Welcome): Wales Gas Board, first published 1953, 1966 ed.

Farmhouse Fare, recipes from country housewives collected by 'Farmer's Weekly', Countrywise Books, 1966 ed.

Fishlock, Trevor: *Wales and the Welsh,* Cassell, 1972.

Fishlock, Trevor: *Talking of Wales,* Cassell, 1976.

Fraser, Maxwell: *Wales,* Robert Hale (The County Books Series), 1952.

Fry, Pamela: *The Good Cook's Encyclopaedia,* Spring Books, 1962.

Griffith, L. Wyn: *The Wooden Spoon,* Dent, 1937.

Grigson, Jane: *English Food,* Macmillan, 1974.

Grigson, Jane: *Fish Cookery,* David & Charles for the International Wine & Food Publishing Company, 1973.

Hartley, Dorothy: *Food in England,* Mac Donald, 1934.

Hutchins, Sheila: *English Recipes,* Methuen, 1967.

Hutchins, Sheila: *Daily Express Cookery Book,* Collins, 1976.

Jenkins, J.Geraint: *Life and Tradition in Rural Wales,* Dent, 1976.

Lermon & Mallet, Editors for the English edition: *Cuisine du Terroir,* Blenheim House, 1987.

Llanover, Lady: *The First Principles of Good Cookery,* Richard Bently, 1867.

Llewellyn, Richard: *How Green Was My Valley,* Michael Joseph, 1939.

Llewellyn, Richard, *Up into the Singing Mountain,* Michael Joseph, 1963.

Lloyd George's Favourite Dishes: ed. Bobby Freeman, John Jones (Cardiff) Ltd., 1974, 1976, 1979

Owen, George: *Description of Pembrokeshire,* 1603.

Parry-Jones, David: *Welsh Country Upbringing,* Batsford, 1948.

Peate, Iorwerth C.: *Tradition and Folk Life, A Welsh View,* Faber & Faber, 1972.

Reinhard, John R.: *Mediaeval Pageant,* Dent, 1939.

Richards, Melville: *The Laws of Hywel Dda* (trans.), University Press, Liverpool, 1954.

Roberts, Enid: *Bwyd y Beirdd,* North Wales Arts Associaion

Sikes, Wirt: *Rambles and Studies in Old South Wales,* Sampson Low, Marston Searle & Rivington, 1881; reprinted 1973 by Stewart Williams, Barry, South Glamorgan.

Skeel, Prof. Caroline, M.A., D.Lit.: *The Cattle Trade between Wales and England from the 15th to the 19th centuries.* Transactions of the Royal Historical Society.

Thompson, E.P.: *The Making of the English Working Class,* Gollancz, 1963.

Tibbott, S.Minwel: *Welsh Fare,* Welsh Folk Museum, St.Fagan's 1976.

Tucker, H.M.: *Gower Gleanings,* published by the Gower Society for the 1951 Swansea Festival.

Westland, Pamela *A Tale of the Country,* Elm Tree Books, 1974.

White, Florence: *Good Things in England*, Jonathan Cape, 1968 edition.

Warne's Model Cookery: ed. Mary Jewry, (condensed edition), Frederick Warne & Co., 1968.

Williams, Prof. Gwyn: *The Land Remembers*, Faber & Faber, 1977.

Williams, Dr James: *Give Me Yesterday*, Gomer Press, 1971 (3 reprints).

Wilson, C.Anne: *Food and Drink in Britain*, Constable, 1973.

Welsh Language Bibliography (NLW).

Llyfr Cogyddiaeth Newydd, *Caernarfon, c.*1867, 296p, 14 cm. (Instruction in planning nutritious meals rather than meal-by-meal buying of food).

Llyfr Coginio a Chadw Tŷ (A Book of Cookery and Household Management),Hughes and Son, Wrexham, 1880 (?), 328p, 19cm. (In the style of 'Warne's Model Cookery', by the author of 'Llyfr Pawb ar Bob-peth' – 'Everyone's Book about Everything', see below.

Llyfr Pawb ar Bob-peth: Hughes & Son, Wrexham, 1877.

Y Tŷ, a'r Teulu, 'S.M.M.' (The House and Domestic Economy), 366p, 1891. (Distinction drawn between Welsh and English tastes in food in a book of household management aimed at the better-off.)

Y Trysor Teuluaidd (The Family Treasure), 22p, 18 cm. T.J.Griffiths, 1877. (Written for readers of *Y Drych* (The Mirror), a Welsh language paper circulating amongst the Welsh community in Utica, N.Y., U.S.A. A work of general reference in the style of *Pear's Encyclopaedia*.)

Goginiaeth a Threfniadaeth Deuluaidd, Cyfaddas i Anghenion Gweithwyr Cymru: Mrs.Edwards, Corwen, 1887. A compre hensive book of household management and recipes in the Victorian style, including some for traditional Welsh dishes, directed at the 'Welsh working man's wife'.

Index

confectionery, 242-6, r 245, r 246
confits, r 246
Consul, American, 1880's *see* Sikes, Wirt
coracles, 39
crab apples, 44
cranberries,
    tart, r 177
cream:
    in fruit fools, r 179
    in Patagonia,
        cream tart, r 194
    with salmon in milk, 65
    in sauces, 307-8
    sour:
        in cakes, 204, r 209
cree:
    cake, r 213
    see also scruggins
Croeso Cymreig (Wales Gas), 17
    apple ginger, r 247
    bara brith, r 103
    Caerphilly scones, r 279
    cawl, r 110
    cawl haslet, r 127
    Christmas cake, r 279
    ffowlin Cymreig, r 130
    Glamorgan sausages, r 152
    Katt pies, r 239
    lamb pie *(pastai oen)*, r 142
    nettle syrup, r 258
    pig's liver soup, r 127
    pumpkin wine, r 166
    rice pudding, r 184
    shearing cake, r 269
    suryn cyffaith poeth (spiced sauce),
        r 132
    teisen datws sbeis (cinnamon potato
        cakes), r 209
    teisen lap (adapted), r 210
    teisen sinamon, r 211
    toffee, r 246
    trollins, r 190-1

Welsh chicken, r 130
    Welsh curd cakes, r 183
Curiosities of Ale and Beer, The (John
    Bikerdyke), 258
curry powder, r 304

Daily Express Cookery Book (Sheila
    Hutchings):
        scruggins cake, r 122
dairy trade, 33-34
damsons, 44
    and apple jelly, r 247
Davies, Ann,
    her recipe, r 212
Davies, Cdr.John Pendry:
    cockles and eggs, 85
    mackerel, 68-9
Davies, Captain Wil, 81
deep freeze chest *see* freezer
Description of Pembrokeshire (George Owen
    1603):
        herring, 41
        lobster, 42
desserts, *see* puddings and pies (sweet)
diet, Welsh, 19-23, 222-4, 233
    c.f. English, 15-6, 19-23, 222
    invalid, r, 112, 227
    medieval, 19-20, 53-4, 99-100
    poverty, 222-33
    mid 1700's, 31
divorce customs, 31
dowset, (Gower pies),
    two versions, r 191-2
drovers, 32-3, 38
duck:
    stuffing for, r 278
    Welsh salt, r 131
        sauces for, r 131-2
dumplings:
    apple, r 232
    barley meal, r 229
    oatmeal, r 190-1

nomads, Welsh, 35
nuts, 44
  in Patagonian black cake, r   216-7
  almonds:
    as thickener, 45
    in ginger cakes, r   217

oats and oatmeal, 20, 27, 90
  broth, r   225
  dumplings, r   190-1
  flummery, r   232
    thin flummery, r   232
  gruel, 228
  oatcakes etc., r   101
    tools for, 100-1
    with junket, 181
  oatmeal water, r   227
  pancakes, 195-202
  porridge, r   230
  poverty dishes, r   225-6
  siot, r   226
  sowans, r   226-7
  trollies, r   190-2
oil lamps:
  shells as, 44
oranges, 279
Old Memories (Sir Henry Jones) *quoted*, 223-4
olive oil, 31, 68, 70
onions:
  with liver, r   126
  with potatoes, 159
    cake, r   161
  sauce, r   131
  Spring:
    in pancakes, r   202
out-of-doors, food for:
  see harvest food and drink *and*
    picnics etc.
ovens:
  Dutch:
    inadequacies and solutions, r 210

Welsh use of, 24, 210
  cake recipes for, r   2 11
  pot, 27, 90
  recipe for, 94
Owen, George (1603): *quoted*, 41, 42
oysters, 80-3
  fried, r   81
  in loaves, r   82
  in mutton, r   83
  pie, r   83
  sausages, r   83
  soup, r   81

pancakes, 24, 195-202
  in canteen, 195
  eating contests, 196
  green, r   202
  cream, r   297
  savoury, r   202
  sweet, r   198
  with yeast, r   198
  similar recipes, 199-201
Parsley pie, r   164
Patagonia, 193-4
  black cake, r   216-7
  carrot pudding, r   194-5
  cream tart, r   194
patty, r   304
peaches:
  of Troy, 19
peacock:
  stuffed, r   54
Pearson, Mary (1755), 83
peas:
  and potatoes, r   158
  soup, r   289
Peate, Iorwerth C., 96
Phelps, Anne, 287-9
Physicians of Myddfai, The, 48-9
pickles:
  gooseberry, r   70
  pumpkin, r   165

FOR MORE COOKBOOKS, Welsh language tutors, books about Welsh art, music and politics . . .

. . . greetings cards, diaries, T-shirts and much more—send now for your free, personal copy of our full-colour 48-page catalogue! Or simply look it up on the Internet!

TALYBONT, CEREDIGION, CYMRU SY24 5HE
e-mail ylolfa@netwales.co.uk
internet http://www.ylolfa.wales.com/
phone (01970) 832 304
fax 832 782